Your
Dog's
Life

Also Available from PRIMA PETS™ _____

TRACY ACOSTA, D.V.M.

Your DOG'S Life

Your Complete Guide to Raising Your Pet from Puppy to Companion

PRIMA PETS
An Imprint of Prima Publishing

Prima Publishing has designed this book to provide information in regard to the subject matter covered. It is sold with the understanding that the publisher and the author are not liable for the misconception or misuse of information provided. Every effort has been made to make this book as complete and as accurate as possible. The purpose of this book is to educate. The author and Prima Publishing shall have neither liability nor responsibility to any person or entity with respect to any loss, damage, or injury caused or alleged to be caused directly or indirectly by the information contained in this book.

YOUR PET'S LIFE and PRIMA PETS are trademarks of Prima Communications, Inc. The Prima colophon is a trademark of Prima Communications, Inc., registered in the United States Patent and Trademark Office.

Interior photos by Kent Lacin Media Services
Color insert photos © Isabelle Français and Joan Balzarini
Chapter 6 illustrations by Pam Tanzey
Cover photos © Photodisc and Tony Stone

Library of Congress Cataloging-in-Publication Data
Acosta, Tracy M.
Your dog's life : the first two years : your complete guide to raising your pet from puppy to companion / Tracy M. Acosta.
    p. cm.
  ISBN: 0-7615-1543-7
   1. Dogs.   2. Puppies.   I. Title.
  SF427.A324   1999
  636.7—dc21   98-41456
                                        CIP

99 00 01 02 HH 10 9 8 7 6 5 4 3 2 1
Printed in the United States of America

How to Order
Single copies may be ordered from Prima Publishing, P.O. Box 1260BK, Rocklin, CA 95677; telephone (916) 632-4400. Quantity discounts are also available. On your letterhead, include information concerning the intended use of the books and the number of books you wish to purchase.

This book is dedicated to my parents, Rita and Lanny, who provided me with the moral, spiritual, and educational background that has allowed me to achieve all that I have. And Dad, remember to keep that midnight oil burning.

"If you have men who will exclude any of God's creatures from the shelter of compassion and pity, you will have men who will deal likewise with their fellow man."
—St. Francis of Assisi

Contents

Foreword

Your Dog's Life could easily have been written under numerous titles. Many appropriate ones came to mind as I reviewed this manuscript, for example, "The Essential Manual of Dog Ownership," or "From Womb to Tomb and More," or perhaps, "Dog Ownership is Serious Business." It is not often that a reader can get the breath of perspective found in this author's work. It is clear that every phase of dog ownership has been experienced, up to and including the technical and medical detail of most common dog diseases and conditions that only a veterinarian could describe. Few readers will have thought of all the considerations of acquiring a new puppy, nor the geriatric considerations when this animal reaches its golden years. Being a veterinarian for nearly 40 years, I have often been bombarded with questions regarding breed selection, gender selection, training, human-animal bond issues, nutrition, and many other non-medical issues. I would have loved to have had access to a resource such as this text, not only as a reference for my use, but to refer those tedious questions that are difficult to answer in brief conversation, especially on a busy day. Young Dr. Acosta, in addition to her informative medical and technical writing, has also shown a clear understanding of the human factors that are vital to the responsible ownership of man's "best friend."

H. Dwight Mercer,
Professor and Dean Emeritus,
Mississippi State University,
College of Veterinary Medicine.

Acknowledgments ————————————————

I would like to thank the following people for supporting and encouraging me throughout this project: My family; Mary Welby Alexander; Susy Beacham; Ann Cook, D.V.M.; and Lorna Dolley Eby, my patient editor. A special thanks to Todd Thriffiley, my agent, my attorney, and, most importantly, a great friend.

Introduction

The special relationship between dogs and people began to form in the very early days of human society. Archaeologists and anthropologists theorize that dogs were domesticated about 12,000 to 14,000 years ago. People probably first employed dogs to help them in the hunt, to protect their living areas from wild animals, and to herd their flocks. In return, dogs received food, shelter, and acceptance. Somewhere, somehow in time, people realized that providing food and an occasional pat on the head could result in a dog's unlimited loyalty and unconditional love. The unique human-dog bond was born. When naturalist Carolus Linnaeus sat down to classify the various species in 1758, he gave dogs the name *Canis familiaris,* or familiar dog, which indeed these animals had become. Other members of the larger *Canidae* family are wolves (from which the domestic dog descended), coyotes, foxes, and jackals.

Today dogs come in an almost bewildering variety of sizes, shapes, colors, and appearance. They have been tinkered with until man, the engineer, created enough varieties to suit any fancy. Whatever quality you desire—intelligence, ease of grooming, size, guarding ability—you're sure to find the dog you're looking for. She may be a purebred, a mixed breed, or the legendary "Heinz 57" variety, but she'll be just right for you.

Dog Ownership: The Many Sacrifices, the Many Joys

Perhaps dogs and people became such good friends because we are so much alike. We are both social, family-oriented animals. Most dogs are willing to make friends with people to whom they are properly introduced. The really gregarious ones will go around introducing *you* to strangers. On the other hand, not every dog has a natural-born attraction to every person she meets. A dog's keen sense of hearing and smell makes her a finely tuned alarm system that will alert you to the approach of friends, neighbors, or salespeople, or warn you when a prowler lurks nearby.

Dogs are strong proponents of family togetherness. In fact, it's hard for me to imagine a child going through life without a dog. Whether the activity is watching television or going on a picnic, dogs enjoy being involved in everything the family does. If the decision were up to your dog, she'd probably never choose to stay behind, nor would she opt to stay at the kennel. She'd rather be an integral family member, and is usually more than willing to move into the house, share the bedroom and even the bed, with her people. She's thrilled when her owners take her along, whether on quick errands or long trips, often safely secured in a specially designed car seat or seatbelt.

There's no doubt that dogs are good for more than warming your feet on cold nights or keeping you company as you drop off the dry-cleaning. They offer a depth of companionship that is indeed rare. They're able to accurately and immediately sense your mood, and can share your excitement, offer silent comfort, and always give unconditional love. They take on your feelings, becoming similarly fearful if you panic during bad weather. They greet you every day with happiness and love, providing excellent emotional therapy.

For most people, the joys of owning a dog far outweigh the sacrifices. As a dog owner, you'll always have someone to cuddle with; someone who will listen but won't spill your secrets; someone who's ever loving and never demanding; completely accepting, totally non-judgmental. A person who provides a dog with all the necessities and a few amenities, and does so with a willing heart, will enjoy a wonderful companion.

Of course, acquiring a dog brings inherent obligations as well, not so different from having a child. To take a dog into your home requires your honest commitment of time, not simply to give the dog the care she needs, but to give her the attention and friendship she desires. In addition, you must be willing to pay her expenses. Fortunately, she won't demand an Ivy League education or designer clothing (although canine equivalents of both are certainly available!).

A Dog in Your Future?

Look into your future. Are you currently single or childless? Would your commitment to a dog remain strong in the face of a marriage or the birth of a child? A dog is indeed a great child substitute, but she's not a pet who can be set aside in a corner once you do have children. Will you still be willing to make time for your dog and protect her from tail-pulling and clumsy handling?

How's your sense of humor? If your dog ran through the guests at your cocktail party carrying your underwear, would you laugh or cry? Are you flexible—willing to live with dog hairs here and there (or everywhere)? Can you live with never knowing what your puppy may do next, without having complete control?

Like marriage, a human-dog relationship should not be entered into lightly. Dogs, especially the more companionable breeds, become very attached to their people. Adopting a dog should be a commitment for her lifetime, a time frame likely to span 10 years or more.

Fulfilling the Human-Dog Bond

I'll always remember the special memories of my miniature Dachshund, Hanni, who blessed our family from the time I was in fifth grade until my junior year of verterinary school. She truly was a special dog who provided so much love and companionship to every member of my family. Of course, anyone who knows me also knows that my black Labrador, Bacchus, is definitely special to me. I have had him since my first year of veterinary school, and he is one of the main reasons I stayed in shape and survived the stress of school. In fact, to this day, former students and faculty of Mississippi State University, thinking back to Bacchus and me strolling around campus, still remember me as the "little girl with the big, black dog." He is still one of my "babies" today.

My childhood relationships with dogs led me to pursue a career as a veterinarian. Today I fulfill my calling to care for dogs through my small-animal practice. Writing this book lets me share what I've learned and experienced with those who have, or are considering acquiring, a dog. My intention is to provide the knowledge that will enable you and your dog to fully experience the joy of the *Homo sapiens—Canis familiaris* bond.

While I do not intend the topics to be exhaustive, the information will help you make practical and educated decisions about your dog's life. Chapter 1 will help you decide whether dog ownership is right for you and provides tips on how to make your selection. You'll find out how to prepare for your puppy or dog's arrival in chapter 2. Chapter 3 explains how you can satisfy your dog's nutritional needs, while chapters 4 and 5 furnish technical and medical details that will enable you to raise a healthy dog and to recognize when she does require medical attention. Remember, however, that the general knowledge you'll gain in these chapters is no substitute for seeking professional help when your dog needs it.

Chapter 6 contains the training basics that ensure a safe and harmonious relationship with your dog. Chapter 7 presents the basics of grooming so you and perhaps a groomer can keep your dog attractive, clean, and healthy; and chapter 8 describes how you can successfully incorporate your dog into your family life. The final chapter wraps it all up with a few thoughts on your dog's lifetime into her golden years. The various appendixes enhance the usefulness of the text, providing you with a quick and easy reference source offering a developmental chart, common congenital defects, important phone numbers and addresses, lists of poisonous plants, and a glossary of terms. All the information is offered with a single underlying premise: A well-informed dog owner is the key to a joyful and rewarding human-dog experience.

Happy tails to you!

So, You Want a Dog

The human-dog bond is awesome when you really think about it. I have witnessed this bond among people of all ages and both genders. Dogs often provide a best friend who is always there, no matter what is happening in our lives. Children and adults benefit emotionally from having such a constant and loving relationship. A dog offers acceptance while at the same time teaching us responsibility. And the look on a child's face as she smiles and accepts the warmth and love of her dog is simply priceless.

For senior citizens, especially those who are unable to get out much, a dog offers constant companionship. We have all seen pets who give their owners a great reason to get up in the morning and enjoy life. For people of all ages, dogs have proven beneficial to overall health and well-being. Some research indicates that pet interaction helps cardiac patients live longer; can lower blood pressure; and may even temper episodes of anxiety, verbal aggression, and hyperactivity in some Alzheimer's patients. Many studies indicate that dogs have a refreshing effect on human stress. In today's society, it seems that no matter how weak human relationships become, our human-dog bond only continues to grow stronger.

> A dog offers acceptance while at the same time teaches us responsibility.

As we'll see, bringing a dog into your home is a long-term commitment, but the rewards for you and your dog are immeasurable.

Keys to Your Dog's Happiness

Part of developing a great relationship with a dog is providing an environment in which she will be happy. Factors to consider before getting a dog include her needs for living space, exercise, training, grooming, and companionship, which are all discussed in this book. You should also consider how well she'll interact with other pets.

How Much Space Does a Dog Need?

Some dogs are perfectly suited to life in a 500-square-foot studio in Manhattan while others do best in the sprawling environment of a large ranch home on 100 acres. It depends on factors such as the size of the dog and the amount of exercise he needs. A Border Collie, for instance, is happiest when he's herding a flock of sheep, although he can adapt to a city environment if given a regular job to do and plenty of exercise. As an example, he'd be the perfect aide to a parent who volunteers as a crossing guard on a busy street.

How Much Exercise?

Some dogs are couch potatoes and others are nonstop dynamos, but all need some amount of exercise to keep them physically and mentally fit. Exercise keeps weight off, keeps the joints working smoothly, and meets a dog's needs for interacting not only with his owners but also with his environment. Even toy breeds need exercise, because they put on weight easily (and an extra pound could mean an obese Chihuahua!). For most breeds, daily exercise of some sort is a must.

Exercise can be as simple as tossing a ball for a dog to chase (an excellent option for owners confined to wheelchairs) or taking him for a walk. It can also be as active as participation in dog sports such as fly ball and agility (both of which are discussed further in Chapter 6, Basic Training). For little dogs, racing down the hallway, jumping up on furniture, and twirling around in circles count as exercise, too.

How Much Training?

All dogs need training, whether they're the size of a Yorkshire Terrier or a Saint Bernard. Training teaches a dog to look to you for guidance and gives him the discipline he needs to fit into your household without being a nuisance. A good puppy kindergarten class, beginning when the dog is 10 to 12 weeks old, will help you lay the foundation for a mutually respectful relationship. Your dog will learn basic obedience commands, such as sit, down, stay, and come, and you will learn positive, nonforceful ways to provide guidance and discipline. (Puppy kindergarten and other training issues are discussed further in Chapter 6, Basic Training.)

Dogs are smart, but don't expect them to develop perfect behavior simply by attending six or eight weeks of puppy kindergarten followed by another six to eight weeks of obedience class. It's just like playing the piano—if you don't practice, you forget how to do it. You'll need to help your dog practice his skills regularly so that he doesn't get lazy and become disobedient. It's easy to keep up his skills. You can make him sit before you give him meals or a treat, or have him lie down when he's hanging out with you in the kitchen as you prepare dinner.

> All dogs need training, whether they're the size of a Yorkshire Terrier or a Saint Bernard. Training teaches a dog to look to you for guidance and gives him the discipline he needs to fit into your household without being a nuisance.

Can My Dog Stay Home All Day Without Me?

Dogs are social animals and can become lonely, bored, noisy, and destructive if left alone frequently. The amount of time you spend at home is definitely something to consider before you acquire a dog. While you needn't spend 24 hours a day with him, it's not fair to get a dog if you know you won't have time for regular walks, play, and other interaction.

If you must be gone during the day, you may wish to provide your dog with a playmate—a second dog. They can keep each other company during the day as long as you're ready, willing, and able to provide plenty of time for them in the evening. If a second dog isn't possible, you may be able to find a doggie day-care center nearby, where your dog will get attention from people and have supervised play with other dogs. Many boarding kennels now offer this option.

What If I Have Other Pets?

Adding a dog to the family requires considering how well he will get along with other pets. Dogs and cats can get along—despite their reputation for being enemies—but they need to be introduced slowly and taught to respect each other. It's ideal if your new puppy has been raised in a household with cats. If the same care is taken in introductions, dogs can also learn to share their territory with ferrets, birds, rabbits, and other small animals. When you introduce your dog to a smaller pet, make sure your dog is on a leash and under control. One person should hold the leash, while another holds the small pet. Let the dog sniff the animal, and give a tug on the leash or verbal correction if he tries to attack the small pet.

It is important to realize that when a new pet is joining a home that has an established pet (or pets), a "pecking order" will have to be developed among the animals. Usually the pet that has been in the household the longest will be the dominant pet, or at least attempt to be. It is all too common for the original pet to become jealous of the new pet whether of the same species or not. It should be expected for dogs to have a few disagreements as an order of dominance is

Did You Know?

The wolf, from which dogs are descended, was the first animal to be domesticated.

established. Also, when introducing a new pet, special care should be taken to ensure neither pet is seriously injured in any scuffles which might occur. Often, dogs may simply learn to tolerate each other, and not necessarily become best friends. It is also possible, as well, that some pets will reject each other completely, in which case a new home should be sought for the new pet.

Surefire Ways to Make Your Dog's Life Unpleasant

Attention and *activity* are canine watchwords. Without these, your dog will indeed be unhappy, and an unhappy dog is likely to develop behavior problems or even physical illness. No dog deserves to live in conditions to which he's unsuited, so consider carefully whether your home and family life will meet the basic needs of the dog you choose.

> *Attention* and *activity* are canine watchwords. Without these, your dog will indeed be unhappy, and an unhappy dog is likely to develop behavior problems or even physical illness.

What Dogs Simply Cannot Live With

Three situations will, without a doubt, make your dog's life utterly miserable. Let's take a quick look at the living conditions you simply must avoid.

1. *Life on a chain with no human interaction.* While life on a chain was once the only experience many dogs knew, we have

now learned much more about dog psychology as well as humane treatment of animals. Dogs enjoy spending time with their people, and if your dog is relegated to life outdoors, not only will it require a doghouse or kennel run to protect her from the elements, she will also need frequent human interaction and care to be happy. (Doghouses and kennel runs are discussed in Chapter 2, Welcome Home!.) A dog is not a stuffed animal that can be brought out for show, then tucked away again until needed. She needs human companionship, and failing a sufficient quantity of that, she needs canine companionship. Expect a dog to be at your side during the day and in a crate by your bed at night. (Crates are discussed in Chapter 2, Welcome Home!.) If you don't want a dog to sit in your lap or at your side while you read or watch television, or "help" you while you work around the house or prepare a meal, then a dog probably not the right pet for you.

2. *Lack of protection from children and others who do not treat him with care and respect.* Dogs are not toys or dolls; they're living, breathing animals that can be hurt by ill treatment from people of all ages. Even if a dog is big enough to withstand a child's poking and pulling, she can become annoyed by it, just as you might. Because a dog doesn't have a voice she can use to ask the person mistreating her to stop, and she may eventually resort to biting to get her message across. While this isn't acceptable behavior, it's perfectly understandable. A dog, especially a puppy or toy breed, should never be left alone with a young child. There should always be supervision to make sure everyone, children adults alike, treats your animal with respect.

3. *Lack of appropriate space and exercise.* A dog's space and exercise needs vary according to his size and breed history. A dog that is bred for sporting pursuits or energetic work, such as herding, will find city life stifling unless you can arrange frequent off-leash exercise in a safe area. Some of the more placid working or non-sporting breeds will be satisfied with a daily walk and don't mind where they live as long as there's room for them to sprawl on the floor. On the other hand, a small terrier, hard-wired for action, may find life without a yard stultifying. She, too, needs regular exercise and play— lots of it. Be sure you understand a breed's physical needs before you take it home with you. Lack of exercise, boredom, and loneliness are a recipe for behavioral problems.

I *Think* I'm Ready

Before you go about choosing a breed or head down to the animal shelter to see what's available, it's a good idea to take stock of your life and make sure that a dog is what you really want.

> Dog ownership is an enormous responsibility and a long-lasting undertaking, both emotionally and financially. Dogs today live an average of 10 to 12 years.

Dog ownership is an enormous responsibility and a long-lasting undertaking, both emotionally and financially. Dogs today live an average of 10 to 12 years, while some live longer than that. New owners develop an emotional attachment to their dogs quickly, and many come to view their dog as a true member of the family and nothing less. Also, the financial reality of properly raising a puppy is not to be taken lightly. Let's take a look at some of the costs associated with dog ownership.

How Much Is This Gonna Cost Me?

Initially, the costs for bringing a new puppy home include a complete series of puppy vaccinations, licensing, and necessities such as food, bedding, bowls, a collar, and a leash. That's in addition to the purchase price of the puppy, which can range from $20 to $2,000. In addition, you'll want your puppy to be appropriately trained, which also varies widely in cost, from $10 to $75 or more per lesson. After you get through the first puppy year, there's routine preventive care such as vaccination booster shots, flea control, parasite prevention, and costs associated with unexpected illness.

Another significant factor to consider is the cost of routine professional grooming that certain breeds require. Many of these financial obligations continue through each year of the dog's life. One estimate suggests that it can cost a minimum of $6,000 to raise a medium-size dog to the age of 11. That's a lot of dog biscuits, but ultimately it's money well spent to properly nurture a happy and healthy puppy through adulthood.

Hmmmm, Maybe a Dog Isn't Right for Me

If you are reading this book after already acquiring a dog, you may be learning some things you didn't know and perhaps getting a better understanding of the new dog who is sharing your life. All is not lost if you are discovering that there are certain things you should have taken into consideration before getting a dog. They can be easy to adapt to—if you are willing to make the effort. Some changes are obvious: Bring

Did You Know?

The earliest fossil evidence of dogs dates back to 10,000 B.C.

the dog indoors if he has been living outside or in the garage; carefully supervise interactions with young children or other pets; and provide him with appropriate levels of attention.

However, if your allergies are acting up because of the dog's presence, or you've really given it some thought and decided that you can't give a dog the life he needs, your first step should be to contact the breeder from whom you purchased the dog. Responsible breeders will usually take back a dog they have bred, no matter how long you've had the dog or why you're giving it up. If for some reason they can't take the dog themselves, they may help you place it in a good foster or adoptive home. Of course, you shouldn't expect to receive your money back unless you've had the dog for only a week or two; then the breeder may be willing to give you a full or partial refund.

If you've lost touch with the breeder, or acquired your dog from another source, contact a breed rescue group or humane organization in your area. Numbers for these can be found in newspapers, the Yellow Pages, or the Internet, and their volunteers can help you better adjust to living with your dog or try to place him in a more appropriate home. Rescue and humane organizations don't always charge for taking a dog, but their costs in time, boarding, and veterinary expenses are high, so it is a gracious gesture to give them a substantial donation for their efforts.

How Do I Choose the Right Dog for Me?

The selection of a dog is more than just a matter of looks. In fact, there are many things to consider. In this section, you'll learn more about the type of dog that will best suit you and your lifestyle. Some of the questions we'll examine are:

1. Do you want a pedigreed pooch or a Heinz 57?
2. Do you want a puppy or adult dog?
3. How much space do you have?
4. How much dirt and hair can you live with?
5. How much time do you want to spend grooming?
6. What types of activities do you enjoy? (Do you want a jogging partner or a couch potato?)
7. Do you have children? If so, how old are they?
8. How much time do you have for a dog?

Pedigreed Pooch or Heinz 57?

So, what makes one dog pedigreed and another not? A pedigreed dog is one that is recognized by an official kennel club as being an offspring of registered, purebred parents. Any dog that does not have such papers is not considered a true pedigree. Dogs that are the result of two different breeds or dogs of unknown ancestry are called mixed breeds or "Heinz 57" dogs.

Now, how do you decide which type is right for you? It all depends on what you are looking for. If you want to pursue the dog show circuit, you must acquire a pedigreed dog. Or if your family simply desires a good, loyal companion and pet, a mixed dog can be just as good of a choice as a pedigreed. There are pros and cons to each.

> A pedigreed dog is one that is recognized by an official kennel club as being an offspring of registered, purebred parents.

Pure Breeds

While all dogs share the distinguishable characteristics of attentive and energetic demeanors, a reliance on pack leadership, and a highly organized social structure, each breed has individual qualities that make it special. There are more than three-hundred recognized dog breeds throughout the world today. Initially, different dog breeds were developed out of the needs and demands of humans in particular areas of the world, with one of the oldest recognizable breeds being the Chow Chow, which is more than 2,000 years old. With time and selective breeding, people developed specific characteristics unique to each breed of dog and began recording breed standards in the mid-19th century. Breed clubs were formed and members decided what the perfect dog of a particular breed should be and then wrote a breed standard. Kennel clubs were eventually formed to help ensure that these breed standards were registered, preserved, and recorded. Many of these breed standards have withstood the test of time and are still used today by breeders and dog show judges. In fact, each breed has its own dog club which sets and enforces the standards of the breed. The American Kennel Club (AKC), established in 1884, forms its legislative body with delegates from each of these breed clubs, whose originators recorded the desired features of their breed and ultimately set the breed standards. As the breed numbers grew, stud books and registration books were developed.

The result of all this is that with a purebred puppy you usually have a good idea of how the puppy will develop both mentally

> Different dog breeds were developed out of the needs and demands of humans in particular areas of the world, with one of the oldest recognizable breeds being the Chow Chow, which is more than 2,000 years old.

and physically and what its temperament and normal disposition will be since each breed has a standard for physical conformation and temperament. If you can see these desired characteristics in the puppy's parents, then you can feel better when choosing a puppy from their offspring. By choosing a purebred, you eliminate much of the element of surprise regarding your puppy's size, appearance, and, to an extent, behavioral characteristics.

Mixed Breeds

As mentioned, a mixed-breed is the result of mating between two different purebred dogs or a mating between dogs of unknown ancestry. A constant question I receive from owners is, "What kind of dog is she?" in reference to their dogs. Sometimes there does appear to be a predominant breed, but other times the puppy will be a virtual melting pot of many breeds, making it difficult to distinguish any one or two specific breed characteristics.

If you were to put dogs of several breeds together and let them reproduce for a few generations, you would end up with a dog which was probably very similar to the first dog. Or, you might cross two specific breeds, such as a Poodle and a Cocker Spaniel, or a Collie and a German Shepherd. The results of such indiscriminate breedings are known as mixed breeds, mutts, or if the two breeds are known, cross breeds. Outside of working breeds, mixes were probably the most commonly found dogs until the rise of the middle class during the Victorian era, when ownership of purebred dogs became a status symbol. Mixed breeds are still plentiful and popular

Did You Know?

The fastest dog in the world is the Cape Hunting Dog, which can reach speeds of 45 mph. The greyhound is second at 39.65 mph and the whippet is third at 35.50 mph.

today, with many people valuing them for their unique appearance and characteristics.

When it comes to health, temperament, character and personality—such things as shyness, aggression, friendliness, ease of training—some people think the mixed-breed dog wins paws down. Many people believe that mixed breeds combine the most desirable characteristics and are all around heartier than any purebred, with less health problems, better behavior, and unparalleled owner loyalty. Dogs are individuals, though, and just like purebreds, mixed breeds can inherit bad qualities as well as good. Also, with a mixed breed it's difficult to predict what the dog will be like as an adult. This is especially true when a puppy is taken in as a stray or adopted from a humane society. In either case, you usually won't know what either parent looked like. For example, one puppy adopted from a shelter was classified as a Pomeranian mix, but as she grew it became clear that she was really a Husky mix. What a difference! With a mixed breed there are rarely guarantees as to the dog's eventual looks, size, or temperament.

The decision of purebred versus mixed breed is a matter of personal choice. This issue could be debated for hours; but the reality is that any dog, purebred or mixed breed, can have serious behavioral and physical problems. And dogs are like people in that they all have different personalities. Just because you have

had a certain breed in the past or know the personality of the litter's parents, there is no guarantee with a mix or purebred that the offspring will fully exhibit the same desired traits.

One of the most common questions asked of veterinarians is whether they can recommend a particular breed. Veterinarians see a lot of different dogs, and if you are considering a particular

Looks Aren't Everything

My favorite true story demonstrates that love between the dog and the owner is the most important aspect in the relationship and has nothing to do with beauty or physical appeal. Many years ago, some members of my family bought two standard poodles, beautiful large black animals full of energy. Over time, they produced several wonderful puppies who were allowed to roam freely in the bayou community. Inevitably, one of the females produced a litter from a union with a large Deerhound.

The offspring looked, well . . . different, to say the least. My great uncle Arthur adopted one of the strange-looking dogs. Jack had the body shape of a Deerhound, covered in a coat that was long and slightly curly, yet stringy at the same time. His floppy ears were covered with the same long, curly, stringy hair and hung on either side of his face, which wore a permanently funny-looking expression. An instant and absolute love affair began.

The loyalty of the dog to Arthur and Arthur's love for the dog became the talk of the small village on the bayou. Then disaster struck. In 1965, Hurricane Betsy crashed into the Louisiana coast. A 20-foot tidal surge washed most of the village away, including Arthur's home. After the fury of the storm subsided, my uncle returned home to evaluate the damage. His greatest sadness came not from losing his home but from the loss of his dog. Miraculously, two weeks after the storm, the dog found his way back to the land where the house had been and Arthur cried with joy. You can fall in love with a mixed breed—even a funny-looking mixed breed—just as easily as with a purebred.

breed, your veterinarian can tell you about his or her experiences with it. Only you, however, can determine exactly what you're looking for in a dog.

What's the American Kennel Club? Founded in 1884, the American Kennel Club (AKC) is a nonprofit organization dedicated to the advancement of purebred dogs. Composed of over

500 dog clubs from across the nation, the AKC's objectives include maintaining a registry of purebred dogs, promoting responsible dog ownership, and sponsoring events, such as breed shows and field trials, that promote interest in (and appreciation of) the purebred dog.

To be eligible for AKC registry, a puppy must be the offspring of individually registered AKC parents, and the breeder must obtain the proper paperwork before the puppy's sale. Once registered, a dog is eligible to compete in AKC-sanctioned events and, if bred with another AKC registered dog, to have his/her offspring registered.

The AKC has created an official breed standard for each of the 147 breeds currently eligible for registration. The breed standard describes the ideal dog of each breed; it lists the physical qualities a breeder should attempt to instill in his dogs. The AKC derived its breed standards largely from the standards used by the individual breed clubs that make up its constituency. Judges of AKC-sponsored events and competitions use the breed standards as the basis of their evaluations.

> Avoid making the mistake of choosing a certain breed for its fleeting popularity rather than first learning the truth about what the breed is like to live with.

Because of the AKC's emphasis on excellence and high standards, it is a common misconception that "AKC registered" or "AKC registrable" is synonymous with quality. However, while a registration certificate identifies a dog and its progenitors as purebreds, it does not necessarily guarantee the health or quality of a dog. Some breeders breed for show quality, but others breed for profit, with little concern for breed standards. Thus, a potential buyer should not view AKC registration as an indication of a dog's quality.

Pop Culture Pooches— Not Always the Best Choice

When Jack Russell Terriers became popular a few years ago, thanks to their exposure on the TV sitcom Frasier and in other media, many people rushed to acquire them, only to discover that without an outlet for their energy and intelligence, the cute little dogs could be demons in dog suits. Dog breeds, like anything we might choose to acquire, are subject to trends relating to what is fashionable or popular. Popular breeds are often those seen in movies, commercials, and television shows, such as the crush in demand for Dalmatians with the release of the movie 101 Dalmatians. People rushed out to get a cute Dalmatian pup, only to discover Dalmatians aren't always good with kids. Avoid making the mistake of choosing a certain breed for its fleeting popularity rather than first learning the truth about what the breed is like to live with.

Puppy or Adult Dog?

Puppies are a delight. They're funny, playful, and loving. Few things in life are more fun than watching a puppy trip over his feet, roll and tumble, then get up, dust himself off, and continue exploring his world. On the other hand, few things in life are as exasperating as cleaning up after the same puppy's housetraining mistakes or picking up the pieces of a prized possession, destroyed in the wake of his sometimes disastrous energy. Puppyhood doesn't last for just a month or two, but instead continues for up to two years. Before you get a dog, make sure your store of patience and humor is well stocked, for both are important characteristics of a successful puppy owner.

If you're not sure you're ready for the lengthy antics of puppyhood, you needn't give up your dream of owning a dog. Thousands of wonderful adult dogs are available for adoption.

Acquiring an adult dog is often a far better decision for a busy family. Adult dogs have the advantages of being past the destructive teething and exploration stages, they may already be spayed or neutered, and sometimes they even come fully trained. Bella, a three-year-old Cavalier King Charles Spaniel, came to her new owners with a Canine Good Citizen certificate and the good manners she learned in puppy kindergarten and basic obedience class. She was car-trained, crate-trained, and housetrained. She adapted beautifully to her new home, with no transition problems at all. Even if an adult dog doesn't come "fully loaded," as Bella did, he's still accustomed to family life and is capable of learning whatever you're willing to teach.

How Much Space Do You Have?

Some of the following factors will be helpful in deciding what dog will best fit your lifestyle.

Among the first criteria to keep in mind are the environmental surroundings that you can provide to meet the dog's inherent needs. For example, if you live in an apartment, be realistic about the size and activity requirements of the dog you choose. Many of the larger or more active breeds should have at least a large fenced yard in which to play and exercise. However, don't be fooled by some small- or medium-size breeds such as the Border

Collie or Jack Russell Terrier. Even though these dogs are not large in stature, they are truly happy only in an environment that allows them freedom to live out their instincts, such as herding and hunting. If you do live in an apartment, it's only fair to pick a breed that is small and requires minimal space for exercise—unless you're willing to go for daily walks or runs that would adequately meet the energy level of an active breed. While living in an apartment during veterinary school, I had a Labrador Retriever, whom I walked or ran on an almost daily basis, keeping both of us in good shape. My Labrador was a happy and well-behaved indoor dog.

The bottom line is that you must be committed to providing what is best for your puppy when it comes to space requirements. When researching different breeds, be sure to acknowledge what is considered the normal environment and activity level for each particular breed and be honest about what you are willing or able to accommodate.

> All dogs, regardless of whether they live indoors or outdoors, must be provided with a safe and secure place.

All dogs, regardless of whether they live indoors or outdoors, must be provided with a safe and secure place. Be sure to read more about puppy-proofing your home later in this book.

How Much Dirt and Hair Can You Live With?

This is definitely a question to consider before choosing your puppy. If you are a neat freak, you probably should avoid breeds that have a lot of hair, shed regularly, or love romping through mud puddles—especially if you plan on having your dog indoors. Dogs who have longer hair coats can track in a lot of dirt even when only going outside to potty. A lot of hair or a long coat does not necessarily mean a lot of shedding, though. For example, Poodles remain a popular choice among people who detest shedding. Also, many small breeds that live indoors hate to get dirty. Some don't even want to get their feet damp from the morning dew.

Often when people look at a dog's hair coat, they mistakenly consider only the length. Just because a certain breed has short hair does not mean shedding will be minimal or nonexistent. Breeds with a short hair coat, such as the Labrador Retriever, do shed—and shed quite a lot (as I know from firsthand experience!). When studying the different breeds, inquire about the type of coat and whether shedding is excessive or minimal. You may be surprised!

How Much Time Do You Want to Spend Grooming?

Some dog owners enjoy the daily grooming routine of certain breeds, but I'd be willing to bet that the majority of us prefer breeds with low-maintenance needs. Regardless of hair coat type, all dogs should be brushed on a regular basis. Every dog's coat benefits from a good brushing because it stimulates the skin's natural oils and distributes them throughout the coat.

Dogs whose coats require daily maintenance can develop skin problems if they're not cared for properly, so if you choose one of these breeds, be sure you can either devote the grooming time required or pay for the cost of professional grooming. Even if your dog doesn't need professional grooming, it can be a good idea to pay for a half-hour to an hour of a groomer's time so she can guide you in the basics of your dog's grooming needs and advise you on the grooming tools you'll need. You may even decide that it's worth the price to have a groomer do any routine bathing, even if you have an easy-care breed such as a Labrador Retriever.

What Types of Activities Do You Enjoy?

Other factors to examine prior to selecting a puppy include your interests. Most people choose a dog to be simply a trusting and loving companion. Others wish to pursue showing, breeding, or hunting their dogs. Naturally, you'll want to choose a dog who's suited to your interests. For instance, if your goal is to have a dog you can play Frisbee with, or even compete in flying disc events, a Border Collie or Whippet is a better choice than a Dachshund or Basset Hound. In certain sporting or hound breeds, some lines are bred strictly for hunting, others for the show ring, and never the twain shall meet. Among the breeds for which this is a consideration are Beagles, English Springer Spaniels, and Labrador Retrievers.

The best advice is to seek out a breed that will fit into your lifestyle and your idea of the perfect dog concerning exercise requirements. The ideal dog varies from one particular person or family to another. Fortunately, a number of breeds are available to suit every need.

> The best advice is to seek out a breed that will fit into your lifestyle and your idea of the perfect dog concerning exercise requirements.

Should you wish to select a dog who has exercise needs that coincide with your current exercise habits, it is helpful to consider the type of dog. For example, if you enjoy daily walks or runs, think about selecting a dog who's bred to be on the go for long periods of time, such as a Labrador or Golden Retriever, or a working dog such as a Boxer or Siberian Husky, to name only a few. On the other hand, if you normally come home exhausted from long hours at work, you may prefer a Basset Hound, a Maltese, or a Yorkshire Terrier, who would also prefer to take it easy.

Do You Have Children? How Old Are They?

Children and puppies can be a wonderful combination. Puppies thrive on the constant love and attention they receive, while children can learn respect and responsibility by helping to care for a puppy. However, a critical consideration when choosing a puppy who will be compatible with children is the temperament that a particular breed is known to have. In most cases, puppies raised in a home with small children tend to develop a more patient and tolerant disposition. If your family is contemplating the purchase of a puppy, consider the ages of your children and the personalities of each family member, as well as the temperament and size of the dog. Some breeds are definitely better suited to life with children than are other breeds. For instance, Mastiffs and Bloodhounds love kids and are big enough to withstand roughhousing; on the other hand, they can knock over a toddler with a swish of their tail. A Golden Retriever is also loving toward children but isn't quite so huge. Research your breed choice thoroughly to make sure the dog you choose is well suited to life with your children. Whatever the breed, it's ideal if the pup you select has been raised with children in the home or at least has been exposed to them on a regular basis.

How Much Time Do You Have for a Dog?

How much time you have to dedicate to raising a healthy and happy dog is important to consider before you actually acquire a puppy. The first year of a puppy's life can be extremely time-consuming since this period is critical in establishing a puppy's daily routine, training, and providing necessary health care.

An easy way to determine how much time you will need to devote to a puppy during the first year of life is to compare it to the time required to care for a two-year-old child. Puppy training takes patience and devotion.

Be honest when examining your normal work schedule and your actual time at home. If your schedule does not allow for much commitment, do yourself and the puppy a favor: wait until life's demands allow for it, or consider adopting a mature dog. Remember, too, that the puppy came from a litter full of mates, and now is alone for the first time, which can be quite difficult and trying. Loneliness can lead to behavioral problems. Puppies have emotional needs, as well as exercise and playtime requirements, that must be met daily for them to attain a happy and fulfilled life. Dogs thrive on attention, and the payoff is usually well worth your investment. Consider the time spent with your puppy as a step to creating an inseparable human-animal bond.

Also consider the family's day-to-day routine. If you work long hours, you still must come home and tend to the dog's basic needs of feeding, exercising, grooming, and playing, activities that typically require more time during the first year of a puppy's life.

If your life is hectic, but you still want a puppy, put your thinking cap on. Could a neighbor or responsible student come by during the day to give your pup some playtime and food if necessary? Would you be able to take the puppy to work with you? Some offices have become more relaxed about pets in the workplace, and if your pup is crated and doesn't cause problems for allergic coworkers, this may be a feasible solution. One man, whose wife was out of town for a week during a time he was working 12- to 14-hour days, found a boarding kennel with a daycare program only a block from his office. He dropped his dog off there every morning and picked her up on his way home. This was

Did You Know?

The United States and France have the highest rates of dog ownership in the world (for countries in which such statistics are available), with almost one dog for every three families. Germany and Switzerland have the lowest rates, with just one dog for every ten families.

Boy or Girl?

With each gender comes advantages and disadvantages. Some people believe that females tend to be less aggressive and more loving than males. However, both genders are equally capable of outpourings of affection and aggression.

Females tend to be slightly smaller in stature and body weight than their male counterparts. If you have not had your female puppy spayed, then you will have to deal with the regular estrus (heat) cycle, which occurs every six to twelve months, depending on the breed. A female in heat will attract every male dog for miles around to your house, which can be quite a nuisance. During the heat cycle, which lasts approximately three weeks, you must keep a constant watch on your dog to avoid an unwanted pregnancy. You should have your puppy spayed before her first heat cycle, which can occur as early as six months of age. The importance of this will be addressed later in the book.

Unneutered males are inclined to roam in an effort to establish as large a territory as possible, so they tend to be escape artists. Besides the desire to prove themselves big dog in the neighborhood, intact male dogs can become so overwhelmed by the scent of female dogs in heat that they are at high risk for getting hit by a car while in search of a potential lady love, as well as for contracting transmittable diseases. I have seen male dogs who have been gone for days at a time, only to return home thin and often injured. For these reasons, it's best to neuter a male unless he's part of an established breeding program and can be securely confined to his own home and property.

If you already have a dog at home, most experts advise you to acquire a puppy of the opposite gender. Dogs of the opposite sex tend to get along better than dogs of the same sex. If you do bring a dog of the opposite sex into the home and do not plan to breed them, then each dog should be spayed or neutered. Of course, some dogs are mellow enough to tolerate a second dog of the same gender. The best way to help with this decision if you are bringing a puppy into a home with an established dog is to consider how your current dog has responded to dogs of the same and opposite sex. For a majority of dogs, it does matter.

a perfect short-term solution for a family that had no yard where their dog could go for bathroom breaks during the day.

Researching Breeds

Without a doubt, all puppies are adorable. With maturity, however, certain traits of each breed become apparent, some of which may not suit your lifestyle or perception of the "perfect" dog. A good way to examine breeds and narrow your choice is to browse through a book that offers a brief description of each breed's unique traits and demands.

Once you have limited the choice to several breeds, you should do in-depth research into each breed. By reading books devoted to each breed, attending dog shows, and talking to several breeders, you can get more detailed and pertinent information regarding each breed. Internet searches also offer a wealth of information. For example, at the Purina online site (www.purina.com), you can find a personality test and questionnaire that are extremely helpful in making this decision. (See Appendix 3 for more helpful addresses and phone numbers.) Contacting breeders or owners of particular breeds is a great way to learn the true characteristics and time requirements inherent with each type of dog. They can also inform you of how easy or difficult it is to work with a breed and what can truly be expected.

Where Do I Find the Perfect Puppy?

It might seem as if buying a puppy is as simple as looking in the newspaper, going to a pet store, or getting one from the local animal shelter. For the best results, however, you'll want to exercise patience and do some serious interviewing of several sources before you bring any puppy home.

Several options exist for obtaining a puppy: private breeders, pet shops, animal shelters, and rescue organizations. Each has advantages and disadvantages that you should weigh before purchasing a puppy. As a veterinarian who regularly sees puppies from different sources, I have seen the best results from private breeders. This is *not* to say that no great dogs come from animal shelters or rescue organizations, or that poor-quality dogs are never obtained from private breeders. However, when people ask where they should look, I recommend they go to a private breeder.

> Several options exist for obtaining a puppy: private breeders, pet shops, animal shelters, and rescue organizations. Each has advantages and disadvantages that you should weigh before purchasing a puppy.

Buying from a Breeder

Once you have decided on the breed you want, it's important to investigate several breeders and the quality of dogs they produce. Bloodlines and registration papers are not the only factors that guarantee a good puppy. For the most complete evaluation, you need to see the parents and the offspring in person to judge size, personality, and overall body composition.

Remember that even within specific breeds, anything from the dog's size to temperament can vary from the standard, so be sure that a breeder's dogs meet your wishes or idea of the breed you want.

A good breeder will be able to provide pertinent information about her puppies, such as family pedigree, family medical and behavioral history (the good *and* the bad), referrals to past buyers, vaccination status of each litter, and any guarantees offered. Also, by using a private breeder, you will have the opportunity to observe at least the mother (dam), which is greatly beneficial in predicting the final outcome of conformation and personality. You are also able to inquire about, if not observe, the father (sire) as well. Remember, the more information you have about the ancestors, the better you can predict the health, life span, and behavior of a puppy. A lot of this information can often be obtained well in advance of the birth of each litter.

Reputable breeders are usually quite choosy about the homes in which they place their puppies. They expect many questions from you and will have their own questions as well, such as what you expect of the breed, what other pets you have or have had, how their health was, and how long their life span was. Rather than be offended by probing questions about your lifestyle and intentions toward the dog, respect the breeder for her concern about the pups' welfare.

When you go to see a breeder's puppies, don't expect to go home with a dog that day. Most breeders do not send puppies to their new homes before they reach at least seven and preferably eight weeks of age. Many well-documented studies support this practice as being beneficial to the puppy for its lifetime. If puppies are separated from their mother and littermates too soon, especially before six weeks of age, the separation can lead to poor growth rates and numerous behavioral problems later in life. In fact, if a breeder attempts to place your puppy with you earlier than seven weeks, you may want to reevaluate your choice. In addition, by the time your puppy comes to you, he will already have been started

Did You Know?

The Saluki, a hunting dog raised by ancient Egyptians, is the oldest known breed.

on his vaccination series and a regular deworming protocol.

Another benefit of buying from a reputable breeder is that most will and should provide proof that the parents have been declared free of eye problems by the Canine Eye Registry Foundation (CERF) or of hip/elbow dysplasia by the Orthopedic Foundation for Animals (OFA), if applicable to the specific breed. All credible breeders will also offer some type of guarantee regarding birth defects and hereditary problems for a limited time period. (See glossary of terms for more details on hip/elbow dysplasia.)

Breeders should also provide a contract or some written, signed conditions of sale. You should receive a copy of your puppy's pedigree, and you should be able to see a copy of the AKC registration application form. A respected breeder will also give you a reasonable period of time, usually 48 hours, to have your new puppy examined by a veterinarian to determine her state of health. Many dedicated breeders will ask that the puppy be returned to them or placed with new owners who meet their approval if for some reason you are ever unable to continue ownership.

What may seem to be a disadvantage of dealing with reputable private breeders is the cost of their puppies. However, as with many other things in life, you often get what you pay for. Before ever producing a litter, reputable breeders put a lot of money into their dogs through entry fees for shows to have their dogs evaluated by experts, pre-breeding health checks, and high-quality foods. Puppies from pet stores often cost as much as or more than those from breeders, but they don't have the breeder's high standards behind them.

There is a considerable range in what you can pay for a puppy through a private breeder. Prices vary depending on what part of the country you're in and the availability of the breed you want. In most cases, a Labrador or Golden Retriever—both highly popular breeds—will cost less than a Mastiff or a Bloodhound, breeds that are considerably less common. Consider several breeders and what each has to offer in terms of price and quality.

Keep in mind that the pick of the litter, if he's even available, is going to cost more than a perfectly nice puppy with a mismarking or light eye that disqualifies him as a show dog but doesn't affect his health or temperament in any way. Most breeders charge less for these "pet-quality" puppies, although others note that the same amount of time, effort, and money went into each puppy and charge the same price for all of them. If you buy a pet-quality puppy, be prepared for the breeder to require you to spay or neuter it, or to sell it with what is called a limited registration, which means that the puppy can be registered but any puppies it produces will not be eligible for registration.

The American Kennel Club can refer you to breeders in your area. Other ways to find breeders are through Internet searches, local veterinarians, specific clubs devoted to each breed, and from rescue league organizations. Please refer to Appendix 3 for important addresses and phone numbers of many such organizations.

> The American Kennel Club can refer you to breeders in your area. Other ways to find breeders are through Internet searches, local veterinarians, specific clubs devoted to each breed, and from rescue league organizations.

Buying from a Pet Shop

A second option is the multitude of pet shops. These include both local and franchise businesses. Keep your head firmly in control of your heart whenever you enter one of these business establishments. An impulse purchase of a sad-looking puppy is a common event. Despite the fact that these purebred puppies are

Interviewing a Breeder

1. Ask to see the dam and, if he's local, the sire.

2. Inquire about the litter's family history—medical and behavioral.

3. Ask to see the AKC pedigree, and ask the breeder to explain his goals for his breeding program.

4. Ask to see OFA or CERF certification if necessary.

5. Ask about the guarantee for their puppies (what it covers and its duration).

6. Ask about any vaccinations or other medical treatment that the puppies have already received.

7. Discuss what you are looking for (such as size or temperament) in that particular breed.

8. Ask what the breed's negatives are. A good breeder will tell you honestly about the downside of living with his breed.

often AKC registered, you do not have the luxury of observing the parents' size or gauging their temperament. (Remember, AKC and other registries do not guarantee quality.)

Additionally, you will not be able to know the living conditions in which the pup was raised or how the puppy was treated before arriving at the pet shop. Nor do you have access to critical knowledge of the puppy's family medical history. Commercially bred puppies are often sent to the pet shop at a very early age and miss out on critical interaction with their mother and littermates. If they aren't sold immediately, they languish in the pet store past the usual eight- to ten-week age range when most pups go to new homes. Therefore, they miss out on a lot of early socialization with people.

Puppies who are kept in a pet shop environment for extended periods are highly stressed and thus more prone to contracting contagious diseases such as kennel cough and ringworm. Most important to consider, these puppies tend to learn inappropriate elimination habits and can be difficult or impossible to retrain.

One Papillon never overcame her habit of urinating and defecating in her food bowls, a habit she picked up as a puppy when she was never removed from her cage to eliminate. Other pet-store puppies eliminate in their crates, just as they did in their cages, so this normally effective method of housetraining doesn't work as well with them.

> Most pet shops offer proof of vaccinations and some type of guarantee against serious birth defects.

Most pet shops offer proof of vaccinations and some type of guarantee against serious birth defects, but generally the prices they charge are exorbitant for the quality of puppies they provide. I never recommend that any of my clients purchase a puppy from a pet store. I have seen too many dogs with problems come from these establishments.

Before purchasing a puppy from a pet shop, investigate the store's reputation thoroughly. Contact your local Better Business Bureau (BBB) to inquire about any problems that may have been reported in the past about a particular pet shop. The BBB will be happy to help you with your investigation. It's also a good idea to ask the shop for references from other customers who have bought puppies from them. Obtaining business and personal references can help you decide whether this is where you want to buy your puppy and can help prevent the disappointment of a bad deal.

Adopting from an Animal Shelter

If you don't require a purebred and have an interest in saving a life, the local humane society or animal shelter is a great option.

Unfortunately, with the large animal overpopulation problem, these shelters are filled with many puppies and dogs of all ages, sizes, and varieties—even many purebreds. Most shelters charge an adoption fee. It may be minimal, covering only the costs of vaccination, or it may run as high as $100 and cover vaccinations, licensing, and sometimes early spay/neuter procedures. Each shelter has different fees and policies. If a puppy isn't already neutered, many shelters require sterilization either before he or she leaves for a new home or at least within a few weeks after adoption. This practice is a major step in the effort to reduce the many unwanted pets that are euthanized each year.

> If you don't require a purebred and have an interest in saving a life, the local humane society or animal shelter is a great option.

It's important to realize that puppies obtained from shelters have been in a stressful environment where a large number of dogs in a wide variety of health states are housed together. Some of the most common problems that can spread quickly throughout a shelter are upper respiratory infections such as kennel cough and parasites such as ear mites. Most of these health problems are easily cured once a puppy has left the shelter and receives appropriate medical treatment. Occasionally, a serious viral disease such as distemper or parvovirus may be contracted. Such serious diseases are usually the exception in shelters where the animals are carefully monitored.

By going to a shelter to seek out a new puppy, you can do a great deed by saving a puppy from euthanasia and by offering it a quality and happy home. In fact, some people truly believe these puppies make the best pets. In many instances, the puppies seem to realize how lucky they are and are eternally grateful to their new owners.

Whether or not you choose to acquire a puppy from your local shelter, these organizations have a difficult job and always welcome any support you can give them, either financially or by volunteering a few hours a week.

Adopting from a Breed Rescue Organization

A breed rescue group is another excellent place to look for a dog. You can usually find rescue information from a breed's national club. The national rescue coordinator can direct you to a rescue contact in your area.

Evaluate a dog from a rescue group the same way you would one from a breeder or shelter. If you're considering an adolescent or mature dog, ask ahead of time if you can take the dog for a walk through the neighborhood or at a nearby park. Note the dog's reaction to the approach of bikes, cars, or strollers, and to sudden sounds or movements. Ideally, he will be confident and relaxed, recovering quickly from a startling situation and proceeding with tail and ears up.

As you approach people, pay attention to the dog's response. Be wary of taking home a dog that shrinks away from people, tail between his legs, or tries frantically to climb up into your arms. This dog will require lots of socialization. Acceptable reactions range from indifference to caution to friendliness and curiosity.

Be sure to ask what type of situation the dog came from. If he was given up because he didn't get along with a family's children or other pets, you don't want to take him home to your children or other pets. Some dogs simply want to be the center of attention, and they do best with childless or older couples who can give them the time they need. On

Puppies Versus Older Dogs

There's nothing more fun than watching a puppy grow up, but there can also be nothing more frustrating. Puppies chew on expensive shoes, urinate or defecate on expensive rugs, and must be kept under constant surveillance to make sure they don't hurt themselves or destroy something you value. Puppies require a strict feeding and elimination schedule so they can be housetrained. Someone who's not home during the day would find it difficult to provide a puppy with the number of meals and outings she needs during the day.

On the other hand, puppy antics are pretty entertaining, and there's a lot of pleasure to be gained from bonding with a puppy. If you wouldn't miss that experience for the world—messes and all—then a puppy is the right choice for you.

Adolescent or adult dogs have advantages that puppies don't. They may already be housetrained or have some obedience training. Because they've already been through the destructive chewing stage, you are less likely to fear for your possessions. Sometimes, they're already spayed or neutered, which will save you money. Older dogs don't require as many meals during the day. An adult dog is more likely to be reliable in the house without the minute-by-minute supervision a puppy demands.

An adult dog requires fewer initial veterinary visits and vaccinations than does a puppy. Usually, by the time a dog reaches maturity, any health problems she may have are evident. Adopting an older dog allows you to select one you know is healthy, or at least to go into dog ownership knowing what health problems your pet faces rather than being surprised by them down the road. You also don't have to guess what size she's going to be.

It's not true that an older dog won't be able to bond to new people. Dogs are adaptable; if they weren't, they wouldn't have been so successful as a species. If you can set aside the fleeting joys of puppyhood for the greater pleasure of teasing out a relationship with a dog retired from breeding or the show ring, or whose first home didn't work out, then an adult dog is for you.

the other hand, if the dog was given up for behavior problems caused by lack of attention, that's something you can remedy with training and time.

Adopting from an animal shelter or breed rescue group is not as simple as going in and saying, "I'll take that one." Expect to be required to spay her or neuter him and to return the dog if she or he doesn't fit into your home. Oftentimes, you will be asked to fill out an extensive application form and go through an interview just as grueling as that given by the most careful of breeders, and for the same good reason: Shelter personnel and rescue groups want to make absolutely certain that the animals they place are going to appropriate homes where they'll be loved and cherished.

Finding your ideal puppy will take some research and looking around, but by doing this thoughtfully instead of impulsively, you are sure to make a rewarding decision. No matter what source you choose to purchase a puppy from, taking the puppy to the veterinarian for a thorough physical exam within the first few days is always important. The veterinarian will be happy to provide this service and can get the puppy started on the proper disease prevention programs.

How Do I Choose the Pick of the Litter?

Once the time comes to actually choose that perfect puppy, you'll need to make a powerful effort to listen to your head instead of your heart. All puppies are adorable and difficult to resist, but if you pay attention to the following criteria, you're sure to make a decision that results in acquiring a puppy that's a lifelong companion instead of a disappointing experience.

The Signs of Good Health

Obviously, a puppy must be the picture of good health. Look for a puppy that is bright, alert, and lively. Examine the puppy's eyes, ears, and nose to check that they are clean and free of any discharge and have no sign of odor or inflammation. A puppy's coat is an excellent indicator of her overall health. The coat should be soft and shiny, indicating good nutrition and a reduced likelihood that she has any intestinal parasites. Carefully inspect the puppy's coat for any evidence of flea, tick, or lice infestation. The body condition should appear well balanced. If she is thin over the rib cage with a large potbelly, problems probably exist. A potbellied puppy may have intestinal parasites. Inspect the puppy's anus for any evidence of worms. She should be extremely playful with the desire to be handled. Puppies that are shy or scared of contact usually don't grow out of it.

Temperament Tests

Everyone wants a puppy that will be easy to train and have a friendly personality with any person he encounters. So when you are examining a litter of puppies, you want to look for a puppy that is temperamentally well balanced, even at such an early age.

The puppy should approach people with no apprehension and want to be handled. Some puppies will hang back at first, studying you and evaluating the situation, but will eventually decide to check things out. The puppy who runs and hides may look cute, but his shyness is a drawback.

When the puppy is picked up, he may struggle at first but should soon relax and let you cradle him on his back without too much fuss. If a puppy allows you to hold him in your arms and on

his back, it's a good sign that he's secure and will likely not be one to challenge you later in life. A more dominant puppy won't give up the struggle to be free from the submissive position of being on his back. I always advise people to avoid puppies who, at an early age (eight to ten weeks), are overly shy or aggressive; both these behaviors usually only intensify with age and are often difficult to overcome later in life.

Open the puppy's mouth and handle his feet. He'll no doubt squirm a little, as puppies do, but should be reasonably willing to allow you these liberties with his body. It's a good sign that he's used to being handled by people. Again, the puppy who struggles excessively or even bites when you try to examine him is probably not a good choice, unless you are already an experienced dog owner who's willing to provide the extra structure, training, and discipline this pup will require.

> If a puppy allows you to hold him in your arms and on his back, it's a good sign that he's secure and will likely not be one to challenge you later in life.

No specific temperament tests can guarantee that a puppy will have a balanced temperament later in life, but the above exercises can help you avoid choosing a dog who's prone to certain behavior problems such as shyness or aggression. Rely on the breeder's advice as well. She has spent a lot of time with the puppies and knows their unique personalities, so she can be helpful in picking the puppy who has the traits you want.

Make an effort to look at several litters before making your final decision. By doing so, you'll get to know several members of the breed you're interested in and will be better able to compare temperaments, health, and looks. Then, you and your new puppy will be well on your way to the start of a wonderful human-animal bond.

I Just Have to Feed Him, Right?

Before the puppy arrives, decide who will be responsible for each duty such as feeding, cleaning, exercising, and, of course, the dreaded poop scooping. Involving children with each task is a wonderful way to teach them compassion and responsibility.

Setting Boundaries

Besides delegating daily responsibilities, an important issue to decide *before* the new puppy arrives is the boundaries she will have. For example, if you decide that she will not be allowed on the furniture, then you must enforce this from day one, along with all other established boundaries. This is important when teaching a puppy because, just as with a child, consistency is the key to avoiding confusion and enhancing learning.

Avoid giving your new puppy unsupervised access to the entire house. That's just asking for trouble. Always keep the puppy under your watchful eye. Block off areas of the house with baby gates or keep doors shut. Eventually, as a puppy matures, these boundaries can be removed, but do so gradually.

Another big decision is where the puppy will sleep. Some people don't mind allowing the puppy to sleep on the bed with them, while others would never think of it. Just as with the furniture issue, decide how you want to raise the puppy and stick to the rules. Most young puppies should learn to sleep in a confined area such as a dog crate to start off with, especially until they are completely housetrained. The use of dog crates is discussed further in Chapter 8, Family Life.

Boundaries are important outdoors as well. If your dog will be spending part of his day outside, he will need an appropriately sized fenced area to protect him from traffic and prevent him from roaming and getting lost. Make sure the fence is sturdy and high enough to contain a large breed if applicable. Another option to a fenced yard is an underground fencing system. The underground wires are placed wherever you desire and your dog wears a collar that provides a negative stimulus as he approaches the established boundaries. I have seen both great and poor results with such systems. Some dogs learn their boundaries quickly, while others don't seem to care about the jolt they receive and run right through the established boundaries. Since these systems can be quite expensive, it's a good idea to choose one from a dealer who offers quality installation and training, and a money-back guarantee.

When he's outdoors, your dog will also need a doghouse or other shelter that will protect him from the elements. He'll need shade in the summer and sturdy walls and a roof to keep out wind, rain, and snow. In the next chapter, you'll find more information about what to look for in a doghouse to keep your dog in the comfort and style he deserves.

All puppies should learn from an early age that the street is no place to play. Never trust your puppy or dog at any age to be near a busy street without being under the control of a leash. Far too many tragedies occur when owners trust that their puppies will stay close and not stray to the street. One can never know when a tempting cat or squirrel will catch a puppy's attention and make her forget her boundaries. Even the best trained puppies and dogs can become statistics. For more information on training your puppy, see Chapter 6, Basic Training.

If you want your puppy nearby but are too busy to hold on to a leash, one of the many different tie-outs may offer the best suggestion. They allow the puppy to have a fairly large area to play, but with security. Just be sure to never place a tie-out near steps or a hill where the puppy could get caught and hang itself. Most tie-outs can be easily moved from one area to another.

Remember, consistency is crucial to teaching your puppy his boundaries, so make them clear and easy for your puppy to understand. This will allow you to enjoy playing with your puppy without seriously restricting his freedom.

It is not unusual for one person to take the primary responsibility of seeing to it that all of the puppy's needs are met. The puppy will usually bond more closely and respond better to that person than to the other family members. Dogs are intelligent and will always know who consistently takes care of their needs, especially feeding. This is not meant to imply that the rest of the household should be left out of caring for and training the puppy. An entire family can share in the experience and thereby gain a loyal companion. Some families rotate the daily doggy duties so that no one person is always responsible for taking care of the puppy. By doing this, the family truly creates a "family

dog." Even through some of the less pleasant duties, everyone gets to bond to the puppy and take responsibility for providing only the best care.

The Ten Commandments of Responsible and Joyful Dog Ownership

Every puppy deserves to be raised in a healthy and loving environment. Puppies are totally dependent on their owners for all of life's necessities, including proper food, complete medical care, and lots of love and attention. Under the care of a capable and loving owner, all of a dog's needs are met throughout her life so she can be happy and disease-free. It is the owner who ultimately decides the extent of care a puppy receives. When little or no value is placed on the quality of a puppy's life, she is often sentenced to a life of neglect and disease. The best way to show your puppy you care is to abide by the following commandments:

1. Take your puppy to the veterinarian for a complete set of puppy vaccinations, fecal exams, and physical exams. Continue to bring the dog to the veterinarian every year for annual vaccinations and a physical exam as a part of essential preventive medicine.
2. Spay or neuter your dog. (Learn about the many benefits in Chapter 4, Medical Care Every Dog Needs.)
3. Provide proper nutrition for your dog as a puppy and then as an adult. Consult your veterinarian about which food is best for your dog's life stage. Never feed table scraps or natural bones to your puppy or dog.
4. Always provide fresh water that is changed daily.

5. Equip your dog's collar with both a rabies tag and an identification tag. Dogs may now even be provided with a permanent identification microchip injected between the shoulder blades by a veterinarian.

6. Exercise your dog every day. Just think, both of you will reap the benefits of regular exercise.

7. Start obedience training early. Be consistent with all rules and commands so you don't confuse your puppy. Remember, a well-behaved dog is a joy to live with instead of a nuisance.

8. Provide your dog with a fenced area in which to play and exercise for its utmost safety.

9. Spend quality time every day with your dog. At the same time, examine the dog for any evidence of problems or illness.

10. Keep your dog out of harm's way by never allowing access to dangerous chemicals such as antifreeze and toilet bowl cleaner. These can permanently damage or even kill your dog.

Lots of responsibilities go along with dog ownership, but most involve simple common sense in helping a puppy to attain a fit and content life. Providing loving care is a joy and not a burden for the dedicated owner.

> ### Did You Know?
>
> The word for "dog" in the Australian aboriginal language Mbabaran happens to be "dog."

Dog Ownership—A Lifetime of Fun, Happiness, and Good Times

The depth of the human-dog bond is magical. Today, dogs play many roles: companion, hunter, rescuer, worker, and aide for people with disabilities. We love dogs because of their boundless loyalty and unconditional love. Between humans and dogs there is a unique bond, with both sides benefiting physically and emotionally. What a great deal!

It's hard for me to imagine going through life without a dog. A child without a dog is missing out on a great experience, and the same could be said about most adults. The human-dog bond is an emotional relationship that is a win-win situation. Just think about how many dogs have evolved into being integral family members. And it's amazing how accurately and immediately dogs are able to sense the moods of their owners. If you've had a bad day at work, your dog will sense it and offer silent comfort. When you are excited, happy or fearful, he'll know, and respond accordingly. Your mood will become your dog's mood. The good news is that even when you are down or in a terrible mood, your dog will continue to give you unconditional love. Often the happiness of your dog can overwhelm the bad feelings that you are experiencing. What great emotional therapy it is to be greeted every day by a happy, loving dog.

> Bringing a dog into your home is a long-term commitment, but the rewards for you and your dog are immeasurable.

Gone are the days when our dogs lived their entire existence in the backyard. Most dog owners will tell you that when they first brought their dog home, the thought of having the dog in bed with them was not even a consideration, but after watching the dog grow and experiencing his unfailing love, they soon changed their minds. The next thing they knew, the dog was waking up with them in the morning and going with them on errands, usually in the front seat of their sometimes very expensive automobiles, safely secured in their specially designed carseats or seatbelts. The majority of dog owners would not have their faithful companions anywhere but by their side. Bringing a dog into your home is a long-term commitment, but the rewards for you and your dog are immeasurable.

2

Welcome Home!

In This Chapter

○ Preparing for Your Dog's Arrival
○ Which Supplies Do You Really Need?
○ The First Night with Your Puppy
○ Making an Older Dog Feel Welcome

The big day is almost here. In just a week or two, your new dog will be arriving to spend the next ten or so years with you. Starting off on the right paw will help ensure that the coming years are happy ones. Before the pup arrives, your family needs to sit down and discuss how the new dog will fit in, and who will be responsible for such things as meals, grooming, play time, and poop patrol. You

> Starting off on the right paw will help ensure that the coming years are happy ones. Before the pup arrives, your family needs to sit down and discuss how the new dog will fit in, and who will be responsible for the dog-related chores.

also need to prepare a puppy layette—which is just as important for older dogs—so your dog will feel right at home.

Preparing for Your Dog's Arrival

Whether you are adopting a puppy or an older dog, try to bring your new pet home over a long weekend or during a vacation when you and your family will have several days to spend establishing a routine schedule. Just as with newborns, life with dogs usually goes more smoothly when they have a set schedule for everything from eating to sleeping to playing. Dogs of all ages learn from repetition, and abiding by a schedule reinforces their early lessons in housetraining as well as the proper times for meals, play, and sleep. At least take a weekend to welcome your dog into his new home. You won't be able to potty-train a puppy in these first few days, but you can definitely start things off right from the start. An older dog may already be housetrained, but he'll still need to learn the household routine, and if he's feeling insecure he may have a few accidents, so be patient and put him on the same housetraining schedule you would a puppy. Dogs need a very structured, consistent environment—especially in a new situation. They like to know what the rules are and where they stand in the order of the household.

> **D**ogs of all ages learn from repetition, and abiding by a schedule reinforces their early lessons in housetraining as well as the proper times for meals, play, and sleep.

Bringing Your Puppy Home

By the time puppies are eight to twelve weeks old, they have learned the basics about doghood from their mother and littermates. They're weaned off mother's milk and are chowing down on solid food. They've survived the microbes that can cause illness and death in young puppies, and their immune systems have been boosted with the first in a series of vaccinations. A puppy this age is ready to take on the stressful yet exciting task of learning to be a companion to his new people. His brain is at its peak learning stage, and he's capable of soaking up new sights, sounds, and experiences and internalizing them. Most medium to giant breeds go to their adoptive families at eight weeks of age, while toy breeds are often kept by their breeders until 10 or 12 weeks of age, to ensure that they're strong enough to face the stresses of a new home.

Puppies can be adopted as early as seven weeks of age with no detrimental effects, but the more time they spend with their mother and littermates, the better adjusted they are. Puppies taken from their mother before seven weeks often develop behavioral problems—usually aggression toward or fear of other dogs—that are difficult to overcome. A puppy needs his mom to teach him how to be a dog and learn how to handle situations as well as how to interact with people and other dogs.

It is important for both the puppy and your family to establish the rules of the household from day one. As already discussed in chapter 1, everyone must agree to the puppy's boundaries and enforce them from the beginning. While a puppy's antics may be cute in the beginning, they won't be so funny when he weighs 70 pounds and is destructive or ill-mannered.

Dog-Proofing Your House and Yard

Before you bring your new dog home, take a look at your house and yard from a curious animal's point of view. The few minutes it takes to secure wires, breakables, and other dangers will help prevent the mishaps that an inquisitive dog can get himself into. While it's likely that an older dog is past the destructive chewing stage, never assume anything until you get to know him.

To make sure you don't miss anything, get down on your hands and knees and go throughout the entire house, poking your nose in every place that might hold interest for a pup. Among the hazards to watch out for are small objects that could be swallowed or cause choking, cleansers, medications, electrical cords, and even some common household or outdoor plants.

> It is important for both the puppy and your family to establish the rules of the household from day one.

Dogs don't have hands to examine things, so when they find something new, they pick it up in their mouth to see how it tastes and feels and whether it might be good to eat. Dogs have been known to swallow needles and razor blades. An American Eskimo puppy named Rebel snacked on a glass Christmas ornament. He survived, and now his owner, Betsy, doesn't leave anything the slightest bit dangerous within his curious reach. It's a good idea to secure cupboards with child locks before you bring your new dog home, and place obvious dangers such as poisons and small or sharp objects far out of reach.

Household Hazards

Cleaning products, especially those such as toilet bowl cleaners, can burn a dog's esophagus and stomach or at least make him very ill. Lots of dogs like to drink out of the toilet, so if you use drop-in toilet bowl cleaners that provide continuous release of a cleaning agent, be sure to keep toilet lids down at all times.

Common Hazards

- ○ Cleaning products
- ○ Antifreeze
- ○ Cigarettes and cigarette butts
- ○ Batteries
- ○ Electrical cords
- ○ Alcohol
- ○ Plants

- ○ Insecticides
- ○ Rodenticides
- ○ Fertilizers
- ○ Human medications (prescription and non-prescription)
- ○ Pins and needles
- ○ Chocolate

One serious hazard for dogs that people often overlook is alcohol. Besides alcoholic beverages, alcohol is also found in significant concentrations in mouthwash, perfumes, and some cooking extracts such as vanilla. Just as in people, alcohol acts as a depressant on a dog's central nervous system; but even a small quantity of alcohol can be enough to prove fatal to a puppy. Don't try to get your dog "tipsy" by offering him alcohol, and don't let your friends do it "to see what will happen." The results are likely to be serious and possibly deadly. Be sure that all products containing alcohol are stored safely out of a curious puppy's reach, bottle caps are secured tightly, and alcoholic drinks aren't left where your dog can sample them.

Medications for you and your family can be dangerous to your puppy. Just because a medication is safe for people doesn't mean it's safe for your puppy. And remember that childproof bottles are usually not chew-proof. Some human medications, such as aspirin or Kaopectate, can be given to dogs; but because a dog's body processes drugs differently than the human body, you should always ask your veterinarian first whether the medication is okay to give your dog, as well as what the proper dosage would be.

If you or another family member smoke or have frequent visitors who do, remember to keep cigarette packages and butts out of a puppy's reach. Puppies can suffer from nicotine poisoning if they ingest tobacco in any form, including smokeless tobacco products.

If you sew, keep your needles and thread safely stored. These items can cause serious problems with the digestive tract if swallowed. If your dog ever ingests any of these, take him to your veterinarian immediately.

Houseplants, both indoor and outdoor, are often a particular favorite of puppies who like to chew. Some plants are highly toxic and can be fatal, while others cause less serious side effects. Refer to the sidebar on page 50 for a list of the most common toxic plants found around the house. If you have doubts about whether one of your plants is toxic, give your veterinarian a call for more information.

One common household fixture that can prove dangerous to dogs is the electrical cord. Cords need to be covered with foil or coiled and secured with twist ties so the dog can't chew on them, which could prove a shocking experience, indeed, and could even result in serious burns to the mouth or death by electrocution. This can be especially challenging around the holidays or in rooms containing a lot of electronics, such as computers, stereo systems, VCRs, and televisions.

The flickering light of fire is intriguing to dogs as well. Maybe the flame elicits ancestral memories of creeping round human campfires to snatch a bit of dropped meat. Or maybe fire is just plain interesting to look at. In any case, to keep little Ginger's whiskers from getting singed, place candles up high where they can't be reached or knocked over, and place screens in front of your fireplaces.

Puppy-Proofing Advice

Bringing home a puppy is a life-changing experience in more ways than one. If you've never experienced firsthand the depredations of either a toddler or a puppy, Peggy Sue, a breeder of Cavalier King Charles Spaniels, recommends you get a little practice before puppy comes home. Her tongue-in-cheek advice holds more than a grain of truth. Ask some accommodating friends or relatives to bring over their young children for a day. Follow them around, and put anything in which they show interest well out of their reach. Follow this by inviting a bunch of junior-high-age boys over. Anything that doesn't survive this group wouldn't survive a puppy either. You are now probably ready to bring in your puppy. Be sure to spend the next two weeks following him around to pick up anything the kids missed.

Yard Hazards

Most lawn-proud homeowners have a stash of useful but hazardous products, such as fertilizers and insecticides. Besides keeping them well out of reach, always follow the instructions on each label concerning proper use and prevention of toxic exposure to animals. Most labels recommend some time frame during which both people and animals should avoid direct contact with a treated area.

Among the most deadly products used in and around homes are rodenticides. It often takes a smaller amount of these products to kill a puppy or dog than it would take to kill a mouse or rat. If there is any possibility that your puppy or dog has consumed any amount of rodenticide, take him to the veterinarian or emergency hospital immediately.

Garbage is perhaps the most tempting hazard a dog faces. Spoiled food can give your pup a bad case of food poisoning; and bones, corn cobs, or fruit pits can cause intestinal blockage. Be sure garbage cans are securely covered. This is especially important if your dog is a member of the chowhound group:

Common Poisonous Plants

This list contains some, but not all, of the common plants that can harm your dog. Consult a plant book or a nursery if you have any doubts about a plant in your home or yard.

Alfalfa

Amaryllis

Asparagus (Sperengeri) fern

Azalea

Beach tree

Belladonna

Bird of paradise

Black locust tree

Caladium

Castor bean

Chinaberry

Coriaria

Crown of thorns

Daffodil

Daphne

Datura

Dieffenbachia

Elephant's ear

Euonymus

Foxglove

Henbane

Honeysuckle

Hydrangea

Iris

Ivy (especially English, heart, needlepoint, and ripple)

Jack-in-the-pulpit

Jerusalem cherry

Jessamine

Jimsonweed

Larkspur

Lily-of-the-valley

Mistletoe berries

Monkshood

Moonseed

Morning glory

Mums (spider and pot)

Nightshades

Oak trees (acorns)

Oleander

Periwinkle

Philodendron

Plant bulbs (most)

Potato (green parts and eyes)

Poinsettia

Precatory bean (rosary pea)

Rhododendron

Rhubarb (leaves, upper stem)

Skunk cabbage

Tobacco

Tomato vines

Tulip

Umbrella plant

Water hemlock

Wisteria

Yew tree (Japanese, English, Western, American)

Beagles, Bassets, Bloodhounds, and Greyhounds. Many other breeds qualify as chowhounds as well.

Just as you did in the house, go along your fences at dog level to ensure that they are free of any sharp objects, such as nails or protruding wire. Barbed wire is not recommended as fencing for dogs. Patch up any holes that a dog could wriggle through or dig under, and remove any sticks or other objects that could cause injury.

The Garage

This is an area where many hazardous products are often haphazardly stored, just waiting for a nosy dog to seek them out. Problem products include paints, sealants, strippers, and antifreeze. Unsealed antifreeze containers and areas where it has collected due to a spill or leak are often the sources of deadly poisoning incidents. If you replace your own antifreeze, be sure to thoroughly wash away any that spills onto your driveway or other surfaces for your dog's and other animals' protection. Antifreeze has a sweet smell and taste, but only a few drops can be deadly. Even "environmentally safe" antifreezes are toxic when ingested, so ensure safe handling and storage of all such products.

You can't be too careful when it comes to providing your dog with a safe environment. Be alert to dangers and double-check inside and outside your home for any perils before your dog arrives.

Did You Know?

According to the American Animal Hospital Association, over half of all dog and cat owners give their pets human names.

Which Supplies Do You Really Need?

Most of a dog's needs can be taken care of by a few basic essentials: food and water bowls, collar, leash, bed/doghouse, crate, toys, and proper grooming supplies. If you buy high-quality equipment from the beginning, you'll be more likely to avoid the cost of frequently replacing items.

Feeding Dishes

There are probably as many choices of bowls as there are foods, from basic stainless steel to colorful ceramics and plastics. Each has advantages and disadvantages.

Stainless-steel bowls are dishwasher-safe, easily disinfected, and can withstand chewing during the puppy phase. They're often lightweight, though, and a rambunctious puppy will play hockey with them, spilling food and water. So, you may want to look for a non-tip or heavy-weight model. If you have a large dog or a puppy who will grow large, it's a good idea to choose elevated stainless-steel dishes that come in an adjustable stand.

Ceramic bowls are another popular choice. They are dishwasher-safe, come in a variety of colors and designs, and are heavy enough to withstand most puppy play, although they are breakable. Make sure they are made in the USA. Some foreign-made ceramics contain high levels of lead and should not be used for food or water.

Plastic dishes are lightweight, inexpensive, and easy to clean, but over time, they can discolor a dog's nose, changing a black nose to light pink, for instance. Some dogs may be allergic to a component in the plastic bowls that causes this unattractive cosmetic alteration. In most such cases, the normal color returns shortly after the dog is switched to a stainless-steel or ceramic bowl. Plastic can also retain odors, which may be unpleasant for you and the dog unless they're washed frequently and thoroughly.

Another consideration is the design of the bowl. Manufacturers have designed a large number of no-tip bowls, elevated bowls for large breeds and bowls for dogs with long ears. For instance, a good choice for Spaniels, Beagles, or other long-eared breeds is a ceramic or stainless-steel bowl that's just wide enough for the dog's muzzle to fit inside, so the ears hang outside the dish and don't drag through the food. You may also want to consider self-feeders/waterers or automated feeding dishes. These are useful if you work irregular hours and don't want your dog to miss a meal, or if you have a dog with a medical condition, such as diabetes, that requires him to have access to food at regularly scheduled times.

Some of these feeders hold a large amount of food or water that automatically falls into the bowl as the dog empties it, allowing free feeding. This is not a good choice for a dog who will eat even after his hunger is satiated. A better choice in such a case is a feeder that holds a specific amount of food and operates on a timer that opens the dish at a set time. Timed feeding dishes suitable for small dogs are available at most pet supply stores, but those for larger dogs are usually available only by mail order or from online pet supply stores such as coolpetstuff.com or pet-expo.com.

Collars and Leashes

A good collar and leash, plus an identification tag with your name and phone number, are essential tools in your dog's safety and basic training. Your puppy will probably have a wardrobe of collars, from a buckle collar for everyday wear to a chain or nylon training collar to a harness for car travel. Never leave a training, or choke, collar on an unattended

Did You Know?

The smallest dog ever documented was a Yorkshire Terrier measuring 2.5 inches tall by 3.75 inches long fully grown and weighing only 4 ounces.

puppy or dog. These types of collars can easily get caught on something and kill the dog by hanging or choking it.

As a puppy grows, so does her neck size. Be sure to choose a collar that fits comfortably around her neck and allows at least two fingers to be placed easily between the collar and the puppy's neck. Check the comfort of the collar on a weekly basis as the puppy grows to adult size. Most collars are adjustable; but depending on the dog's size, you may need to purchase one or two new collars as the puppy matures. When you first place a collar on the puppy, you can expect some squirming and scratching at the collar until the puppy gets used to wearing it.

Harnesses and halter-type devices are also popular. A harness can be a practical alternative to a collar for small dogs who are sensitive to being corrected or whose necks are too fragile for correction with a collar. Harnesses encourage pulling, so they are best used on small dogs that are easily controlled. A powerful working dog or a Nordic breed that's bred to pull is better off with a regular collar or a head halter.

Halters for dogs are quite similar to those used on horses. Several types are available, but all work on the principle of having more control over the dog's head while walking. The idea is that if you have control of your dog's head you will have control of its entire body. The halter isn't a muzzle, and the dog can still bark or take a drink while it's on. I use one on my Labrador and find it extremely practical and helpful. In fact, I find it a lot more humane than any choke collar, and it actually works better with my dog.

Choosing the perfect collar, harness, or halter device may take some trial and error, and every dog trainer has an opinion on this issue. Go with what works best for your particular dog's size and temperament.

Leash options are numerous as well, and are usually a matter of personal preference. Choose a leash that is the most comfort-

How much is all this going to cost me?

The basic supplies for your new dog can come with a hefty price tag depending on size and quality, and often it's a price you'll be paying more than once. Remember to factor in these costs when making the decision to get a dog. Prices likely will vary depending on where you live, but the following should give you a good idea of what to expect.

Item	Low Price	High Price
Crate	20.00	200.00
Food and Water Bowls	3.00	60.00
Collar	4.00	40.00
Leash	4.00	50.00
ID Tag	3.00	15.00
Pet Stain/Odor Remover	4.00	10.00
Brush	4.00	20.00
Toys	1.00	40.00
Food (8 lb. bag)	4.00	9.00
Bed	10.00	200.00
TOTAL	57.00	644.00

able for you and easiest to use with your dog. The shorter the leash, the more control you have with your puppy or dog. Usually a six-foot leash is appropriate for training class. If you will be walking your dog through highly trafficked areas and need to keep close control, buy a four-foot leash. When your pup has learned basic manners and is ready for more freedom, you may wish to purchase an extendable leash that will allow him to roam 12 to 16 feet ahead of you yet be reeled in quickly as needed.

Leather leashes are lightweight, durable, and classic in appearance, but some dogs enjoy chewing on them. Nylon leashes are also lightweight and durable, and they come in many colors and patterns. With nylon, you can have a whole matching ensemble of collar, leash, and car harness. Chain leashes tend to be heavy and noisy.

Bedding and Shelter

Every puppy deserves and truly appreciates having a place of his own to rest. Your dog can sleep in a wire or plastic crate lined with a mat or blanket, or you can purchase any of a variety of dog beds in a range of fabrics, shapes, and sizes. Most dog beds are equipped with washable covers to help keep odor down. While puppies are young and going through the chewing stage, the dog bed may suffer some abuse, so it might be a good idea to purchase a relatively inexpensive bed to start off with and switch to one of the finer and more expensive choices once the puppy matures.

Dogs need shelter outdoors as well. Doghouses have come a long way in design and durability since the era of the homemade wooden doghouse. These prefabricated doghouses are made of insulated, smooth, and nonporous plastics that are easy to clean

and help to prevent flea and tick infestation. Most doghouses are equipped with a ventilation system and can be used in both warm and cold weather. Some doghouses come with optional flaps to keep out wind, rain, and snow. The perfect doghouse is not too big and not too small. Your dog should be able to stand up and turn around inside it. Anything larger won't hold in heat, and anything smaller will be uncomfort-

Benefits of Crating

Jayne learned the hard way about the benefits of a crate. "My first Lab, Tess, came to live with us about 17 years ago. Tess was a lovely, outgoing, and happy little ten-week-old yellow Lab girl. I picked her up from her breeder on a Friday afternoon so I could spend the entire weekend with her before having to leave her alone when I went to work on Monday. The weekend was filled with the usual new puppy routines of running outside to potty and playing and admiring her. At the time, I was naive and thought crates were cruel, so when I went to work Monday, I left Tess in my kitchen with the entry gated off. I thought she would be safe and secure, but she was a lot more clever than I gave her credit for. When I returned home that evening, Tess was sitting happily in the family room admiring her accomplishments. She had apparently jumped the gate, and during her eventful day knocked over three huge potted plants, spread the dirt from one end of the room to the other, chewed all the leaves off the plants (fortunately, all were nontoxic), dragged the remains through the dirt, and pooped and peed in the dirt a few times. To top it all off, she dragged a white afghan my great aunt had made through the whole mess. After spending hours cleaning up this mess (the carpet was destroyed and had to be replaced), I went straight to the pet supply store and bought the one truly indispensable item a pet owner needs: a crate. I have never since had a dog without a crate."

able. Place the doghouse in the shade or in an area that provides some protection from weather extremes. For your dog's optimum comfort, provide some type of bedding such as a blanket, hay, or cedar chips, and change it regularly. Be sure to clean the doghouse as often as needed.

Crates are Great!

One piece of equipment that I consider a necessity is the dog crate, especially for indoor puppies. A crate is invaluable in housetraining, and it's a great way to keep your puppy—and your possessions—safe when you're not around to supervise his activities. Far from being cruel, a crate represents a safe and secure den to a puppy, a place where he can go to take a nap, eat dinner, or just relax away from a busy or noisy household. Specifics of crate training and its use are discussed in detail in Chapter 6, Basic Training.

The Joy of Toys

Toys, especially chew toys, are an important part of every puppy's life. They're a great way for you to interact with your puppy, and chew toys serve a practical purpose by helping your puppy get through the painful teething stage and preventing him from choosing other objects, such as furniture, to chew on. Hard rubber or rawhide chews satisfy a puppy's desire to chew, relieve boredom, and are good for the teeth.

Always purchase rawhide and similar chews that are made in the United States, since some imported chews contain dangerous preservatives. Puppies also enjoy playing with balls, stuffed items, and squeaky toys. Most veterinarians and trainers discourage tug-of-war toys. Such toys can teach a puppy unwanted aggressive behavior by encouraging him to challenge you, his owner. Whatever you choose, make sure toys are too large to be swallowed, and don't give any play-

things that have buttons, bows, or bells that could be chewed off and swallowed. While it might seem like a good idea to toss a pup your old shoes or socks to play with, a puppy isn't able to distinguish his "toy" from your brand new shoes, which look and taste the same.

Toy Safety

Amber's puppy HipHop loved playing with Beanie Babies. Amber spoiled him, and bought him a new one every week. One day, when Amber wasn't home, HipHop tore open one of his Beanies and ate the pellets inside it. They wouldn't pass through his system, and at first the veterinarian was afraid the pup was going to require surgery at a cost of $300. Fortunately, HipHop was able to pass the pellets before surgery became necessary. Now Amber avoids stuffed toys that her dog can destroy.

Grooming Supplies

The grooming supplies you need will depend on the type of coat your dog has. But whether he's a furry wonder or of sleek physique, you'll need to brush him daily. Brushing him encourages replenishment of his skin's natural oils and helps keep his coat shiny and healthy. If your puppy requires professional grooming, ask the groomer what you can do at home for daily maintenance.

Because canine skin has a different pH level than human skin, your bottle of Prell or Suave is too harsh for your dog's needs. Bathing should always be done with a shampoo formulated for dogs. On that same note, use ear cleaners designed for the sensitive ear canal of dogs, rather than such products as alcohol or hydrogen peroxide.

Keeping your puppy's nails trimmed is an essential part of proper grooming for all breeds. Your veterinarian or groomer will be happy to show you how close to cut the nails and can recommend a good nail clipper that you can use at home.

Additional details on grooming and grooming aids will be covered in Chapter 7.

A Special Note About Children

When Christopher's parents brought him home from the hospital, Rebel was very curious. Mike and Betsy set Christopher on the floor so Rebel could sniff him and see that he was part of the family. Rebel slept by Christopher's crib, and barked to alert Betsy if he started to cry. When Christopher entered toddlerhood, he and Rebel became best buddies, "skiing" together across the floor and "sharing" meals, with Christopher dropping cookies and vegetables from his high chair to Rebel who waited below.

Children raised with pets as part of the family develop a deep and lasting regard and compassion for animals and people, but that sensitivity isn't innate; it must be nurtured. If children are going to be a part of the puppy's life, they must first learn to respect the puppy as a delicate living being that can be harmed if not handled properly. When that notion is instilled in the child, then a puppy can become a best friend who is there no matter what is going on in the child's life. Children benefit emotionally from having another living being dependent on them. A puppy offers a child acceptance and at the same time teaches responsibility and affection.

To ensure that this lifelong relationship gets off to a good start, begin by teaching small and young children how to gently

pet a puppy. Explain that it's not acceptable to pull on the puppy's ears or tail. Express it in terms the child will understand, by asking "Would you like it if I pulled your hair or ears?"

Only older children should be allowed to pick up and hold a puppy. Younger children should only be permitted to handle the dog while they're sitting on the floor. Demonstrate how to properly hold a puppy by placing one arm under the chest and the other arm supporting the back legs while keeping the puppy close to the body. No child—or adult—should ever be allowed to pick up or carry a puppy around by the ears or the scruff of the neck, since this is painful and risks causing serious neck and/or neurological problems for the puppy.

While puppies and kids are great playmates, all their interactions should be supervised until the child is of an age to treat the dog carefully and with respect, usually at six years of age or older. Nor are dogs appropriate babysitters. No matter how loving and careful they are, dogs should never be left alone with very young children. Dogs only know how to discipline puppies, not toddlers, and they can seriously injure or even kill a child without meaning any harm at all.

Finally, teach your kids to always wash their hands after handling the puppy to prevent transferring harmful parasites and unwanted germs.

The First Night with Your Puppy

Your puppy's first few days with you will be exciting and scary for him. He may be shy at first, even if he was outgoing at the breeder's home. That's only natural. He was comfortable there, and it may take him a few days to adjust to you and your home. Before you leave, ask the breeder for advice on making a smooth transition. He or she will probably have some good sug-

Things will go more easily if you've bought all your supplies beforehand. That way you don't have to run out at the last minute to get food or some other necessary item.

What's In a Name?

At times the behavior of the new puppy will help in selecting a name that really fits his habits and personality. Once we were given a cute little Dachshund puppy by a good friend. Not just for the first few nights, but for his entire life, this puppy would sing and sing, especially at night. His howl was so musical that the whole family agreed that his name must be Caruso. Rather than be bothered by his propensity to "sing," we came to enjoy this trait and his song. We still enjoy his memory. (Caruso taught us the importance of puppy-proofing as well. In addition to his vocal talents, he loved to chew. One night he chewed a large hole right through a flat sheet-rock wall.)

gestions, such as using a blanket that's the same size or texture as the one the pup is used to sleeping on or using similar food dishes.

Things will go more easily if you've bought all your supplies beforehand. That way you don't have to run out at the last minute to get food or some other necessary item.

When you get home, let the puppy potty before you take him inside so he'll be less inclined to have an accident. For now, keep him confined to one room, such as the living room or den, where everyone is most likely to be. There's plenty of time for exploration later. Let the puppy get to know everyone, but don't overwhelm him with a lot of people. Your friends, relatives, and neighbors should meet him a few at a time, not all at once. Show him where his crate is, lined with familiar bedding. He may be so exhausted from the trip or the excitement that he'll crawl right in for a nap. That's a good sign. Let him rest undisturbed. You don't want him to sleep too much during the day, though. Make sure he gets plenty of playtime in the evening so that he'll be tired and more likely to sleep through the night.

The first night away from his mother and littermates can be traumatic for a puppy. When you first brought him home, he was excited and playful and probably too busy to realize that his mom and littermates were missing. Unfortunately, this becomes all too apparent when bedtime comes around and he doesn't have his littermates to cuddle up to as he has for the past eight weeks.

More than likely, your new puppy will whine and cry out of loneliness. You can help him feel more at home by placing his crate by your bed so he can hear and smell you during the night. That comforting scent will help lull him to sleep. Your puppy may be anxious or restless those first few nights, but if you're patient and prepared to put up with some inconvenience, he'll soon adjust.

Although you'll want to comfort him, it's not a good idea to let him sleep in the bed with you or the kids, especially if that's not something you would permit an adult dog to do. Young puppies aren't even close to being housetrained, and accidents are bound to happen. The crate gives the pup a feeling of security and allows him to remain close to you while still being confined so he can't roam the house and have potty accidents. See more details on crate training in chapter 6, Basic Training.

To help the puppy feel more secure when you're not around, leave something nearby that will provide constant sound, such as a radio on low volume tuned to a soothing classical station or a clock with a loud tick.

Did You Know?

Researchers are almost positive that dogs dream. If you look at a sleeping dog, sometimes you'll notice its eyes move beneath its eyelid. Because this is what humans do when they dream, researchers believe it is an indication of dreams in dogs, too. No word yet on what they dream about.

Making an Older Dog Feel Welcome

The move to a new home is stressful for a dog of any age, but most dogs adjust well given a little time. Knowing as much as possible about the dog's previous home will help.

You can help an older dog feel at home using methods similar to what you would do for a puppy. If you know his background, try to make the dog's new environment as much like his previous one as possible regarding bedding, food, and type of dishes used. Make changes slowly whenever you can. Just as with a puppy, don't overwhelm a dog by introducing a lot of new people all at once. Instead, give him plenty of opportunities to do what he enjoys, such as going for a walk or playing fetch. This will help him relax.

Your new dog is probably already familiar with family life, so the best thing you can do for him is to provide some structure and consistency. Take him outside to eliminate on a schedule similar to the one you'll be following during the workweek. This will also help you gauge his "holding capacity." You may need to arrange for more frequent outings depending on his needs. Going for a walk is a good way for for all of you to get to know each other. Feed him in a quiet area away from household hustle and bustle, and show him where his sleeping quarters are. Just like a puppy, he'll be comfortable in a crate or you can provide him with some other type of bed. Sleeping in a crate next to your bed will give the dog a feeling of security and help him feel at home

Remember to take a lot of pictures from day one so you can look back through the years for happy, lifelong memories. I still

> Remember to take a lot of pictures from day one so you can look back through the years for happy, lifelong memories.

enjoy looking back through pictures of my past and current dogs. It is hard to imagine that my Lab was ever really that small! For sure, bringing home a new puppy is definitely a time of great fun and excitement. Congratulations! You are off to a great start with your new dog.

Did You Know?

The average cost per year for owning and maintaining a dog in the United States is $1,220.00.

3

Food for Thought

In This Chapter

❍ Why Good Nutrition Matters
❍ Choosing the Best Food for Your Dog
❍ How Often and How Much Do I Feed My Dog?
❍ What's All The Fuss About Supplements?

What your dog eats is every bit as important as how much he eats. A high-quality diet can positively affect his appearance, energy level, resistance to disease, and overall well being.

Why Good Nutrition Matters

Proper nutrition is the foundation from which all good health stems, therefore it's among the most important needs of every dog throughout each stage of life. The correct food choice greatly contributes to maximizing the health, performance, and longevity of your dog. Many veterinarians regard wholesome diets as an essential part of preventive medicine, along with vaccinations and annual physical examinations.

A good diet is one that provides the essentials: water, fats, proteins, carbohydrates, minerals, and vitamins. These nutrients work in combination to keep the body functioning at peak levels. When a dog's level of nutrients is low—because of a poor diet, for instance—her body functions less efficiently. Hair becomes dull or falls out, teeth become loose, eyes lose their shine, and the skin loses its elasticity. It's easy to tell at a glance when a dog is or isn't eating correctly.

> What your dog eats is every bit as important as how much he eats. A high-quality diet can positively affect his appearance, energy level, resistance to disease, and overall well being.

Each nutrient plays a specific role in the body's maintenance and function. Protein contains amino acids, which the body needs for tissue growth and repair. The body itself produces some amino acids, but others—the ten "essential" amino acids—must be obtained from food. Meat, eggs, and dairy products are high in protein and contain all the essential amino acids. Grains and vegetables also contain protein but are lacking in some of the amino acids. They are known as incomplete proteins. Both animal and non-animal sources of protein are important to a dog's well-being.

Carbohydrates provide the energy your puppy uses to pounce on a toy, run barking to the door when a delivery is made, and jump up to greet you. Quick energy comes from simple sugars such as glucose, while starches and complex sugars give more long-lasting energy. Corn, rice, wheat, and oats are common sources of carbohydrates, and they also add fiber to the diet, which is helpful for smooth-functioning intestines.

Animal or Vegetable?

We often think of dogs as carnivores, the big-time meat eaters of the animal world; but strictly speaking they are omnivores, which means they can make a meal from both animal and plant sources. Wild dogs such as wolves and coyotes enjoy all parts of their prey, including the stomach with its grassy contents. Our dogs don't dine that close to the food chain anymore, but now you understand why the labels on their bags of food include grains such as corn, wheat, and rice.

Fat is also a source of energy, but it has other purposes as well. Fat cushions the internal organs and helps the body conserve heat, move nutrients, and send nerve impulses. Oleic, linoleic and linolenic acid—known as the fatty acids—contain vitamins A, D, E, and K and are necessary for such bodily functions as gastric acid secretion, inflammation control, and muscle contraction. Fat has a bad reputation; but in the right amounts, fat is a must for every dog's diet.

Dogs need only minute amounts of various vitamins and minerals, but without them they would suffer serious health problems. Vitamins and minerals are involved in almost every aspect of the body's operation, from tissue formation to cell maintenance and growth to the transformation of proteins, carbohydrates, and fats into energy. Most veterinary nutritionists agree that a high-quality balanced diet contains all the vitamins and minerals your dog needs.

Water is the most important nutrient of all, making up about 70 percent of your dog's body weight. Lack of water can of course lead to dehydration, but water is also a vital element of cell and organ function. Without it, the body couldn't maintain proper temperature, transport nutrients, circulate blood, digest food, or eliminate waste products. A dog can survive several days without food, but as little as a 10 percent loss of body water can make him very ill. It's easy to see that fresh water daily is a must for your dog. Recent news reports have cast doubt on the quality and safety of some municipal water supplies, so consider giving your dog the same bottled or filtered water you drink yourself.

> Water is the most important nutrient of all, making up about 70 percent of your dog's body weight. Lack of water can of course lead to dehydration.

Choosing the Best Food for Your Dog

No one food is appropriate for a dog's entire life. Just as with people, dogs' nutritional needs change with age and activity levels, so choosing a food that's appropriate for your dog's particular stage of life is important.

Puppies and Expectant Mothers—Puppies need foods that are high in fat and protein for optimum growth. This type of food is also given to pregnant bitches, who need extra nutrients for fetal development and milk production.

Mature Dogs—They eat what are called maintenance foods, which provide enough calories for the normal activity level of the average pet. Most dogs can be switched to a maintenance food when they're about six months old.

Working Dogs—High-energy diets are suited to working dogs who expend lots of calories hunting, herding, or pulling sleds. They aren't meant for pets that spend their days playing in the yard or going for walks and can lead to obesity if the animal isn't active enough to work off all those calories.

Less-Active and Overweight Dogs—Less active dogs, or those who are overweight, may need a low-calorie or high-fiber diet. This type of food provides all the nutrients the dog needs while still cutting calories. Fiber is added to help the dog feel full.

Older Dogs—Some older dogs with health problems may need a geriatric or senior food that's formulated for their special dietary needs.

If a food's label claims to offer complete and balanced nutrition for all dogs regardless of life stage, be wary. Multiple studies have shown that this "all-purpose" concept isn't effective for all dogs of different ages and needs. Research into canine nutritional requirements has enabled the development of many commercial dog foods that provide optimum nutrients for all stages of a dog's life. It may seem hard to choose from among all the bags and cans that line store shelves, but the decision is easy once you know what to look for.

Unlike, say, canned vegetables or drugs, there is no generic version of a dog. Each is an individual, with unique needs. Just as not every food is tasty or agreeable to us, not every formulated diet is best for all dogs. Choosing the right food is a matter of experimenting to find a high-quality diet that suits your dog's nutritional needs and tastes.

When evaluating dog foods, consider the quality of ingredients, the digestibility, the amount of energy the food provides, and the food's taste, or palatability—that is, does your dog like it? Price and availability are important as well, but shouldn't be the primary factors in your decision.

Any food you are considering should be labeled "complete and balanced." Such a food is formulated to contain the correct levels of all the nutrients a dog needs. The Association of American Feed Control Officials regulates these nutrient levels and requires pet food manufacturers to prove their claims through feeding trials or chemical analysis.

Feeding trials are preferable to chemical analysis because they provide physical evidence of a food's nutritional value. If a food hasn't been tested on dogs, there's no way to know whether dogs are able to digest and absorb the nutrients. For instance, the label on a food might state that it contains 25 percent protein, but if only 10 percent can be used by the dog, the extra 15 percent is not doing the dog any good. Look for foods that carry the phrase "feeding tests," "AAFCO feeding test protocols," or "AAFCO feeding studies."

> When evaluating dog foods, consider the quality of ingredients, the digestibility, the amount of energy the food provides, and the food's taste, or palatability.

Nutritional balance is key. Most often, we only worry about dietary deficiencies, but too much of a good thing can be harmful as well. In fact, most problems seen in puppies today result from excesses in their diets rather than deficiencies. These excesses can be caused by the amounts provided in some commercial dog foods as well as through supplementation by well-intentioned owners. The problem with commercial dog foods is that the regulations for production require only that they meet or exceed established minimums. Some manufacturers produce foods that contain far more of the nutrients than are recommended by the National Research Council (NRC). Be wary of those products claiming to exceed NRC recommendations. These companies realize most people believe that more is better, and their marketing strategies play off consumers' lack of nutritional knowledge.

After making sure the label states that a food is complete and balanced, take a look at the ingredient list. The label must list ingredients by weight in decreasing order. That is, the amount of the ingredient listed first—usually some form of animal protein—is not exceeded by the amounts of any one of the following ingredients. That seems straightforward enough, but manufacturers can get around this requirement by a practice called split-ingredient labeling, in which ingredients of the same type are spread out so they will appear farther down on the label. For instance, a grain such as corn, wheat, or rice might appear on the label in several different forms, such as flour, flakes, middlings, or bran. A food labeled this way might actually contain more protein from grain sources than from animal sources.

Quality ingredients, which should appear first or second on the ingredient list, include animal protein, eggs, or cheese. All the added vitamins in the world can't turn a food with poor-quality ingredients into a product that's nutritionally sound.

Labels also include a guaranteed analysis of the percentages of crude protein, crude fat, crude fiber, and moisture the food contains. This information has only superficial value, however. The guaranteed analysis doesn't list exact amounts of nutrients, only minimum and maximum percentages.

It's not enough to simply read the label the first time you buy a food. Check it regularly to see if the formulation has changed. Ideally, the manufacturer is using a fixed formula, which means that the ingredients remain the same from batch to batch, rather than

Did You Know?

Veterinarians estimate that between 30 and 50 percent of today's dog population is overweight.

fluctuating based on availability of ingredients and market prices. A change in formula could cause stomach upset in a dog with a sensitive digestive system.

Digestibility is another important factor in your choice. The amount of usable nutrients a food contains determines its digestibility. Nutrients that aren't absorbed by the body are eliminated as waste. A food's digestibility is not something you can find on the label; the proof is in your dog. A highly digestible food is evident in a healthy dog that produces small, firm stools. Food that isn't being well digested often results in flatulence (gas), loose or large stools, or even diarrhea.

Choosing a food requires being aware of your dog's energy needs. Different dogs need different amounts of energy. Working dogs need more energy than toy breeds, and puppies need more energy—to fuel their growth—than mature dogs. Like nutritional quality and digestibility, the amount of energy a food provides—its metabolizable energy—is determined through feeding trials. Labels must include a nutritional adequacy statement advising consumers for what life stage a food is appropriate, such as puppy, adult, active dog, or senior.

Palatability is another factor that can only be tested by your dog. No matter how great a food's ingredients are, if your dog won't eat it, then it won't do the dog any good. Of course, just because your dog scarfs up a particular food doesn't necessarily mean the food is good for him. That's where reading labels comes in handy. Since your dog can't read them, you need to do it for him.

Freshness is important as well. Change your dog's food daily, throwing out anything that's left uneaten from the day before. Clean food dishes also make meals more appetizing. Rinse them off or toss them into the dishwasher after the dog eats to prevent food from crusting on the surface. Besides providing a great growth spot for bacteria, encrusted dishes simply aren't pleasant to eat from.

Once you've chosen a food, stick with it as long as it's right for your dog's life stage. If your Max or Rufus or Lady has bright eyes, a shiny coat, and good health, the food is doing its job. Your dog doesn't need variety or regular changes in his diet. This only leads to a finicky disposition, not to mention such unpleasant side effects as diarrhea or excess gas.

Premium Foods Versus Grocery Store Foods

Commercially prepared diets fall into several categories: generic, private label, popular brands, and premium brands. Although exceptions exist, in general the quality of foods increases from generic to premium foods.

Premium foods are usually found in pet supply stores or through veterinarians. They claim top-quality ingredients and a high nutritional value. Grocery store foods run the gamut from well-known national brands to private-label store brands to no-label generic foods. They claim to meet a dog's nutritional needs at a fair cost. Which is better? Like so many issues involving dogs, there is no single correct answer. Each dog is different, and no one food can meet the needs of every dog. However, knowing the differences between the two can help you come to the decision that's right for your dog, as well as for your pocketbook.

The primary advantage of premium foods is the guaranteed consistent quality of the ingredients used. These diets are developed to provide optimal balanced nutrition for a particular life stage based on specific ingredients, regardless of cost. With this type of production, premium diets never provide excesses or deficiencies of nutrients.

Since the ingredients used are not chosen based on cost or availability, premium foods cost more per unit of weight, but they have a higher density per volume. That is, a tablespoon of a premium food usually contains more digestible nutrients than a tablespoon of a regular food. You can usually see that difference in stool volume. Dogs fed premium diets usually produce smaller, firmer stools. Although it may cost more initially to purchase a premium food, the dog eats less of it—so it lasts longer—and is able to absorb more nutrients from it. This helps to bring the actual cost of feeding a premium food close to that of a popular food. Your veterinarian can probably show you a breakdown of the actual feeding cost per day of different brands.

> Your veterinarian can probably show you a breakdown of the actual feeding cost per day of different brands.

A premium food is a good choice if your dog needs to put on a little weight—for instance, if he's been unwell—or if he's just a picky eater. But can a premium food actually make a difference in a dog's health? Many veterinarians, breeders, and pet owners believe it can, citing examples of improved health, coat quality, and digestibility. On the other hand, just as many veterinarians and breeders say that national brands sold in grocery stores will meet a dog's nutritional needs just fine. These foods are produced and marketed to pet owners whose goal is to provide a nutritious, tasty, yet inexpensive food.

Whether you choose a premium diet or a national brand, you can be reasonably sure of its nutritional quality; but couldn't you save a little money by buying a generic or private-label food? You might, in the short term, but your pocketbook would eventually flatten as you pay for the greater amount of food your dog would have to eat to get the same nutritional benefits he would from a better food.

Generic foods are often produced locally and contain the least expensive ingredients available in the area. Even though this results in lower cost per volume, hidden costs may be involved when you buy a low-quality food. Dogs who eat generic foods often experience slow or retarded growth and skeletal abnormalities, and are more likely to suffer from poor skin condition and coat quality. The manufacturer's quality-control standards may be low or nonexistent. And even if a generic food is labeled complete and balanced, its nutritional benefits may have been determined through chemical analysis or calculation rather than feeding trials over extended periods, which more accurately assess a diet's nutritional value. Thus, these foods may contain nutrient excesses or deficiencies. The potential health problems your dog would face—not to mention the resulting veterinary bills—simply aren't worth the savings.

Most of these same factors apply to private-label foods, which are often produced by manufacturers of generic brands but sold under a particular store chain's name. Most nutritional experts agree that generic and private-label foods generally provide the poorest quality among commercially produced foods since the manufacturers of such products have little regard for proper nutritional content and consistency.

> ## Did You Know?
>
> Dogs and cats in the United States consume almost $7 billion worth of pet food a year.

Cost Differences: Why They Exist, What They Mean

Corporations that make pet food—whether premium or national brands—all spend big bucks on nutritional studies, feeding trials, and consumer hotlines. The price differences in their products generally are based on types and amounts of ingredients. For instance, a premium food might contain turkey or venison rather than the more common beef or chicken, or grain that's grown organically instead of being treated with pesticides. It may contain more animal protein than grain protein, or be free of dyes or preservatives. As mentioned previously, one reason popular brands are less expensive is that their ingredients may fluctuate from batch to batch, depending on the cost and availability of the components. This may affect a dog's digestive system if a new bag of food contains ingredients to which he's not accustomed.

Choosing a food is one of those instances in which you get what you pay for. The bottom line is that dogs will require less total food when fed a high-quality diet. Be guided by the food's performance rather than its cost.

Canned Versus Dry

In addition to choosing a particular brand of food, you also need to decide whether to feed dry, canned, or semi-moist meals. Each has advantages and disadvantages, and you'll want to weigh your needs against those of your dog when making the final choice. You can find excellent and poor-quality foods among each type.

Dry foods are the most popular by far, for a number of reasons. Their main advantage is lower cost—one-half to one-third less than canned or semi-moist foods of the same quality. This relatively low cost makes dry food a particularly good choice for people with large or giant breeds, or with multiple dogs. Next, they're suited to a free-choice feeding regimen since they can be left out all day without spoiling. Dry

The Importance of Water

Water is important to every living creature, and your dog is no exception.

Water makes up around 70 percent of your adult dog's body and even more of your puppy's constitution. Dogs need water to help their cells function properly and to aid in proper digestion. Basically, dogs need water to live. Without water, a dog will die within only a few days.

The water in your dog's body needs to be replenished on a regular basis, since it is routinely lost through respiration, digestion, and urination. On hot days or when exercising heavily, your dog needs even more water to keep his body running smoothly.

To keep your dog at optimum health, provide him with constant access to plenty of cool, fresh water.

foods also have an abrasive effect on the teeth that helps promote better oral hygiene.

Dry foods do have some drawbacks. They don't taste as good as canned or semi-moist foods, they contain limited ingredient types, and they have low levels of essential fatty acids. The way dry foods are processed eliminates the use of fresh animal tissues and limits the amount of fat that can be used. This makes dry foods lower in essential fatty acids, which are important for healthy skin and coats. On the other hand, that lower fat content makes dry food a good choice for dogs prone to obesity.

Canned foods are the next most popular choice. Without a doubt, they're more palatable than their dry counterparts, but they're much more expensive to feed, especially considering that as much as 75 percent of a canned food is water. In addition, canned food must be refrigerated to maintain its freshness. The major advantage of canned foods is that they can be made with a wider variety of animal tissues, since the drying process isn't a factor. Canned foods usually contain more fat and deliver more calories per pound, and their high nutrient density is beneficial for dogs who are stressed, ill, or working hard. It's also a good choice for picky eaters, dogs with poor dental health who find it painful to crunch down dry food, or older dogs whose sense of smell has deteriorated, as canned food typically has a much stronger scent than dry.

Semi-moist foods are often more palatable than dry foods, but they are also considerably more expensive. This type of food often comes in individual packets, which makes preparation convenient. Semi-moist foods contain preservatives to prevent spoilage so they don't require refrigeration. They also include fair amounts of corn syrup as the major carbohydrate source, which is not always the best for a dog's overall health.

Of course, there's always room for compromise. There's nothing wrong with using a little canned food to add flavor to a dry meal or keeping a little semi-moist food on hand for a treat.

All-Natural Foods

With the increased interest in the link between healthful eating and a longer life, it's not surprising that pet owners are demanding higher quality meals for their dogs as well. Certain types of

foods and supplements are gaining a "magic bullet" reputation for their ability to improve health; and in the past decade, manufacturers have increasingly begun providing diets touted as being "all-natural."

When it comes to pet foods, there's not really a good definition for what makes a food "natural." Generally, however, a natural food is defined as a commercial diet made without preservatives or with natural preservatives such as vitamin E or ascorbic acid. Some foods calling themselves natural contain organic meats and grains or human-grade ingredients.

Most pet foods falling under these definitions are premium products that are available only in pet supply stores, natural-food grocery stores such as Wild Oats or Mother's Market, at dog shows, or on the Internet. They include brands such as Flint River Ranch, Innova, Balance Diet, and Solid Gold. Many dog owners turn to natural diets when they're not satisfied with the performance or ingredients of premium or grocery store brands but are unwilling or unable to feed a homemade or raw diet. As long as such a food has been proven in feeding trials, it can be an excellent choice for your dog.

Did You Know?

Dogs are mentioned 14 times in the Bible.

Preparing Your Dog's Meals Yourself

The commercial market provides dog foods that are convenient with low feeding costs and good performance in regards to overall health. However, a small number of owners prefer to prepare homemade diets, either so they can control the ingredients or because their dogs are suffering from allergies or other health problems which are best supported by a home-prepared diet. For example, older dogs who develop early stages of kidney failure should eat a prescription diet, which is often home prepared. Your veterinarian can offer specific recipes that are nutritionally balanced and appropriate for your dog's needs. However, with the great advances made in nutrition for dogs, a variety of commercially prepared diets are appropriate for particular disease states.

Use your common sense if you decide to go the home-prepared route. Remember that just because a certain diet is adequate for humans doesn't mean it will meet a dog's nutritional needs. For example, pet foods often contain more fiber and calcium than the typical human diet. Homemade diets are one of the most common causes of improper nutrition in dogs, so be guided by a well-respected source such as your own veterinarian or one of the many recipes found in health and nutrition books written by veterinarians.

Use the freshest ingredients, not old foods or your leftovers. Freeze portions you don't use so the food will remain at its peak level of nutrition. Supplement as directed so your dog doesn't develop any deficiencies. Introduce any new food gradually, over a period of at least a week. And be willing to experiment to find the foods and combinations that work best for and are most pleasing to your dog. Just as with any other food, you should be able to tell by looking at your dog whether the meals you're preparing agree with him. And keep in mind that homemade diets can sometimes create finicky eaters that are difficult to satisfy.

> One of the interesting findings of recent canine nutritional research is that large and giant-breed puppies have different nutritional requirements than medium-size or small-breed puppies.

Feeding Large/Giant Breeds

One of the interesting findings of recent canine nutritional research is that large and giant-breed puppies have different nutritional requirements than medium-size or small-breed puppies. This is especially true during the rapid growth phase that encompasses the first six months of life.

A large- or giant-breed puppy is one that will weigh 65 pounds or more at maturity. Among the many breeds that fall into this category are Rottweilers, Labrador Retrievers, Golden Retrievers, German Shepherds, Great Danes, and Mastiffs. Because these breeds grow so rapidly, they are prone to developmental bone problems if they don't consume carefully balanced amounts of fat and protein. These young Goliaths need a well-balanced diet that provides just the right amounts of fat, calories, protein, calcium, and phosphorus.

Too often, owners believe that the more food and supplements they give their large or giant-breed puppies, the bigger and the healthier they will be. That's a dangerous assumption. Such a diet often contributes to the formation of developmental bone diseases that can be crippling and sometimes irreversible. They include hip dysplasia, elbow dysplasia, panosteitis, osteochondritis dissecans (OCD), hypertrophic osteodystrophy (HOD), and wobbler syndrome. (Please refer to the Glossary for definitions of these diseases.)

Some of these diseases also have a genetic contributing factor, which is not to be ignored; but there is a proven link between a puppy's genetic heritage and environmental factors such as food intake. While you can't change your puppy's genetic makeup, you can control his diet by simply decreasing food intake and controlling certain nutrient components. This will effectively slow the growth rate and reduce physiologic and pathologic bone changes. By limiting intake of food during growth, you promote proper development with no reduction in adult body size, and greatly decrease the chance of obesity and developmental bone diseases.

The most important factors to monitor in a large/giant breed puppy's diet are fat, protein, calories, calcium, and phosphorus. Dietary protein levels from 15 to 32 percent have no adverse effect on bone development, with the optimum level being about 27 percent. Protein levels that are too low can cause a decrease in body condition.

Fat is an important source of energy, but it's more than twice as high in calories as protein and carbohydrates. Limiting the amount of fat in a puppy's diet decreases the incidence of developmental bone diseases.

The idea that large/giant breed puppies need extra calcium is false. Many commercially prepared dry dog foods contain several times the required amount of calcium, but studies have shown that excess calcium greatly increases the chance of developmental bone disease. It has also been suggested that the prolonged intake of high quantities of calcium in combination with too much food may contribute to gastric dilatation and volvulus, better known as bloat, a life-threatening concern for large, deep-chested breeds.

> Young puppies, aged six weeks to six months, should be fed two to three meals per day at regularly scheduled times.

Phosphorus levels should also be carefully balanced with the amount of calcium. Phosphorus is required at levels lower than that of calcium. The desired ratio of calcium to phosphorus is usually 2:1. To help your large/giant breed puppy grow to a healthy maturity, resist giving supplements and avoid overfeeding him. It's preferable to keep your puppy lean rather than pudgy during the growth phase. If your friends or neighbors make comments about your "skinny" dog, you can tell them that your breed won't be full-grown until he's 18 to 24 months old and that the restricted diet won't affect his size at maturity. Indeed, several studies have shown that slightly underfeeding doesn't have any effect at all on size at maturity or musculoskeletal development.

Several diets have been specially formulated for large/giant breed puppies. These diets contain less calcium and phosphorus to help contribute to a controlled rate of growth. A puppy should be started on this type of diet when he's about six weeks old, usually around the time he's being weaned from mother's milk. If you have a large/giant breed puppy, this type of food is the best diet you can give him until he is six months old. Your veterinarian can advise you about these diets and other ways to provide a balanced diet for your puppy.

How Often and How Much Do I Feed My Dog?

One of the questions new dog owners most often ask is how frequently their puppy or dog should be fed. Young puppies, aged six weeks to six months, should be fed two to three meals per day at regularly scheduled times. Because of their rapid metabolism, most toy breeds need three meals daily until they're six-months old. Obviously, some owners can't leave work during the day to feed a puppy his lunch, but with the help of a friendly neighbor or a timed feeder, which allows you to provide scheduled meals when you can't be home, you can ensure that he receives all the meals he needs, when he needs them. Even after a dog has matured, most behavioral specialists recommend

Did You Know?

The world's heaviest, as well as longest, dog ever recorded was an Old English Mastiff named Zorba. In 1989, Zorba weighed 343 pounds and was 8 feet 3 inches long from nose to tail.

feeding two meals a day so the dog won't feel hungry or anxious until his next meal shows up.

What Should I Feed My Puppy?

A well-nourished puppy is vigorous and has a strong resistance to disease, so choosing the right food is important. With your veterinarian's help, you can choose a diet that will best suit your puppy's changing needs as he grows into adulthood.

> A well-nourished puppy is vigorous and has a strong resistance to disease, so choosing the right food is important.

The growth phase is the most important nutritional time in your puppy's life. For all breeds, the most rapid growth occurs during the first six months of life, but depending on their breed or mix, dogs continue to develop until they're 12 to 18 months old. The breeder and your veterinarian can advise you about how long your puppy's growth phase will last.

The goal for all puppies is to achieve an average growth rate for that particular breed. A high-quality, growth-formulated puppy food will provide your new friend with all the nutrients he needs to develop properly. The trick is to avoid overfeeding him.

In fact, slightly underfeeding your puppy is better than feeding him too much. When it comes to puppies, bigger is definitely not better. Excess weight puts stress on growing bones, and puppies who put on weight too quickly, especially large or giant breeds, are more prone to debilitating orthopedic problems such as hip or elbow dysplasia, osteochondritis dissecans, and patellar luxation. And just like people, dogs who are fat in puppyhood are more prone to obesity as adults.

When you bring your new puppy home, ask the breeder or animal shelter what he was being fed and how much. Even if you decide to change foods, you'll want to do so gradually to avoid the mild diarrhea that can occur when a dog switches to a new food. To prevent any gastrointestinal upset, purchase a small bag of what the puppy was eating and a bag of the food you plan to feed. Over a seven- to ten-day period, gradually increase the amount of new food as you decrease the old food.

> When you bring your new puppy home, ask the breeder or animal shelter what he was being fed and how much. Even if you decide to change foods, you'll want to do so gradually.

The Importance of Routine

Establishing a feeding schedule early in a puppy's life has many advantages. Puppies on a schedule are easier to housetrain, and they're less likely to overeat. Dogs like a daily routine, and they quickly learn to appreciate set feeding times. A schedule is also good for adult dogs, who learn to eat on their owners' timetables. There are a variety of feeding practices, each with advantages and disadvantages. Choose the one that works best with your daily schedule and is most beneficial to your dog.

A lot of people simply leave food out all the time, allowing the dog to eat as much as she wants whenever she wants. Free-feeding requires the least amount of work and works best for dogs who are nibblers rather than gobblers. It sometimes discourages coprophagy (eating of feces) and helps more submissive dogs to get their fair share when dogs are group-fed. With these advantages come several disadvantages. Left to their own devices, some puppies will eat too much and get fat. Certain breeds, among them Dachshunds and Beagles, are predisposed to obesity, which is something you should ask the breeder or veterinarian about when you get the puppy. Another disadvantage of free-choice feeding is that you don't know when or how much the puppy has eaten, so it's difficult to predict when she's likely to have a bowel movement. Save free-choice feeding for mature dogs who aren't obsessive about food.

A system that works well for feeding dogs of any age is limiting meals to specific times, amounts, and durations. At whatever time you choose, set down your dog's food for 15 to 20 minutes. Your puppy might not eat the entire meal when you first begin this method, but rest assured that she'll quickly learn to eat what is offered during her dinnertime. Restricting meals this way allows you to better determine when the puppy will need to relieve herself and gives you more control over how much food she eats. Dog trainers prefer this method because it helps move housetraining along, with less confusion for both the owner and the puppy. It also allows you to monitor your dog's appetite level. Loss of appetite is often an early warning sign of illness. If you own a large/giant breed puppy, you'll want to pay particular attention to the amount of food your pup eats. Remember, in any breed, a leaner puppy is preferable to a pudgy puppy.

> Dogs are individuals when it comes to serving size. The serving portions listed on food labels are merely guides, which you can use in conjunction with advice from the breeder or your veterinarian.

Dogs are individuals when it comes to serving size. The serving portions listed on food labels are merely guides, which you can use in conjunction with advice from the breeder or your veterinarian. Your dog may do better with more or less than the recommended daily amount.

Don't be afraid to experiment. If your puppy is getting too fat on his puppy food, try a brand with a lower fat and protein content. If he's not putting on weight but is otherwise healthy, keep him on puppy formula a little longer than you might normally. Most dogs make the switch from puppy to maintenance food at six to eight months of age, depending on size or breed. An older dog usually has a lower activity level and metabolic rate than a younger dog, so he may eat less food and still maintain a good body weight. He still needs the same amount of nutrients, though, so it's especially important that the senior dog get a high-quality, nutrient-rich food.

Dogs also vary in their eating styles. Some are nibblers while others are gobblers. Some are of the opinion that anything that can be swallowed should be eaten. And some like to have company—human or canine—while they eat. Take these factors into consideration when you're deciding whether to free-feed or at what times to serve meals.

Is It Okay to Share My Food?

Feeding table scraps is rarely a good idea. Giving a dog food off your plate encourages begging, which is cute the first couple of times but quickly becomes annoying. Take Muffin, for instance. This long-haired Dachshund—whose name is definitely appropriate for her rotund body—hates dog food but loves pizza and other "people" food. Muffin was so determined to have her favorite food that one day she grabbed a slice of pepperoni pizza right out of her owner's hands, leading to a messy tug-of-war.

Did You Know?

Greyhounds have the best eyesight of any breed of dog.

On a more serious level, people food is usually high in fat and too rich for a dog's sensitive digestive system. And what might

Training a Finicky Eater

When you switch your dog to a new food, even if you do it gradually, your puppy may refuse to eat some or all of his food for a day or more. This adjustment period is normal—remember, dogs are creatures of habit—but it's not a good idea to prime the puppy's dish with tasty treats in an effort to get him to eat. Puppies are smart, and it only takes once for them to realize that if they hold out long enough, you'll give in and provide something they like better. Your puppy won't let himself starve, and if only one particular food is offered, he will eventually resort to eating that food. If you have a toy breed that's prone to hypoglycemia—low blood sugar—consult your veterinarian or the breeder about dealing with picky behavior. A healthy addition such as yogurt or cottage cheese may be necessary to get these dogs to eat.

seem like a small amount to you could be a huge amount for your dog. Besides resulting in obesity and pickiness, some rich, fatty foods—even in tiny amounts—can cause a life-threatening condition called pancreatitis. Little Binks, a Yorkshire Terrier, was diagnosed with this condition after becoming very ill. Her owners wracked their brains trying to think of the cause. She hadn't gotten into the garbage, and as far as they knew hadn't eaten anything besides her regular dog food. Finally, one of them remembered slipping her less than a teaspoon of cooked steak from the previous night's meal, thinking that such a small amount wouldn't hurt her. That was all it took. Binks had to stay in the hospital for a week to receive IV fluids and antibiotics.

You don't want to risk a trip to the emergency room just for the sake of giving your dog a special treat. On the other hand, some people foods are perfectly fine to give your dog—on special occasions and in reasonable amounts. The following section on treats suggests healthy foods your dog will enjoy.

Healthy Treats

It doesn't take a rocket scientist to figure out why people enjoy giving dogs treats. The look of anticipation on a dog's face and her pure enjoyment of a special food make giving treats more than worthwhile. Treats are also invaluable during the training process. The trick is in giving dogs treats that are both healthy and tasty.

There are plenty of treats that are fine for a dog to enjoy. The best ones are hard biscuits, which are great for keeping a dog's teeth free of tartar buildup. Rawhides and dental-type chews are also popular with dogs and can be invaluable during the teething stage, saving your furniture and giving your pup's gums some relief. Some dog owners recommend against feeding pig ears and rawhides because of the possibility of choking, but let your own dog be your guide. If she doesn't gobble them but rather gnaws on them slowly without trying to eat them, they are probably safe to give under supervision. Be sure you buy high-quality American rawhide; foreign-made rawhide is sometimes treated with dangerous chemicals.

Offer soft, salt- or sugar-laden treats in small amounts. They are best saved for training sessions, which require a reward that can be eaten quickly.

Other healthy treats most dogs enjoy include fruits and vegetables, such as bits of baby carrot, chopped apple, or banana. Some will even eat broccoli florets and frozen mixed vegetables. Apples are good for stabilizing blood sugar, so they're handy to have around if your dog is hypoglycemic. Fruits and veggies are low in calories, so you can give them without a guilty conscience. Don't give too much, though. An excess of fruit—especially

fruits that are high in sugar and water, such as grapes—can cause diarrhea. It took fewer than a dozen to give the runs to Savanna, a Greyhound. And some vegetables—broccoli, for instance—can give dogs gas.

> If you do offer a treat on a regular basis, be prepared to continue this practice. It doesn't take a dog long to learn when to expect and demand it.

Most owners develop some type of routine of when they give their dogs treats. For example, you may give your dog a treat when you come home from work. If you do offer a treat on a regular basis, be prepared to continue this practice. It doesn't take a dog long to learn when to expect and demand it.

When you give treats, reduce by a little bit the amount of regular dog food you give. That way, you don't have to worry about your dog gradually packing on the pounds. A good rule to remember is that treats should never make up more than 5 to 10 percent of your dog's daily intake.

Toxic Treats—Dangerous Foods for Dogs

While dogs are like us in many ways, they differ physiologically, especially in the way they process food. Foods that are harmless to people, such as chocolate or onions, can have serious consequences in dogs. Objects that are closely associated with dogs, such as bones, can be problematic as well. These and other potentially harmful foods should never be offered to any dog of any age.

At the top of the list is natural bones. Dogs love chewing on bones and without a doubt consider them a great treat, but bones can splinter. If bone fragments are swallowed, they can get lodged in the mouth or digestive tract, causing serious injury or even death. When a large bone is found in the digestive tract, it must be removed surgically to prevent intestinal rupture or blockage. Another risk of chewing on bones is broken teeth. So do yourself and your dog a favor and give him rawhides or chew toys instead.

Dogs are known to have a sweet tooth, but their craving shouldn't be met with anything containing chocolate. That goes for ice cream, candy, and chocolate chip cookies. The problem with chocolate is that it contains theobromine, which is quite toxic to dogs because their bodies are slow in removing it from their system. The different forms of chocolate contain varying amounts of theobromine. Milk chocolate usually contains the lowest amounts and unsweetened baking chocolate the highest. If your dog overdoses on chocolate, the signs of illness will range from vomiting and depression to lethargy, muscle tremors, diarrhea, and even death. If you suspect your dog has gotten into your chocolate stash, call your veterinarian or the emergency clinic right away. Store chocolate well out of your curious dog's reach, especially during the holidays when gifts of chocolate are everywhere.

A lot of people like to feed eggs to their dogs in the belief that they help produce a shiny coat. Eggs are fine in moderation, but they should always be cooked. Raw eggs, poultry, and other animal products may be infected with salmonella, *E. coli*, or other bacteria. Just as in people, a case of food poisoning can cause diarrhea and vomiting; and some bacterial infections, such as salmonella, can be passed between dogs and people.

One common mistake people make when they first bring a puppy home is to offer it milk to drink or to mix the puppy's dry

Did You Know?

Houston topped the 1998 list of cities with the highest number of postal workers bitten by dogs, with Chicago a close second.

food with milk. Cow's milk is high in lactose, which is not compatible with a puppy's digestive system. The result is diarrhea. If you want to soften the food, add water instead of milk.

Other foods that can be harmful to dogs are raw or cooked onions. A chemical in onions can destroy a dog's red blood cells, causing a serious or even fatal case of anemia. There's an old wives' tale that garlic prevents worms and fleas. Some people swear by it, but formal studies haven't proven that it really works. If you decide to try it, though, give garlic only in small amounts. It's a member of the onion family and can have the same serious consequences if a large enough amount is consumed all at once. Ask your veterinarian about more effective ways to ward off fleas and worms.

> Other foods that can be harmful to dogs are raw or cooked onions. A chemical in onions can destroy a dog's red blood cells, causing a serious or even fatal case of anemia.

Preventing Obesity for the Life of Your Dog

Obesity is one of the most common health problems seen by small-animal veterinarians, affecting about one out of every four pets. Among the reasons for this outbreak of obesity are the appetizing flavors of commercial pet foods, owners who leave food out all the time, and a sedentary lifestyle. Heredity, breed type, sex, and age can also play a role, but the overwhelming cause is overeating.

A dog is considered obese when he weighs 15 percent more than the optimum weight for his breed and sex. Just as in humans, obesity can lead to serious life-threatening medical conditions. Obesity and diabetes go hand in hand. Carrying too much weight also causes orthopedic problems, and is linked to heart disease. Besides seriously decreasing your dog's enjoyment of life, obesity reduces your dog's overall life span by as much as two to three years.

Eye your dog objectively and give him the hands-on test: Can you feel his ribs (but not see them) or are they well padded with fat? From above, your dog should have a visible waist behind his ribs. A rounded or bulging abdomen and no waist are signs that your dog has been eating a little too much and not exercising enough. When a dog takes in more calories than he expends, obesity is inevitable.

> A dog is considered obese when he weighs 15 percent more than the optimum weight for his breed and sex. Just as in humans, obesity can lead to serious life-threatening medical conditions.

If your dog is a chowhound instead of a nibbler, you need to take steps to keep his weight at an appropriate level. The following tips will help you get started. Be sure to check with your veterinarian first to make sure your dog has no health factors that would preclude a dietary change or increased exercise.

The first step requires getting the entire family committed to the plan. It takes only one family member to ruin the whole effort. The dog usually knows the "weak link" and will seek him or her out diligently. It becomes quickly apparent when someone is not doing his or her part because dogs do not lie!

Next, if your dog could earn his way begging on the streets, keep him out of the kitchen while you are preparing and eating your meals. This will help eliminate incessant begging. If you have more than one dog, feed them separately so the fat one doesn't mooch off the other's bowl.

Regular exercise is a crucial element of the plan. Add more activity to your dog's routine, from throwing

More Weight-Loss Tips

○ Reduce the amount of food you give. Something as simple as giving a level half-cup instead of a heaping one reduces the number of calories your dog gets.

○ If reducing the amount of food isn't practical, switch to one of the many reduced-calorie dog foods on the market. Your veterinarian can recommend the best choices for your particular dog.

○ Introduce the new food gradually, over a 7- to 10-day period, and be patient but firm during the change. Expect that your dog may eat less or not at all for the first few days but will eventually make the switch.

○ If you change foods, don't switch to a type to which your dog isn't accustomed. For example, if he's used to eating canned food, switch to a canned diet food, rather than to a dry diet food.

○ Increase the amount of fiber your dog gets in his diet. Adding canned green beans, pumpkin, or carrots to his food will help him feel full without adding a lot of extra calories.

○ Offer several small meals daily. More frequent meals will help satisfy your dog's desire to eat and help prevent him from realizing that he's getting less food.

a ball to increasing the length of his daily walks. If he's seriously overweight, start slowly and keep exercise sessions brief. As he loses weight, you can increase the length and intensity of exercise. Think of it as a good reason for you to get off the couch as well. If your dog is extremely overweight, ask your veterinarian to outline a safe exercise plan.

Many of us equate giving food with an expression of love, but too much of anything can be detrimental. If you're concerned that putting your dog on a diet or cutting down the treats is reducing your expression of love, consider the situation from a different point of view: You're showing even more love by ensuring that your dog lives a long and healthy life.

What's All The Fuss About Supplements?

Nutritionists know that vitamins and minerals are necessary to maintain good health, but there's not a lot of evidence yet about the optimal amounts of vitamins and minerals the human body needs, let alone the canine body. They do know, however, that an imbalance of vitamins and minerals—whether too many or too few—can cause serious health problems. Because commercial dog foods already contain what is believed to be an appropriate level of vitamins and minerals, most veterinarians and veterinary nutritionists recommend against giving supplements to a dog who's eating this type of food.

Exceptions include dogs who have been ill or are suffering from malnutrition, in which cases your veterinarian may recommend a supplement to help build the dog back up.

Fatty acid supplements can help certain dogs maintain a healthier skin and coat and are commonly recommended by veterinarians.

Dogs who eat homemade diets also require supplements. The appropriate amounts should be included in any recipe used. If they're not, don't guess. Enlist the help of a qualified veterinary nutritionist.

Does My Puppy Need Supplements?

A puppy who's eating a well-balanced diet shouldn't need supplements of any kind. Calcium supplements, especially, can cause skeletal abnormalities in

How Obesity Begins

Obesity in puppyhood results from an increase in the size and number of fat cells, while obesity in adult dogs occurs only from an increase in the size of fat cells. Once the number of fat cells is established, it's difficult to decrease. Therefore, excess fat deposits made during a puppy's growth phase increase the total number of fat cells and predispose the puppy to obesity throughout life.

a growing puppy. Check with your veterinarian before giving your puppy any kind of supplement.

What About My Older Dog?

In most cases, a healthy older dog doesn't need supplements. Your veterinarian may recommend one, however, if your dog is starting to show signs of age-related problems. Supplements of B vitamins are important for dogs with reduced kidney function. A calcium carbonate supplement may be necessary if your dog's teeth are in bad shape, making it difficult for him to eat enough of a balanced diet. Your veterinarian can recommend an appropriate supplement if your older dog needs one.

4

Medical Care Every Dog Needs

In This Chapter

○ Going to the Vet
○ Preventive Medicine
○ Spaying and Neutering
○ Sick Calls and Emergencies

Your dog counts on you to take care of him. In addition to providing him with the appropriate food and exercise, he also needs proper medical attention and care. By gaining a basic understanding of your dog's requirements for good health, you will be better prepared to assist the veterinarian of your choice in giving him the best possible care.

Going to the Vet

The veterinarian is your partner in your dog's health care. Through regular exams, inoculations, and expeditious treatment during the hopefully rare emergencies, your veterinarian will provide the foundation for your dog's physical well-being. You can build on that foundation through your observations of your dog's normal behavior—and your quick response when something isn't right. Together, the two of you can work toward ensuring your dog a long and happy life.

> The veterinarian is your partner in your dog's health care. Together, the two of you can work toward ensuring your dog a long and happy life.

By establishing and maintaining a relationship with the veterinarian early in your dog's life, such as during regular checkups and puppy vaccinations, you'll feel comfortable asking your veterinarian questions about different aspects of dog care. That way, you'll be better prepared in the face of an emergency. Many veterinarians will see only their own clients for after-hours emergencies. Waiting until an emergency arises to find a veterinarian for the first time could delay proper treatment. It's always best when your veterinarian, who knows your dog's medical history, is able to treat your pet in the event of an illness or emergency. Make sure you know beforehand whether your veterinarian takes after-hours calls or refers emergencies to a local emergency clinic. Either way, have the appropriate phone numbers handy at all times.

Selecting the Right Vet

If you don't already have a favorite veterinarian, it's a good idea to tour several clinics to find the one you're most comfortable with before you get your dog. Ask dog-owning friends or neighbors for recommendations, and call to schedule a clinic tour. The receptionist or office manager should be happy to set one up for you.

Special Services

Many veterinary clinics offer far more than just shots and surgery. During your introductory visit, ask whether any of the following services are provided:

○ Boarding

○ Grooming (including bathing and dipping)

○ Puppy day care (convenient and practical for some busy owners)

○ Early morning drop-offs for vaccinations/treatments

○ House calls or pickup and delivery services

○ After-hour emergency services. (If yes, find out the protocol you need to follow. If no, ask what local emergency hospital they recommend.)

○ Obedience and/or "puppy kindergarten" classes

○ Behavior counseling

During this informal visit, ask about office hours; fees for routine procedures such as annual exams, vaccinations, and spay/neuter surgery; and how and when payments can be made: cash, check, or credit card. Note whether the clinic is clean, reasonably odor free, and well equipped. Ask to see the surgical suite, the x-ray unit, and the quarters for hospitalized patients. Anywhere animals are treated, boarded, or hospitalized should be sanitary and clean. Find out whether the clinic has separate wards for critically ill or infectious patients.

Of course, you'll want to meet the veterinarian and make sure he or she has a friendly yet knowledgeable "petside" manner. Don't be afraid to ask about educational background, continuing education, and practice philosophy. Most veterinarians are happy to discuss these details with you. If your dog is a breed that's prone to particular health problems, ask whether the veterinarian has experience treating those conditions and how he or she handles them. Once you find a practice that meets your needs, you won't have any qualms about bringing your new dog in for an introductory exam.

Your Puppy's First Visit

Diane, a veterinary technician, welcomed the Johnson family and their new Golden Retriever puppy, Cricket, to the clinic. As she asked the owners about the puppy's background, she weighed him and noted the information on the chart she was setting up. She then went over these puppy basics with the family: a vaccination schedule and other routine veterinary care, feeding schedules, potential emergency situations, and grooming advice (nail trimming, bathing, and dental care).

Dr. Long, who'd just finished examining another patient, was now ready to examine the squirming Cricket. During the exam, he answered a few questions on subjects Diane hadn't gotten to and discussed the benefits of spay-neuter surgery and early training classes. By the time he'd finished, Diane gave the Johnsons a packet she'd assembled, containing information about Golden Retrievers, spay-neuter surgery, and local puppy kindergarten classes. The Johnsons scheduled a follow-up appointment for Cricket's vaccinations and left the clinic with new respect for both the veterinarian's and the technician's knowledge and abilities. They felt confident knowing Diane was there to help them with any problems should Dr. Long not be immediately available.

The Johnsons' experience was typical for a first puppy visit. Normally, your clinic will schedule a 15- to 20-minute visit for vaccinations only, but many clinics schedule about 30 minutes for the first visit. This allows them time to take a complete medical history, provide information about important aspects of your puppy's care, answer questions you may have, and conduct a careful and thorough physical examination. This first visit should begin a solid, long-term relationship between you and your dog, and the veterinarian and technician. Together, you can develop an education and health-care plan that will benefit your puppy for his lifetime.

What to Expect

Usually, a veterinary technician will call you and your puppy into the examination room, confirm the reason for the visit, and perform some initial procedures. Normally that includes weighing your dog; taking his temperature, pulse, and respiration; doing ear swabs if indicated; and setting up a fecal flotation to check for intestinal parasites. The technician may discuss all the aspects of dealing with a new puppy—behavior, diet, the dog's place in the family, and your expectations of the dog, as well as routine veterinary care and advice on handling emergencies. Sometimes the technician performs routine procedures such as cleaning the ears, brushing the teeth or trimming the nails, and should carefully instruct you on how to perform these maintenance procedures at home. Because puppies are usually acquired just before their permanent teeth start to come in, this first visit is a good opportunity to discuss what to expect during teething and how to prevent destructive chewing. Other topics the technician may touch on include feeding schedules;

Did You Know?

Shelters in the United States take in nearly 11 million cats and dogs each year. Nearly 75% percent of those animals have to be euthanized.

whether to add vitamins, food supplements, and treats to the pet's diet; and using feeding times to teach your puppy (more on this in Chapter 6, "Basic Training for Your Dog").

Next comes the complete physical exam by the veterinarian. You may wonder what your veterinarian is looking for as he or she thoroughly examines your new puppy. The exam involves a search for congenital defects like cleft palates, heart murmurs, and disorders of the eye. On young dogs, umbilical hernias are common. Some of these will repair themselves with time, but sometimes require surgical repair later. Your veterinarian will normally check to be sure that the testicles of male puppies have descended. Since your veterinarian also serves as your dog's dentist, a careful oral examination is part of the normal procedure. As in humans, good dental care and hygiene are important to a dog's overall good health, even when they are puppies. The veterinarian may also go over the areas discussed by the technician to make sure all your questions have been answered. This first visit gives the veterinarian a baseline from which to judge your puppy's development on future visits.

By monitoring your pup's weight at each visit, your veterinarian can gauge the growth of your puppy. Only when the physical examination shows that your puppy is in good health will he receive vaccinations; otherwise, they'll be postponed until he's in

peak condition. Your puppy may yelp a little when he gets his shots, even though he's probably been through this at least once at the breeder's. Your veterinarian and the technician are both well trained to administer injections that cause minimal pain, but it's normal for your puppy to react with displeasure to receiving injections.

During the first visit, the veterinarian will also discuss the importance of preventive care. Be-

Questions to Ask

Remember, the only stupid questions are those that are never asked. And there's a good chance that your veterinarian has heard all your questions before. Among the typical questions you might ask are whether the veterinarian detects any defects or problems, what his recommendations on diet are, and what suggestions he has for housetraining and puppy kindergarten classes.

sides vaccinations, preventive medicine includes heartworm prevention, spaying and neutering, and good nutrition. Take notes or ask for informational pamphlets if necessary. Being a well-informed dog owner will enable you to better care for your dog.

Because your puppy will need a series of vaccinations, expect to make a couple more visits after this initial one. Booster vaccinations are generally recommended every three weeks up to 4 to 6 months of age.

During each examination, your veterinarian will assess whether your puppy is developing and maturing at a normal rate. You can also get a better idea whether your puppy is developing normally (and probably get some reassurance!) by referring to the "Developmental Chart" in Appendix A. Remember that your puppy's growth and development is controlled by genetic and environmental factors. A puppy goes through different phases of maturation until he reaches adulthood. The most rapid growth phase is during the first six months of life. Just like teenagers, puppies go through an awkward rapid-growth phase where their bodies don't seem to fit and they bumble around clumsily. Some puppies are downright ugly. Don't panic or run to the breeder to demand your money back if your puppy doesn't look or act exactly the way you imagined. Most likely your puppy will emerge

What Your Vet Might Ask You

Your veterinarian depends on getting information from you. Be prepared to answer questions such as these:

○ In general, how are things going? Do you have any concerns or questions?

○ How long have you had the puppy?

○ What diet are you feeding? Has the puppy's appetite been good?

○ Has there been any vomiting or diarrhea/loose stools?

○ Have you observed any worms in your puppy's stool?

○ Is your puppy indoor, outdoor, or both?

○ Are you having any behavior problems?

○ Have you had problems with external parasites such as fleas or ticks?

from adolescence looking like the fine specimen of doghood he's meant to be.

Mention everything you can think of, even details that seem unimportant. You'll be helping your veterinarian make a more accurate initial assessment and diagnosis. Sneezing, scratching, and coughing, or visible lumps or bumps may seem trivial but could prove to be meaningful symptoms to your veterinarian. All should be addressed during your dog's physical examination. It's better to be too informative than not informative enough.

Preventive Medicine

An annual exam is much more than just an opportunity for your dog to get his vaccinations. Even though your dog may appear to be in perfect health, his annual exam provides the veterinarian a chance to thoroughly examine him to make sure no unseen problems exist. Veterinarians are highly trained observers who can often spot details that even the most conscientious owners don't notice. Health problems that are detected early are often less damaging as well as less expensive to treat.

Annual Visits: What to Expect

A typical visit to your veterinarian should be a pleasant and informative experience. Schedule an appointment so the veterinarian is prepared to meet your dog's needs and allows enough time for your visit. At times, your veterinarian will have to deal with emergencies, and the actual time spent with your dog may be delayed or shortened. Be patient and remember that you would certainly want your veterinarian's immediate and complete attention if your dog were experiencing a medical emergency.

If you are taking your dog to a new veterinarian for his annual physical examination and routine vaccinations, bring along records of any previous vaccinations administered by the breeder or any other veterinarian. It's a good idea to keep complete records of all medical care your dog receives throughout his lifetime. Just as you keep receipts for tax-deductible items in a specific place or file, your dog's medical records deserve the same care. Something as simple as a file folder or shoebox will do, as will something more elaborate, such as one of the many puppy keepsake books on the market.

Before you enter the clinic, prepare your dog for the visit, especially if he's aggressive toward other animals. Keep him on a leash, and muzzle him if necessary to ensure everyone's safety. Use common sense in deciding whether to bring your children. If your kids are likely to cause disruption in the clinic, be considerate and leave them with a babysitter; or arrange beforehand to drop Spanky off at the clinic before his exam and to pick him up afterward. If necessary, you can talk with the technician or veterinarian by phone.

A veterinary clinic is full of unusual smells and strange animals. Such distractions can cause your dog to forget his usual polite behavior, so keep a close eye on him and a firm grip on the leash. Once in the exam room, you may be asked to help restrain your dog. If you're uncomfortable doing this, ask that the technician restrain your dog instead. Most veterinarians actually prefer having their trained technicians hold or restrain your dog during examinations and procedures. Some dogs bite out of fear when they're in strange situations, so it's not uncommon for the veterinarian or technician to muzzle the dog before performing the exam. Don't be offended by this. Instead, realize that most if not all veterinarians have suffered serious bites at one time or another and must take precautions to protect themselves. If your dog experiences extreme fear when he enters the clinic or at any time during the examination, your veterinarian may prescribe calming sedatives to be given before the next visit.

During the exam, you'll be "speaking" for your dog since he can't speak for himself. The veterinarian's careful and complete physical examination—along with your own observations—is crucial to ensure an accurate diagnosis. Before the visit, write down what you've noticed about your dog's behavior or appearance, as well as any questions you want to ask (and remember that all questions are worth asking!). It's not unusual for dog owners to forget to express a serious concern or ask a crucial question once they focus on what's going on. As in all medicine, you must be an aggressive consumer.

During the examination and treatment of your dog, be supportive but stay out of the way unless you're asked to help. If you try to pet or soothe your dog while the examination is going on, your veterinarian may not be able to hear your dog's heart and lung sounds clearly. Ask your questions at appropriate times during the examination, not when he's listening with his stethoscope.

A thorough veterinary exam begins with a check of temperature, pulse, respiration rate, and body weight, followed by a hands-on, head-to-tail body check. Careful scrutiny of the head area can reveal myriad conditions. Eye appearance can indicate such problems as anemia, infections, and jaundice, as well as glaucoma, corneal abrasions, and other eye diseases and injuries. If your dog has been shaking his head, scratching his ears, or giving off an unpleasant odor, he may have an ear infection.

Your veterinarian will look for inflammation or unusual discharge from the eyes, ears, and nose; changes in color, texture, moisture, or shape of the nose; nasal obstructions or foreign objects in the mouth; and dental disease, bad breath, or abnormal growths in or around the mouth.

Moving on, the veterinarian will listen to the heart and lungs with a stethoscope. Early heart disease is often discovered during an annual health exam. Then the veterinarian will palpate the entire body, feeling for organ position and size, abnormal lumps or bumps, and any areas that seem painful. Palpation also indicates condition of the joints, muscles, skin, lymph nodes, and hair. The genital area will be checked for discharges and growths.

At the same time, the veterinarian will be giving your dog a visual

Did You Know?

Tests conducted at the Institute for the Study of Animal Problems in Washington, D.C., revealed that dogs and cats, like humans, are either right- or left-handed.

Keeping a Pet Diary

Writing down your daily observations of Spanky's eating, elimination habits, behavior, and activities is a great way to keep track of what's normal for him. This will help you see patterns develop and notice changes, such as his choosing an unusual spot to sleep, which may indicate something's wrong. And if Spanky becomes ill, your diary will be invaluable to the veterinarian—serving as a quick, easy reference about your dog's behavior, including when the symptoms started. A simple spiral-bound notebook is all you need to get started. Write a paragraph each night, and you'll soon have not only a great veterinary resource but also a record of your dog's days.

going-over—seeing how he moves; looking at the condition of the skin and coat; and checking for fleas, ticks, and other external parasites. She may discuss how much your dog weighs and whether he needs less food and more exercise.

If all is well, Spanky will get a clean bill of health, and you can take him home, knowing you've been doing a great job of caring for him. But sometimes even the best-cared-for dogs get sick or injured. Unless the problem is external—an abscess, for instance—some form of diagnostic test will probably be required. Based on the findings of the exam, your veterinarian may suggest performing a complete blood count, a chemistry profile, a urinalysis, a chest x-ray, ultrasonography, endoscopy, or an electrocardiogram. These diagnostic aids can help the veterinarian identify what's troubling your dog.

Vaccinations

The control of so many viral diseases that affect puppies and dogs is considered a prominent success of twentieth-century veterinary medicine. Part of being a responsible owner is providing your puppy with preventive care through a series of vaccinations as a puppy and throughout life as an adult.

Why Vaccinate

Vaccination is the most effective method of preventing viral diseases, which can lead to serious illness and even death. Many of these viruses are ever-present in the environment and can be contracted through direct or indirect contact. This is a danger to dogs as well as to the human population if a zoonotic disease—a disease that can be passed from animal to person—such as rabies is involved.

Young puppies are at great risk for contracting many serious viral diseases because their immune systems are immature. That's why they need a series of vaccinations to confer complete immunity.

> Part of being a responsible owner is providing your puppy with preventive care through a series of vaccinations as a puppy and throughout life as an adult.

Young puppies are initially protected from disease by the immunity they receive from their mothers while still in the womb and from the maternally derived antibodies (MDA) that are present in her milk during the pups' first 48 hours of life. This immunity lasts until the puppy is six to eight weeks old. While the protection conferred by the MDA is important for puppies during the first weeks of life, it can also block the response from their immune system to initial vaccinations. If the MDA levels are too high when the first vaccinations are given, the vaccinations can fail. Levels of MDA can be too low to prevent infection yet high enough to prevent the vaccines from doing their work. This time frame when pups are most prone to disease is called the "window of susceptibility." The only way to determine MDA levels is by measuring the level of antibodies in the blood. This is expensive and impractical in an everyday animal hospital, so veterinarians instead give a series of vaccinations to reduce the chance of vaccination failure and decrease the window of susceptibility.

When to Vaccinate

In comparison to human medicine where there are definite widely used vaccination schedules, veterinary medicine contains no such consensus. This is because there are so many vaccine manufacturers, each of which recommends a different schedule for its particular line of vaccinations. The guideline is simply this: discuss with your veterinarian the particulars of his or her recommended vaccination schedule, which can vary depending on which diseases are most common in your area.

In general, most veterinarians recommend starting the vaccination series at six weeks of age, eight weeks at the latest. The puppy will need to return at three- to four-week intervals until he's received a total of four to five sets by the age of 18 to 20 weeks. It's critical that these vaccinations be administered on schedule and performed to meet the series requirements. A majority of veterinarians also recommend that the puppy have limited exposure to other dogs of questionable vaccination status and be kept close to home until the entire series of vaccinations has

been given and the puppy has built up sufficient immunity. If you plan to enroll your new pet in puppy kindergarten, which usually begins at 10 to 12 weeks of age, be sure the trainer requires proof of vaccination from all the "students."

Recommended Vaccinations

Across the country and from clinic to clinic, you'll find variations in the vaccinations administered.

Sample Vaccination Schedule

This chart shows a typical vaccine schedule currently recommended by veterinarians. Since each puppy is an individual, the actual schedule your vet designs may be somewhat different, depending on your pup's health and the diseases prevalent in your area.

○ 8 weeks: Distemper, Hepatitis, Leptospirosis, Parainfluenza and Parvo (DHLPP), usually combined in one injection.

○ 12 weeks: DHLPP, usually combined in one injection. Bordetella if pup will be going to kennels, groomers, or shows. First Lyme vaccination if pup will be exposed to ticks. Rabies if state law allows vaccination this early.

○ 16 weeks: DHLPP, usually combined in one injection. Second Lyme vaccination if first given at 12 weeks. Rabies if not given at 12 weeks.

○ 1 year after last vaccination: DHLPP, usually combined in one injection. Bordatella and Lyme if previously given. Rabies.

However, all puppies should be immunized against viral agents that are considered prevalent or endemic in puppies. The following descriptions of each disease are intended simply to provide you with the most pertinent information on those most prevalent and to point out which diseases can be transmitted between people and dogs.

Most veterinarians use combination vaccines that provide protection against a number of different diseases through a single injection. Quite a few different combinations are available, so ask your veterinarian what diseases his or her combination vaccine protects against. Your veterinarian may recommend annual booster shots or a booster one year after the series is completed, followed by boosters every three years.

Canine Distemper Virus (CDV)   CDV is the most deadly worldwide viral disease of dogs. This virus, which is closely related to the measles virus, is a severe, highly contagious disease affecting many organ systems. CDV can affect dogs of any age, but puppies that haven't been vaccinated and whose MDA levels are too low to be protective are most susceptible. CDV poses a danger not only to our domestic canine friends but also to many wild animals, including foxes, coyotes, wolves, ferrets, minks, skunks, and raccoons. Because so many wild animals are susceptible to CDV, they are a constant potential source of infection to family dogs who come in contact with them. Wild and domestic animals spread this disease rapidly because they shed the virus in all body secretions and excretions. Fortunately, CDV doesn't survive long in the environment because it's easily destroyed by dry conditions and by most disinfectants. Areas where dogs are housed together in large numbers, such as pet shops and animal shelters, are high-risk areas. With the widespread vaccination of dogs in industrialized nations, the incidence of this terrible viral disease has been greatly reduced, but CDV should still be taken seriously.

Dogs become infected with CDV by inhaling the virus into the respiratory tract. From there the virus spreads quickly to tonsils and bronchial lymph nodes. Even before clinical signs of disease are evident, the virus travels through the bloodstream to the bone marrow, spleen, other lymph nodes, stomach, and small intestine. Other organs frequently affected include the urinary system, the eyes, and the skin. The central nervous system is often the most seriously affected. The outcome of CDV depends primarily on the dog's immune system. If the dog's body can mount a proper immune response, a mild infection will occur and the dog should be completely free of the virus 14 days after exposure. However, if the dog's immune system is weak and fails to suppress this virus, serious clinical signs will occur.

One effect of CDV is suppression of the immune system, which allows the invasion of many secondary bacterial infections.

Some of the most common clinical signs evident in dogs infected with CDV are depression, anorexia, and a fluctuating fever range. Respiratory signs are common as well, and include a thick discharge from the nose, cough, and difficulty breathing. In severe cases, pneumonia can develop. Gastrointestinal signs involve vomiting and diarrhea. The eyes can also exhibit a thick discharge. All this discharge can result in secondary conjunctivitis and dry eye syndrome. The effects on the central nervous system are the most serious of all. These include seizures, behavioral changes, pacing, circling, muscle twitching, difficulty walking, and partial paralysis. Two classic signs of distemper are discolored, pitted teeth, and hardening of the pads of the feet. The latter symptom contributed to CDV being known as "hardpad disease." Be aware that these clinical signs vary from case to case, with some dogs recovering quickly while others succumb to the disease.

The diagnosis of CDV is usually made through clinical signs in a puppy who has not had proper vaccinations and or who may have been exposed to the virus. Diagnostic tests that can be performed by a veterinarian include blood work, x-rays, cerebrospinal fluid analysis, titer checks, and virology. Even with these tests, a definitive diagnosis of CDV can be difficult.

No single CDV treatment is uniformly effective. For the most part, treatment consists of supportive therapy such as antibiotics for secondary infections; medications to control vomiting and diarrhea; anticonvulsants to control seizures; good fluid and nutritional support via intravenous therapy if necessary;

Did You Know?

In 1957, Laika became the first dog in space, riding aboard the Soviet satellite Sputnik 2.

respiratory support with bronchodilators for pneumonia; medication to control fever; and last but not least, a lot of basic nursing care to keep the puppy comfortable. Despite even the best care, some puppies still die or fail to make a complete recovery.

Young puppies have the highest mortality rates. It's important to realize that symptoms may start out mild but can progress to severe incapacitating neurologic disease. In advanced cases of CDV, euthanasia is a humane option. Vaccination is the only preventive against this terrible disease.

A discussion of CDV must include information on the disease known as old-dog encephalitis (ODE). This is a rare condition in which older dogs may exhibit a wide range of neurological signs. It's possible that CDV has persisted in the brain for years and only shows clinical disease signs at a later age. The exact disease process of ODE is still not fully understood.

Infectious Canine Hepatitis (ICH)   This contagious disease of dogs and other wild animals is caused by canine adenovirus type 1 (CAV-1). It is closely related to canine adenovirus type 2 (CAV-2), which is known to be a contributing cause of infectious tracheobronchitis, also known as kennel cough. Fortunately, vaccination programs have greatly reduced the incidence of ICH, making it primarily a disease of unvaccinated dogs. Wild animals are a constant reservoir for infection.

This virus is found in all body tissues and is secreted in urine, feces, and saliva by infected animals. A dog can be infected by inhaling the virus or taking it in orally. The main organs that can be affected are the liver, the kidneys, the spleen, and the lungs. Carriers of this disease can shed the virus for more than six months in their urine. In addition to this length of "infectivity," the virus can survive in the environment for many months, although it can be killed by bleach.

Clinical signs of ICH vary greatly, ranging from mild fever to fatal illness. Watch for signs of lethargy, lack of appetite, thirst, conjunctivitis, thick discharge from the eyes and nose, abdominal pain, vomiting, diarrhea, bleeding gums, disorientation, seizures, and swelling around the head or neck. If the infection affects the eyes, the classic "hepatitis blue eye"—when the eye appears blue and cloudy—is often a helpful diagnostic tool. With liver involvement, one of the worst consequences is a disruption of the normal blood-clotting mechanism. In severe cases of ICH, uncontrollable bleeding occurs, followed by death. The mortality rate is highest in young unvaccinated puppies.

Treatment must be started as soon as a dog shows signs consistent with this disease. A dog with ICH needs supportive therapy, including intravenous fluids, antibiotics, and sometimes blood transfusions.

Fortunately, if proper vaccinations are administered, the likelihood of contracting ICH is extremely low. Vaccination against ICH should start at six to eight weeks of age, with boosters given three to four weeks apart until four complete sets have been given.

Canine Adenovirus Type 2 (CAV-2)   CAV-2 is one of the many infectious agents responsible for the highly contagious tracheobronchitis, better known as kennel cough. The other infectious agents known to contribute to kennel cough are the bacteria *Bordetella bronchiseptica* and the following viruses: canine parainfluenza; canine adenovirus, types 1 and 2; canine herpesvirus; canine reoviruses, types 1, 2, and 3. Kennel cough spreads rapidly among confined animals such as those housed at animal shelters, boarding kennels, and even

veterinary hospitals. However, close contact with other dogs such as through fences or immediate contact is also a method of transmission. This disease is spread by coughing and sneezing or can be transmitted through animal handlers, bowls, and cages.

In a majority of cases, the disease is mild and self-limiting and is confined to the upper respiratory system. The disease lasts anywhere from seven to 21 days. The major clinical signs noted with this form are a hacking, dry-sounding cough. Owners often report that their dog is choking or has something caught in his throat. Usually, the cough becomes worse with excitement or exercise. The veterinarian can easily elicit a cough by gently palpating the trachea. The dog typically remains active and doesn't run a fever. Some dogs may have a mild discharge from the eyes and nose.

In those few dogs that develop the severe form of kennel cough, the above signs are usually much more pronounced. The dog may also run a fever, have no interest in eating, seem depressed, and have a thick discharge from the eyes and nose, a productive cough, and bronchopneumonia. When signs are this severe, it's hard to differentiate kennel cough from distemper. Dogs can die from the severe form of kennel cough, so don't ignore the symptoms.

The diagnosis of kennel cough is usually based on clinical symptoms and a history of exposure, such as at an animal shelter or boarding kennel. The treatment depends on how serious the signs are. In mild cases, if the cough is infrequent and the dog is active and eating well, many veterinarians may elect to let the disease run its course without any antibiotics or cough suppressants. For those dogs with a persistent cough or more severe signs, veterinarians often prescribe antibiotics, cough suppressants (so you and the dog can get some sleep), and sometimes bronchodilators. Good nutrition and hygiene will help speed the rate of recovery.

Prevention of canine adenovirus type 2 (CAV-2) and its resulting kennel cough disease is obtained through proper vaccination as a puppy and then annually as an adult. Further discussion of the contributing factors of kennel cough are addressed in other parts of this chapter.

Canine Parainfluenza Virus   Canine parainfluenza is a common upper respiratory disease as well as a contributor to the kennel cough complex. It, too, is highly contagious and spread primarily through coughing and sneezing. Generally, the signs attributed to parainfluenza are mild: coughing, sneezing, and discharge from eyes and nose. Sometimes, though, secondary infectious agents are involved, leading to more severe illness. Refer to the above discussion on kennel cough for complete details.

Diagnosis of canine parainfluenza is based on the symptoms the dog shows and whether he's been exposed to sick dogs or hasn't been vaccinated. Treatment usually involves a course of antibiotic therapy. Prevention is provided through the initial puppy vaccination series and carried on throughout life with regular boosters.

Did You Know?

The Chihuahua is the world's smallest breed, while the Irish Wolfhound is the tallest and the Saint Bernard is the heaviest.

Bordetella bronchiseptica   This bacteria has been identified as one of the primary causes of the kennel cough complex. Just as the viral agents that contribute to kennel cough are highly contagious, so is *Bordetella bronchiseptica*, which is rapidly spread by coughing, sneezing, and exposure to infected cages and bowls. Diagnosis relies on clinical signs and recent exposure, such as at an animal shelter or boarding facility. Treatment involves appropriate antibiotics and cough suppressants when necessary. All dogs who are frequently in contact with other dogs such as at dog shows, grooming parlors, boarding kennels, or even the neighbors' dogs should be vaccinated against *Bordetella bronchiseptica*. The *Bordetella bronchiseptica* vaccine is often given intranasally and is highly effective.

Leptospirosis   Leptospirosis is a contagious disease of animals and humans that results in anything from asymptomatic infections to a range of various disease conditions. The organs usually affected are the kidneys, liver, and reproductive organs. Large numbers of this microorganism can be shed through the urine of an affected animal for many months to years. This disease for both people and animals is often waterborne since the microorganisms can survive in water for an extended length of time. Infection occurs when a person or animal comes in contact with leptospirosis-laden water, food, bedding, soil, plants, or any other object that has been infected. The microorganisms are able to penetrate mucous membranes or areas on the body where an abrasion or opening in the skin exists. Leptospirosis can also be transmitted to puppies in the womb, through sexual intercourse, and through bite wounds. Wild animal and rodent populations are constant reservoirs for leptospirosis.

Humans can acquire an infection not only from contact with their infected dog but also from waters contaminated by urine of infected animals. The most common clinical symptoms in people are fever, headache, rash, muscle pain, and depression. As with infection in animals, the most severe risk if not identified and treated appropriately is kidney failure.

With dogs, there are three different types of leptospirosis to be concerned about: *Leptospira icterohaemorrhagiae, Leptospira canicola,* and *Leptospira grippotyphosa.* This disease can affect any dog regardless of age. Clinical signs of leptospirosis are fever, depression, anorexia, vomiting, muscle pain, dehydration, conjunctivitis, bleeding gums, uncontrollable hemorrhaging, and sudden death in some. Since the primary target organs are the kidneys and liver, both kidney and liver failure can result. Other less common clinical outcomes are abortions or stillbirths and meningitis. In the more severe cases, onset of symptoms can be rapid.

Diagnosis of leptospirosis is based on blood work, urinalysis, blood titers, and consistent clinical signs. The goals of treatment rely on rehydration, and steps to repair liver and kidney failure when present. Antibiotics are also crucial to proper treatment. During the treatment period, it is crucial for owners and hospital staff to take precautions with exposure to contaminated urine because of the risk of disease transmittal.

Discuss with your veterinarian whether he or she recommends a vaccination against leptospirosis, which today is relatively uncommon in dogs. Many dogs, especially toy breeds, have reactions to this vaccine, and your veterinarian may choose not to give it unless the disease is common in your area. Practicing effective rodent control is also important for prevention.

Canine Parvovirus (CPV)   Canine parvovirus type 2 has been a major health concern for dogs worldwide since it was identified in 1978. This virus is highly contagious with an acute onset leading to severe illness and often even death. This disease is spread through fecal contact or can be taken in orally. Infected dogs shed tremendous amounts of the virus in their feces, and parvovirus can survive and continue to be infectious in the environment

and on objects for many months, contributing to this deadly disease's continual spread among susceptible dogs.

Dogs of all ages and breeds can be affected by parvovirus, but it tends to strike puppies between six weeks and six months more often. Also, certain breeds seem to have a higher incidence of parvovirus than others: Rottweilers, Doberman Pinschers, Beagles, American Pit Bull Terriers, and black Labrador Retrievers. No one has been able to identify why these breeds suffer more cases of parvovirus than others. It could simply be that the disease is more commonly seen in these breeds because all are extremely popular compared to others.

Parvovirus produces two different disease forms: myocarditis and enteritis. Because most dogs of breeding age these days have been vaccinated against parvovirus, the neonatal myocarditis form is less common. Parvoviral-induced myocarditis results in sudden death of young puppies between the ages of four to eight weeks.

The most common form of parvovirus leads to a severe enteritis. Signs of this form include lack of appetite, fever, severe depression, vomiting, frequent and sometimes bloody diarrhea, hypothermia, severe dehydration, and bacterial infections of the bloodstream (sepsis). Parvovirus attacks the rapidly dividing cells of the intestine, bone marrow, and lymphoid tissue. The intestine is stripped of its ability to properly absorb nutrients, contributing to the severe vomiting and diarrhea associated with this disease.

The severity of parvovirus is often complicated by other stresses on the puppy's immune system such as unsanitary living conditions, and concurrent diseases such as distemper, coronavirus, and intestinal parasites.

Diagnosis of parvovirus may be based on several parameters: clinical signs, low white blood cell count, x-rays to rule out foreign bodies in intestines, and a test that detects viral shedding through the feces of a sick animal. Veterinarians have an in-house laboratory test that can be done within minutes to check for the presence of parvovirus in the feces. This test is extremely accurate if the puppy is shedding the virus. However, false negatives can occur if the test is performed before the puppy begins the virus-shedding process.

There is no cure for parvovirus, only supportive therapy to re-hydrate the animal and correct nutritional imbalances, and antibi-otics to prevent bacterial sepsis. Intravenous fluids containing the proper electrolytes are crucial to therapy since the puppy is un-able to handle any intake by mouth. Many veterinarians also ad-minister medication to help control the vomiting and diarrhea. In severe cases where the bone marrow has been greatly affected, a blood transfusion may be required.

The prognosis for parvovirus varies from case to case. If treated early, and the puppy survives the first three to four days of therapy, the prognosis is much improved; but if treatment is delayed and the puppy becomes severely dehydrated and weak-ened from other complications, the chances for recovery are greatly lessened.

Parvovirus is only preventable with vaccination. The complete series of puppy vaccinations must be administered at the appro-priate ages starting at six weeks of age through the age of 18 weeks. Young puppies that have not finished their vaccination se-ries should be isolated from dogs of questionable vaccination sta-tus. Regular vaccination against parvovirus is recommended for the remainder of the dog's life.

If you have had the misfortune of having a puppy die from parvovirus, it's best to wait at least six months before introducing another puppy into the household. Parvovirus is highly resistant and can remain infective in the environment and on objects for many months. Food dishes, crates, and other objects can be effectively disinfected with a 1:32 mixture of bleach to water. Take all necessary precautions to prevent this disease. Every small-animal veterinarian hates to see any puppy suffer the ill effects of parvovirus.

Canine Coronavirus (CCV)   Coronavirus is very similar to parvovirus in the clinical signs it causes, but it's generally a much less severe disease. Coronavirus infection may often occur without obvious clinical signs. A majority of outbreaks thus far have been linked to boarding kennels and dog shows. A puppy can die from coronavirus if it gets severely dehydrated from the diarrhea that can occur, but this is rare.

Coronavirus, like parvovirus, is spread rapidly orally or from contact with infected feces. Clinical signs include sudden appetite loss, depression, vomiting, and diarrhea. Most dogs don't run a fever, and the duration of symptoms is usually brief.

A definitive diagnosis of coronavirus requires specialized laboratory tests that can detect the virus in a dog's feces. However, even if the virus is detected in the feces, it is important to note that many healthy dogs shed coronavirus in their feces. Therefore, the veterinarian must often base the diagnosis on  clinical symptoms and a recent history of possible exposure.

Treatment is supportive and depends on the symptoms. The dog may need intravenous fluid therapy and medication to control vomiting and diarrhea. Most dogs recover from coronavirus rapidly with timely and appropriate treatment.

Coronavirus can be prevented with a vaccination, but it's not routinely given unless the disease is common in a particular area. Ask your veterinarian about it if your dog is at high risk from being boarded frequently or attending dog shows.

Rabies   Rabies is a disease of worldwide prominence that can affect all warm-blooded animals, including humans, and has a mortality rate of close to 100 percent. In many developing countries of Asia, Africa, and Latin America, dog rabies remains a serious health problem with significant domestic animal and human mortality. In the United States, the main problem with rabies is the persistence of the disease in wildlife populations rather than in domestic animals. Until rabies can be eradicated in wildlife such as foxes, skunks, and raccoons, domestic animals, livestock, and people are at risk of infection. Therefore, your dog's rabies vaccinations are a must. This is a primary reason why officials do not recommend keeping wild animals as pets and using extreme caution in aiding an injured wild animal.

> Rabies is a disease of worldwide prominence that can affect all warm-blooded animals, including humans, and has a mortality rate of close to 100 percent.

In humans, rabies results in fatal encephalitis. Humans can be infected by bites from rabid animals and through exposure to a rabid animal's saliva. Once clinical signs of rabies develop, the disease is almost always fatal. Because of the public health significance of rabies, public health officials must be contacted if there is any question of human exposure. Since the consequences of rabies are so severe, most veterinarians and animal control officers receive pre-exposure vaccinations to offer a first line of protection. Fortunately, the incidence of human rabies is extremely low in the United States.

In dogs, rabies is transmitted via the saliva from the bite of an infected animal. From the bite wound, the virus moves into the animal's peripheral nervous system and then to the animal's central nervous system (spinal cord and brain). The virus then spreads from the brain to the animal's salivary glands and other tissues of the body by way of their nerve supply. This virus travels the body through the animal's nervous system instead of the usual spread via the bloodstream. The time frame for clinical signs to appear is anywhere from two to eight weeks. However, the virus is shed in the animal's saliva in approximately eight to ten days.

There are three recognized phases of rabies: the prodromal phase, the furious "mad dog" phase, and finally the paralytic phase. The prodromal phase is rarely noticed due to the lack of distinct clinical signs. If any change is noted in the dog, it is a subtle change in behavior. The dog may stop eating and go off to be alone. This prodromal phase lasts from two to three days. Next comes the furious phase, characterized by irrational behavior and extreme aggressiveness. The dog loses all sense of fear of any other animal or human and is extremely dangerous to be around. The facial expression is full of anxiety, and pupils are often dilated. Many times the dog becomes unable to swallow water and excessive salivation occurs. The dog becomes extremely sensitive to any noise or light stimulus. As the rabies progresses, the dog soon becomes uncoordinated and disoriented. Dogs rarely live more than 10 days after clinical signs begin. The furious phase lasts from two to four days. The final paralytic phase is classified by paralysis of throat and jaw muscles noted by excessive drooling and change in bark, paralysis of legs, depression, coma, and finally death from respiratory paralysis. The paralytic phase is rapid and death ensues in just a few hours.

The diagnosis of rabies is based on postmortem evaluation of brain tissue. The early diagnosis of any rabid animal is vital to ensure that exposed animals and humans can take necessary precautions. There is no treatment for rabies, and the disease is almost 100 percent fatal in domestic animals. Because of the significant public health risk, all animals suspected of rabies must be quarantined or euthanized and public health authorities notified.

The prevention of rabies in the domestic animal population is crucial. For that reason, every state requires that dogs be vaccinated against rabies. Puppies are first vaccinated at three months and again at one year of age. After the vaccination at one year, dogs are vaccinated against rabies every one or three years. There are vaccines that give one-year or three-year protection, but each state has its own laws about how often the vaccine must be given. Your veterinarian will know what the law is for your state.

Lyme Disease   This multisystemic disease transmitted by ticks affects dogs, cats, horses, cows, wild animals, and humans. It's considered endemic in Wisconsin, Minnesota, and the northeastern United States, and has been reported in most other states, as well as in Canada, Europe, and Australia. Lyme disease is transmissible between dogs and people, with human cases distributed in parallel numbers in endemic regions.

The causative agent of Lyme disease is the spirochete *Borrelia burgdorferi,* which is carried by the deer tick, the dog tick, several other tick species, horseflies, deerflies, and mosquitoes. However, only ticks, primarily the deer tick, have been linked with disease transmission. Infection occurs through the bite of a tick carrying *Borrelia burgdorferi.* Transmission has also been reported transplacentally (through the placenta) or through infected urine.

Did You Know?

A dog's heart beats between 60 and 120 times per minute, compared with 60 to 80 times per minute for humans.

The most common clinical signs include joint inflammation, appetite loss, weight loss, lethargy, and fever; but some dogs just show up lame without any other symptoms. Diagnosis is based on a history of exposure to ticks or a tick-infested area in conjunction with clinical signs. Laboratory confirmation can be obtained through titers on blood or joint fluid.

Treatment of Lyme disease requires antibiotic therapy for at least three weeks. Dogs should show a quick response to the antibiotics. The best way to prevent Lyme disease is to protect your dog against ticks with the use of effective collars, sprays, and other repellents. If you live in an endemic area, be sure to check your dog daily for ticks. A vaccination for Lyme disease does exist, but it's not usually given unless you live in a high-risk area. Your veterinarian can help you decide what is best for your dog.

The Reproductive Cycle

By the time a male or female dog reaches six to nine months of age, her hormones have kicked in and she is able to reproduce, even though she isn't fully mature emotionally or physically.

In females, the reproductive cycle begins when they enter estrus, or heat. Depending on the size and breed of your female dog, you can expect her to reach sexual maturity and come into heat anywhere between six months to one year of age. Estrus usually occurs every six months and consists of four stages. It

starts with a bleeding phase called proestrus, which lasts three to 17 days, with an average of nine days. Signs of proestrus are vulvar swelling and a bloody, mucousy discharge. During this stage, your female will be aggressive toward any males that try to have their way with her.

Proestrus is followed by estrus, during which your Blossom will be even more attractive to male dogs and will eagerly seek out their advances, twitching her tail in invitation. Estrus usually lasts about nine days, but can range from three to 21 days, depending on the individual dog. Ovulation occurs about two days after the onset of estrus, or about 12 days after the onset of proestrus. The estrus cycle can initiate a temporary personality change. It's not unusual for dogs to seem cross or agitated while in heat. During this entire period, you must keep your female away from all male dogs to prevent unwanted breeding. Her scent will draw male dogs from miles away and they'll do whatever it takes to get to her, so she'll need to be confined in your home or in a secure pen or yard that can't be dug or jumped into. After estrus come diestrus and anestrus, which are periods of rest for the reproductive system.

When male dogs become sexually mature, their desire and ability to mate are not confined to a certain period. They are ready, willing, and able at any time, as long as they have access to a receptive female. A male dog will have the urge to roam in search of romance as well as to mark its territory just in case a willing female might be around to sniff his message. Intact males who are not bred lead a life of frustration. If a female isn't available, your dog will satisfy his urges by humping pillows, legs, or anything he can find that seems suitable. Not an attractive habit by any means!

Spaying and Neutering

Not surprisingly, living with an intact dog of either sex can be messy and frustrating, for both you and the dog. Fortunately, surgical neutering is a safe, effective way to prevent embarrassing behavior and unwanted pregnancies. It also provides a number of health benefits for both sexes.

The Road to Puppyhood

Amy loved the idea of raising a litter of puppies; but her concern for the pet overpopulation problem had always taken precedence. She adopted animals that needed a home and made sure all were neutered. Then she acquired Dodger, a show-quality Australian Terrier. Dodger was soon followed by a female Australian terrier, CeCe, and Amy's friends in the breed urged her to take the puppy plunge. Amy was hesitant, but decided to breed CeCe after thinking about it for four years. "If I do it responsibly," she thought, "we might both enjoy the experience."

CeCe was a show-quality dog with a lovely temperament, but Amy knew that wasn't enough. She had CeCe checked by specialists for a variety of hereditary problems, updated her vaccinations, and dewormed her so she wouldn't pass on any intestinal parasites. She chose a father of the same quality who had undergone the same extensive testing. (Dodger had been neutered because he had inherited knee problems.)

At first, CeCe's pregnancy was uneventful, until she passed a blood clot and some discharge. Amy took her in for an ultrasound to make sure everything was okay. On the sixtieth day, right on schedule, CeCe went into labor. After two hours, no puppies had emerged, and CeCe's misery was intense. She looked terrified. Amy wrapped her in a towel and took her to the animal hospital, where the veterinarian recommended a Caesarean section. Out came three puppies, all healthy, but Amy was so unnerved by the whole experience that she asked the surgeon to spay CeCe right then and there.

That wasn't the end of their adventure. When Amy took CeCe and the puppies home, CeCe wanted nothing to do with her offspring. She growled and tried to bite the pups as they tried to nurse. Amy smeared them with some of CeCe's milk, and all seemed to be well—until CeCe developed a bladder infection. That required a urine culture and two types of antibiotics before it cleared up.

Amy loved the puppies, but she was cleaning up after them constantly for nine weeks. Then they went to their new homes, which she had carefully chosen far in advance of the whole ordeal. All in all, Amy's costs for the litter were about $1,800: $300 each for the pre-breeding exam and the stud fee, $100 for the ultrasound, $750 for the C-section, $150 for the cystitis treatment, and about $200 for puppy vaccinations and deworming. Would she do it again? No way, Amy says, and she thinks CeCe would agree.

Spay surgery, which your veterinarian may refer to as an ovario-hysterectomy, is the removal of the ovaries, fallopian tubes, and uterus, thus ending heat cycles and mood swings. A spayed female won't drip blood on your newly cleaned carpet and won't have to be kept away from males while she's in heat. Nor will you have to do the hard work of finding good homes for any puppies she might produce. A spayed female is protected from uterine infections, which can be fatal if not caught early, and the possibility of a difficult or dangerous pregnancy. If your female dog is spayed before her first heat cycle, her chances of developing mammary cancer plummet. Fifty percent of mammary tumors are malignant in dogs, but studies show that fewer than one percent of females spayed before their first heat cycle develop mammary cancer. The risk increases to 25 percent after they have one heat cycle. Spaying also eliminates the possibility of cancers associated with the reproductive tract, such as ovarian and uterine cancer. These are risks hardly worth taking for a beloved dog who isn't intended for breeding.

The neutering of a male dog simply involves removing his testicles, an operation called an orchiectomy. After this surgery, your dog's desire to roam, hump everything in sight, and mark his territory will be diminished or even eliminated; and he'll no longer be at risk of testicular cancer, which is more common when one or both testicles are retained inside the body. Altered males are also less prone to prostate disease—a potentially life-threatening condition that involves blood in the urine, straining, or inability to urinate or defecate, and prostatic abscesses— to painful benign tumors around the rectal area.

In both sexes, an altered dog focuses more on his or her owner, instead of on fulfilling sexual desires. License fees are also less expensive for a dog who can't reproduce, since the county or state is assured that the pet won't be contributing to the cost of caring for unwanted shelter animals.

Spay/neuter surgery can take place as early as four to six months of age. This is before adult reproductive behaviors are learned. If spay/neuter surgery is postponed until later in life, the benefits are not as pronounced or are eliminated.

The surgery is painless, although your dog may be a bit sore for a few days afterward. Your veterinarian can provide medication to keep the dog comfortable during the healing process.

The cost for spay or neuter surgery is about $110 for females, $100 for males. A cryptorchid male—which has one or more retained testicles—usually costs more. This fee covers the veterinarian's time for the surgery, the anesthesia, overnight hospitalization, and suture removal. The cost for surgery may be more or less depending on the economics of maintaining a veterinary hospital in your particular area as well as the size, age, and health of your dog. Given all the health and behavior benefits that result from this permanent surgery, the expense is well worth it. You may even save money over the years, since you won't have to board your female during heat cycles, pay for the cost of raising a litter, or spend several hundred dollars on emergency surgery for a raging uterine infection.

Breeding and Overpopulation—The Facts

There are many myths and misconceptions about breeding dogs. Let's look at a few myths and then at the facts.

Myth: Breeding Rocky or Mitzi will give me another dog just like him or her.
Fact: The purpose behind all responsible breeding programs is to improve the breed and ensure that it remains true to its standard for conformation and temperament. Even if your dog is a fine example of the breed standard, you will never be able to produce an exact replica of the mother or father. Each dog has its own dis-

tinct personality and traits. That is why it is referred to as breeding, not cloning.

Myth: Blossom will be a better pet if I allow her to have a litter of puppies before she's spayed.
Fact: As discussed in the section on spaying and neutering, Blossom will be a healthier, more loving pet if she's spayed before her first heat.

Myth: Rocky will be a wimp if I have him neutered.
Fact: Rocky will still be protective, but if he's neutered he won't have that urge to constantly mark his territory by lifting his leg on your sofa, car, or other possessions. Neutering also takes away his desire to escape any enclosure to find a mate. And he won't be humping the minister's leg when he comes over for dinner.

Myth: The operation will be painful.
Fact: Your puppy is under the effects of anesthesia during the entire surgical procedure and feels no pain. There have been many advances in veterinary medicine, and dogs undergo anesthesia, monitoring, and surgical techniques that parallel those in human medicine. Most puppies have little or no postsurgical pain or discomfort; when they do, it can be relieved with pain medication. Owners are usually amazed that their puppies act as if nothing were done, which is another benefit of performing the surgery at an early age. Just as in people, the young and healthy bounce back much more quickly after surgery.

Myth: I'm afraid my dog will die under anesthesia.
Fact: Pre-surgical blood work should be performed to ensure that your puppy is healthy

and to reduce the risks associated with anesthesia. By performing a pre-surgical blood profile, your veterinarian is able to detect subtle changes in your dog's health that may not be evident on physical examination. The information obtained from the blood work is crucial to ensure that your dog is able to handle the anesthesia and the surgery. The anesthetics used today are much safer than those of the past, but they still depend on a healthy liver, kidneys, and lungs for metabolism and elimination by the body. Veterinarians want to provide the best care and to do everything possible to minimize potential complications that can occur with anesthesia and surgery, so be smart and give your consent when the veterinarian recommends the pre-surgical blood work.

Myth: Purebred dogs are expensive. Just look how much I paid for Princess. I can breed her and make back that money, plus a little extra.

Fact: Many people are excited by the possibility of making a lot of money by breeding their purebred dog, but the truth is purebreds cost a lot because of all the money the breeder puts into producing a litter. When done properly, breeding is a very expensive proposition. Costs include veterinary checks of the female's health and condition before she's bred, stud fees and expenses for transporting her to and from the stud, and an ultrasound exam to confirm the pregnancy and number of puppies.

Remember, too, that pregnancy is not risk-free. Complications, which can result in deformed or dead puppies or a dead mother, are always possible. If whelping doesn't go as expected, Princess may need an emergency Caesarean section in the middle of the night, which could lead to the loss of her or the puppies. If the puppies do make it safely into the world, you'll need to pay for dewclaw removal and tail docking if necessary for the breed standard. The puppies will need to be fed once they're weaned, and dewormed and vaccinated at least once. Finally, responsible breeders pay the expense and spend the time to advertise the litter and screen the buyers.

Not only does breeding involve considerable financial commitment, but a great time obligation as well. Even though a male or female dog can be sexually mature at six months of age, neither should be bred before reaching adulthood at two years of age. Dogs younger than two are not prepared physically or emotionally for the rigors of pregnancy, whelping, and puppy care. Females bred too early in life tend to be poor mothers, and you may wind up raising the litter yourself. Also, dogs cannot be certified free of hip or elbow dysplasia or luxating patellas before the age of two years. That's a long time to put up with a female's twice annual heats or a perpetually randy male.

> **Did You Know?**
>
> Big dogs have larger litters than smaller dogs, but smaller dogs generally live longer.

Myth: Purebred dogs are expensive. I can make back the money I spent to purchase Duke by using him as a stud dog.
Fact: Unless Duke has proven himself in the show ring as a dog worthy of being bred and has passed all his health clearances with flying colors, few if any people will pay big bucks to use him as a stud.

Myth: I know there's a pet overpopulation problem, but my dog's a purebred, and they don't ever end up in animal shelters.
Fact: You're right in one respect. The number of unwanted dogs that must be destroyed each year is in the millions. But as many as one-third of the dogs found in animal shelters are purebreds.

They arrive there for the same reasons most mixed breeds do—because they have behavior problems, got too big, or their people decided they were too much bother to take along when they moved. From Chihuahuas to Greyhounds to Golden Retrievers, all kinds of purebreds have been found in animal shelters.

Myth: My kids will find the birth educational.
Fact: Dogs frequently give birth in the dead of night, and it's a messy, bloody business. The facts of life are best taught through video educational programs.

Myth: My dog will get fat and lazy if spayed or neutered.
Fact: Your dog's metabolism is slowing down right about the time it gets spayed or neutered—usually around six months of age. Their major growth spurt is over, so it's natural that they would start to put on a few pounds, especially if they haven't yet been switched to a maintenance diet. Weight gain is caused by too much food and not enough exercise, not because of spaying or neutering. As long as you watch your dog's diet and give him regular exercise, he won't put on weight.

> Weight gain is caused by too much food and not enough exercise, not because of spaying or neutering.

Myth: My dog's personality will change.
Fact: Most dogs' personalities do not fully develop until they're two years old. By spaying or neutering your dog, his or her personality may actually get better. If the procedure is done before the puppy reaches one year, any aggressive behavior should be completely avoided.

Once they realize the time and expense involved, few people decide to enter the business of breeding dogs. If you are still wondering whether you should breed, ask yourself the following questions. Honest answers will help you make the right decision.

○ Is your dog a purebred? Only registered purebreds should be used for breeding.
○ Did you get your dog from an animal shelter or pet store or did you just find it? Any of these dogs, regardless of registration papers, should be spayed/neutered.
○ Are you knowledgeable about your dog's ancestors? You should be able to tell about your dog's pedigree for at least three previous generations. Your dog's recent pedigree should give evidence of several titled dogs in conformation, tracking, obedience, or some other discipline. If not, spay/neuter.
○ Does your dog have a stable temperament with other dogs and people at all times? If not, spay/neuter.
○ Does your dog meet all requirements of the breed standard? Remember that you want to preserve the breed standard. If not, spay/neuter.
○ Are both breed dogs healthy and free of all genetic disease? If applicable, are both dogs OFA certified? If not, do not breed; have them spayed and neutered.

If your dog can meet all of the above standards and you really want to pursue responsible breeding, educate yourself by reading, talking with other breeders and, of course, consulting your veterinarian. If not, spaying or neutering is truly in your dog's best interest, not to mention your own

Ear Cropping, Tail Docking, and Dewclaw Removal

Certain breed standards require dogs to have their ears cropped, their tails docked, or their dewclaws removed. Each of these procedures must be done at a certain age for good results, as well as for humane reasons. Unless you plan to breed or show a particular dog, all these procedures are optional and have even been declared inhumane and illegal in some European countries.

The dewclaw is the name given to the first toe of the paw on the hind limb. Many people also mistakenly call the first toe of the paw on the front leg a dewclaw as well, but it's not. Most dogs are not born with dewclaws, but they are part and parcel of some breeds, among them the Great Pyrenees, whose standard calls for double dewclaws. Dewclaws are non-weight bearing, so they grow more quickly than the claws on other toes since they receive no wear. Dewclaws that aren't removed must be trimmed regularly or they can grow so long that they curve painfully into the foot pad.

The dewclaws are usually removed when puppies are two to three days old. If the breed also has the tail docked, these procedures are done at the same time. Some breeders dock tails and remove dewclaws themselves, while others prefer to have a veterinarian perform these procedures. Some breeders of sporting dogs also request the removal of the first digits on the forepaws because they can become entangled in brush and get torn.

Many owners do choose to have the dewclaws removed for convenience, since they will no longer have to worry about trimming them often or about their dog painfully tearing one. If dewclaws weren't removed in early puppyhood but you think it's a good idea, you can have it done at the same time as a spay or neuter.

Tail docking is also done to conform to a breed standard and usually takes place when pups are only two or three days old. Just as with dewclaws, some breeders do this themselves, while others prefer that a veterinarian dock the tails. Among the popular breeds that require tail docking are Rottweilers, Cocker Spaniels, Weimaraners, Boxers, Doberman Pinschers, Miniature and Giant Schnauzers, and Poodles.

Unlike tail docking and dewclaw removal, ear cropping is a surgical procedure that should be performed by a veterinarian when the puppy is 10 to 12 weeks old. Popular breeds that often have their ears cropped include Boxers, American Pit Bull Terriers, Great Danes, Doberman Pinschers, and Miniature Pinschers. If you are not going to show your dog, ear cropping is optional. Your puppy will look just as cute with or without its ears cropped.

Ear cropping requires general anesthesia when done correctly by a veterinarian, but even so it is a painful and bloody procedure for a pup to endure. Ask your veterinarian to show you how much of the ear will be removed for a proper cut. If you choose to have the ears cropped, be sure your veterinarian does ear crops regularly and ask to see examples of his or her work on your particular breed. Because some veterinarians do not perform ear crops, you may have to take your puppy to a different veterinarian for that specific surgery.

After the surgery, the puppy will have sutures in the ears for about 10 days, and the ears will have to be taped to help them stand properly. You'll need to help train the ears to stand by using squeaky toys or other methods that strengthen the ears. Don't expect to bring your puppy in only for the surgical procedure. Rechecks and retapings of the ears are necessary for good results.

If you decide not to crop your puppy's ears, that is your decision. Don't let anyone pressure you into the procedure simply because it's the trend.

Sick Calls and Emergencies

If your dog experiences a serious trauma or seemingly life-threatening symptoms, don't wait to see whether the problem cures itself. Call your veterinarian and go to the clinic or emergency hospital immediately. Treating your dog's symptoms or injuries yourself can result in the loss of valuable treatment time, and such delays can lead to permanent organ damage or death.

If an emergency arises, stay calm. Your dog needs your ability to figure out what to do in a timely manner. If he's poisoned, hit by a car, or suffers some other severe trauma, time is of the essence. If possible, one person should stay with the dog while another calls the veterinarian for instructions that may prove life-saving until you reach the hospital.

If you detect signs of poisoning, try to remember any oral or direct contact exposures that might have occurred. When you know what your dog has gotten into, gather any package labels that list ingredients and take them along. They'll help the veterinarian to treat your dog properly.

When the situation isn't an emergency, make an appointment so the clinic can set aside enough time to deal with your dog's problem. For an illness that has just come on, review the dog's symptoms and jot down your observations so you can communicate them clearly to the veterinarian. Important factors to note are appetite (increased or decreased), attitude (normal or lethargic), vomiting, diarrhea, or coughing.

If you think a fecal or urine specimen will be necessary, don't let your dog eliminate before taking him to the vet. Otherwise, your dog will have to stay until a specimen can be obtained. Many owners with the best of intentions bathe their dogs before an examination; but if the symptoms include odors, skin problems, or discharges from the eyes, ears, nose, or other body openings, your veterinarian needs to see exactly what's going on. No matter how ratty your dog looks, his symptoms will help the veterinarian make the right diagnosis. The same advice applies to medicating or cleaning your dog's eyes prior to a visit that pertains to an eye disorder.

When to Call the Vet

You want to give your dog the best of care, but you can't afford to run to the veterinarian every time he sneezes. By developing good observation skills and cultivating a good relationship with your veterinarian, you can solve some problems by phone and learn when Bowser really needs to get to the veterinarian fast and when a wait-and-see stance is appropriate.

Once you get to know your dog's routine, you'll find it pretty obvious when he's not feeling well. Paying close attention to his habits will train you to notice when something isn't right. To ensure your dog's continuing well-being, take him to the veterinarian when you notice any of these signs:

○ *Abnormal behavior, sudden viciousness, or lethargy.* Pets often manifest physical problems through what appears to be misbehavior, and lethargy is a common sign of many diseases.

○ *Abnormal discharges from the nose, eyes, or other body openings.* Discharges often indicate irritation or infection.

○ *Abnormal lumps, limping, or difficulty getting up or lying down.* A lump can be a simple swelling from injury, or a benign or malignant tumor. A soft, hot, or painful swelling is probably an abscess. Limping or difficulty moving may result from an injury or from a painful joint condition such as arthritis.

○ *Bad breath or heavy tartar deposits on teeth; red or swollen gums.* These signs can indicate severe dental disease.

○ *Dandruff, hair loss, open sores, a ragged or dull coat.* Poor coat condition can indicate a diet that's nutritionally deficient, skin disease, or other problems.

○ *Difficult, abnormal, or uncontrolled urination or defecation.*
One sign of diabetes or kidney disease is frequent or excessive
urination. A dog that urinates frequently but doesn't produce
more than a few drops may have a bladder infection or blockage. Diarrhea that lasts for more than a day can signal any
number of problems.

○ *Excessive head shaking, scratching, and licking or biting of any
part of the body.* Parasites, an infection, or skin disease may
have taken hold.

○ *Increased sensitivity.* Depending on where the dog is sensitive,
this may indicate neck or back pain, an internal infection or injury, an abscess, or allergic dermatitis.

○ *Loss of appetite for more than a day, marked weight loss or
gain, or excessive water consumption.* The causes for contin-
ued lack of interest in food can range from dental disease to
cancer. If your dog likes to eat but suddenly loses interest in
food, something may be wrong. Rapid or unexpected weight
loss or gain is almost always significant. Diabetes or kidney disease can cause your dog to drink much more water than usual.

○ *Repeated coughing, gagging, sneezing or vomiting.* Your dog
may have something stuck in his throat, a collapsed trachea, or
heart disease.

○ *Vulvar discharge.* This could signal pyometra, a serious uterine
infection that occurs only in unspayed female dogs.

How to Administer Medication and Pills

Being able to care for your sick dog at home is a plus. Your
dog will feel more secure and recover more quickly if he's
being nursed by loving hands in a familiar place. A very
important skill you'll need is the ability to successfully give
medications.

Getting medication down a dog is both an art and a science, but easily mastered with practice. It takes skill, cunning, and patience. It's a good thing to know, though, because the more confident you are when medicating your dog, the more successful you'll be, and the sooner Bowser will get well. Don't be afraid to experiment until you find a method that works well for you and ensures that Bowser gets the right amount of medication each time. Be sure you give all the medication your veterinarian prescribes. Some bugs are hardy and will come back if they don't get the one-two punch of the complete prescription.

Before you go home, make sure your veterinarian has explained exactly how to give the medication. You should know when to start giving it, how often to give it, how long to give it, and whether it has any common side effects.

Down the Hatch

Your dog is most likely to receive medication in the form of a pill. If you're lucky, he will simply swallow the pill if you mix it in with his food. If that doesn't work, or if Bowser's appetite has gone south, you'll have to try a more direct method.

First, try wrapping the pill in something irresistibly tasty, such as cream cheese, peanut butter, or a favorite soft treat. Bread and marshmallows work well too. With luck, Bowser will gulp it down without even noticing it. Sometimes, however, even the tasty treat method technique fails, and you'll have to give the pill manually.

To do this, kneel or sit with Bowser held firmly between your knees. Hold the pill in your right hand. Using your left first and middle fingers, gently pry Bowser's jaws open, and place the pill far back on his tongue. (If you're a lefty,

simply reverse these directions.) To make sure the pill goes down, hold his mouth closed and lightly stroke his throat until you see him swallow.

You can also try grasping Bowser's head in your left hand and tilting it back until he's looking straight up. With the pill in your right hand, firmly between the thumb and forefinger, open his mouth using the middle finger of your right hand. As you drop the pill into his mouth, use your right index finger to push it over the tongue. Hold Bowser's muzzle closed and gently blow into his nose. The sensation will make him lick and swallow, and down the pill will go. Whichever method you use, remember that some pills taste nasty if they're broken, so don't break the pill unless it's just too big to get down in one attempt.

Liquid medications tend to be the easiest to give to puppies. To give liquid medications, prepare the appropriate amount of medication and restrain your dog between your knees as described above. Using the technique described in the previous paragraph, tilt the head up, open the mouth, and aim the syringe at the cheek pouch. Make sure the mouth is closed around the syringe, and squeeze out the liquid. When it reaches the back of the mouth, Bowser should automatically swallow. If he doesn't, try blowing into his nose to make him lick and swallow.

Medicating Eyes and Ears

To apply eye medication, a good, firm head hold is a must; you don't want Bowser to shake his head and cause you to poke him in the eye. Hold the eyedrops in your right hand, tilt the head upward and place the drops directly on the eyeball at the inner corner of the eye. Try not to let the applicator tip touch the eye. To make sure the eyedrops are distributed evenly, close and open the eyelids.

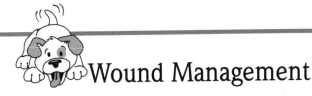

Wound Management

Usually when a wound needs to be protected, a dog is issued what's called an Elizabethan collar—or E-collar—a wide, usually plastic, collar that fits around the dog's head and prevents him from biting or scratching at an injury. Sometimes an Elizabethan collar won't work, though, and that's when you need to get creative.

Jane's Mastiff, Tally, had a lump on her shoulder. Jane and her veterinarian kept an eye on it, and when it grew, they decided to remove it. Happily, the lump was simply an enclosed cyst that wasn't malignant. The vet took it out and sutured Tally. Tally came around from the anesthetic and was sent home. After a couple of days of rest and eating well, the wound began to itch, and Tally decided she didn't like those funny bits of black suture material holding her shoulder together. Jane came downstairs the next morning to discover that Tally had scratched out all her sutures and had a nasty raw patch on her shoulder.

The vet didn't want to anesthetize her again to resuture, so he and Jane came up with a new solution. Jane put a sock on Tally's foot to prevent scratching. Then the veterinarian puffed wound powder liberally on the site and covered it with a large melamine-faced dressing, which was taped to the fur on each side and covered by wide bandages which went all around Tally's body. Since her chest measured 46 inches, that was a lot of bandages. Topping the whole thing was a large open-necked T-shirt, the only kind that would fit over Tally's massive head.

Every two days, Jane took Tally to the vet to check her progress. The wound wept a lot but healed well. An Elizabethan collar wouldn't have worked because the wound was behind Tally's neck. The melamine dressings were not in permanent contact with her skin, so air could reach the wound. It healed pretty well, although Tally had damaged the area so much that she always had a little bald patch. The vet commented that if he had cause to operate in a similar area again, he would make sure the wound was protected so his fine suturing couldn't be destroyed.

To apply an eye ointment, gently pull down the lower lid and apply the ointment to the inside lower lid, avoiding direct contact with the eyeball. You can also pull the upper lid back and apply

Emergency Instructions for the Boarding Kennel/Pet Sitter

What if your dog becomes sick or hurts himself while you are away? If you leave your dog at a boarding kennel, first ask if they have a vet on staff or if they use a veterinarian in the area for emergencies. Either way, it's a good idea to give them the name and number of your dog's veterinarian, especially if your dog has a specific medical condition. If you have hired a dog sitter, leave an emergency list with your veterinarian's phone number, the phone number of the local emergency clinic, and the phone number for the National Animal Poison Information Center, (800) 548-2423. Also leave information on any medications your dog needs or any special medical conditions to watch out for. Prepare for the unexpected to ensure your dog gets the care he needs should an emergency occurs.

the ointment to the white of the eye. Close and open the eyelids to evenly distribute the medication.

If you keep them clean, your dog shouldn't have too many ear problems, but occasionally you may have to administer eardrops or ointment. To do this, tilt the head slightly to the side and apply the appropriate amount of medication. Then use your fingers to gently massage the medication into the ear. Bowser is sure to shake his head after you're done, and less of the medication will fly out of the ears if you've rubbed it in first. Unless Bowser's ears are unusually painful or sensitive, he'll probably enjoy the massage.

Costs

Why Does It Cost So Much?

As we discuss visits to the veterinarian, it's appropriate that we address cost. Quality health care for pets can indeed be expensive. While veterinary care is much less expensive than human medical treatments and procedures, it is certainly not cheap. In the United States, pet owners spend more than three billion dollars annually for their animals' medical care. Just as in the case of human medicine, diagnoses often require x-rays, blood work, and other lab tests. Surgical procedures are time-consuming and require great skill and safe anesthetic protocols. All are expensive. Veterinarians use the same expensive technology and equipment as your local hospital when taking x-rays, analyzing blood and urine samples, and performing pathological studies. The costs of all medicines, whether for people or pets, are high. Many of the same medications prescribed for humans are also prescribed for dogs. And who among us has never paid a high price for dental care? Your veterinarian has been trained in all medical disciplines, including dentistry, cardiology, pharmacology, orthopedics, dermatology, surgery, radiology, anesthesiology, and ophthalmic care. Specialized procedures and quality health care come with a higher cost.

> Most of us would never dream of just letting an auto mechanic proceed with unlimited repairs without a written estimate detailing all parts and labor required.

How to Discuss Finances with Your Vet

It's a good idea to ask for an estimate of charges before any visit. When a procedure or any surgery is recommended, ask for an itemized estimate of charges. You are the ultimate decision-maker in determining the level of care your puppy receives throughout his life. Most of us would never dream of just letting an auto mechanic proceed with unlimited repairs without a written estimate detailing all parts and labor required. Most veterinarians would

How to Make an Insurance Claim

It's your responsibility as a policyholder to make the best use of your insurance plan. Take these steps to get the most for your money:

1. Designate a file for pet insurance forms.

2. Always take a claim form with you to the veterinarian's office. Many companies require a veterinarian's signature.

3. Make copies of receipts. A receipt must accompany every claim form. Some companies require only copies; others require originals. Keep a copy for your records.

4. Make copies of completed claim forms. If a question or payment issue arises, a copy to review on your end of the phone line will be reassuring.

5. Note an acceptable payment period on your calendar. Reimbursement may slip your mind, and it may be delayed in cases where a problem is encountered and you forget to inquire about the payment's status.

6. Mark claims paid and date received. Leave a paper trail that's easy to understand. Looking back a year later, you'll be glad for the notations.

©1999 Solveig Fredrickson

greatly prefer to discuss details before incurring major expenses rather than give you the shock of your life after the treatments or procedures are complete. While most humans have the luxury of health insurance, few dogs enjoy the same.

Savings and Insurance Plans

Along with the many advances in veterinary medicine come higher prices, especially when a serious injury or illness occurs. Many pet owners establish a savings account to cover illnesses that arise, just as they would for one of their children. Another popular option is to acquire pet health insurance. Either of these

10 Questions to
Ask Every Provider

Before choosing a pet insurance or membership plan, be sure to get straight-forward answers to all your questions. If it makes you more comfortable, get the answers in writing.

1. Does your policy follow fee/benefits schedules? If so, please send me your detailed coverage limits. In the meantime, please give me examples of coverage limits for three common feline procedures so I can compare them to my current veterinary charges.

2. Does your policy cover basic wellness care, or does it cover only accidents and illnesses? Do you offer a wellness care endorsement that I can purchase on top of my basic plan for an additional fee? What other endorsements do you offer, and how much do they cost?

3. Under your policy's rules, can I continue taking my cat to its current veterinarian, or do I need to switch to another veterinarian?

4. Does your policy cover hereditary conditions, congenital conditions or pre-existing conditions? Please explain each coverage or exclusion as it pertains specifically to my cat. Is there a feature where pre-existing conditions will be covered if my cat's pre-existing condition requires no treatment after a specified period? What is that period?

5. What happens to my premium and to my cat's policy if your company goes out of business? What guarantees do I have that I won't be throwing my money away?

6. How quickly do you pay claims?

7. What is your policy's deductible? Does the deductible apply per incident or annually? How does the deductible differ per plan?

8. Does the policy have payment limits over a year's period or during my pet's lifetime? How do the payment limits differ per plan?

9. What is the A.M. Best Co. rating of your insurance underwriter, and what does that rating mean?

10. Is there a cancellation period after I receive my policy or membership? How long do I have to review all my materials once I receive them, and what is the cancellation procedure?

©1999 Solveig Fredrickson

methods is helpful when it comes to handling a significant bill from an unexpected problem. Most veterinary clinics can provide you with the information you need regarding pet health insurance programs. These programs are typically not inexpensive, but have proven themselves well worthwhile in many instances.

5

Common Health Concerns

In This Chapter

○ Review of Basic Anatomy and Physiology
○ Fleas, Ticks, and Worms
○ First Aid

When your dog is well, you know it. His eyes are bright and shiny, his ears twitching at the sound of your keys signifying a car ride, and a big grin splits his face from side to side. His coat shines, and his energy level is set at "Go!" But even the healthiest of dogs can experience the occasional health problem, so you'll want to be prepared for any contingency. You can do this by having a good relationship with your veterinarian, having a plan of action in case of emergency, and knowing basic first aid and nursing skills.

Review of Basic Anatomy and Physiology

The more you know about and understand your dog's basic anatomy and physiology, the better able you will be to understand many medical conditions, abnormalities, and their symptoms and treatments. Knowledge of terminology, too, is critical to your understanding. Below is a brief overview of a dog's anatomy and related functions that will be extremely helpful when you communicate with your veterinarian. It's by no means a complete study of the dog, but will supplement your understanding of anatomical terminology. In addition, don't hesitate to ask your veterinarian to repeat something or explain it in terms you can follow.

Skeletal System

The canine skeleton, which consists of about 321 bones, is the body's framework, protecting internal organs and offering attachment sites for muscles and tendons. The bones, then, act as levers for the muscular action required in everyday life. They are also one of the sources of red and white blood cells; and they serve as reservoirs for calcium, phosphorus, and many other elements the body needs.

You can easily see why such great importance is placed on balanced nutrition throughout life to maintain a healthy skeletal system. It can make or break the health of the whole dog.

A dog's skeletal system has five different types of bones: long, short, flat, irregular, and sesamoid. The long bones include those of the leg or forearm. The short bones are associated with the carpal (wrist) and tarsal (ankle) areas. Flat bones are found in the skull and scapula (shoulder blade). Irregular bones are all of those associated with the spinal column (vertebrae), skull, and hip. Finally, the sesamoid bones, which are associated with free moving joints, are formed either in tendons or ligamentous tissue. These bones help to protect tendons at areas of high friction. An example of a sesamoid bone is the patella, or kneecap.

Puppies have growth plates located toward the ends of the bones. These growth plates exist until growth is complete, at which time they unite. The growth plates can be seen on x-rays and help veterinarians determine when a dog has finished growing, a process that can vary in length from dog to dog.

All bones are dynamic, actively metabolizing structures of the body that have a blood supply and contain nerves. Bone is a constantly changing tissue that can undergo adaptation in shape, size, and position based on the constant mechanical and biochemical demands of the body. These characteristics are important when a fracture occurs, but they can also result in orthopedic problems such as hip dysplasia. When such a problem does occur, veterinarians try to use the dynamics of bone to work for the patient's healing.

There are several unique points of interest associated with the dog's skeletal system. One is that three different types of skulls occur throughout the many different breeds of dogs. Think of the many different shapes of heads you see, from Bulldogs to Dobermans to Labradors. For the average size and conformation, such as that seen in Labradors and Beagles, the term mesaticephalic is assigned. For breeds with long, narrow heads such as Collies and Borzois, the term dolichocephalic is given. The brachycephalic breeds, which exhibit short, wide facial components, include Bulldogs and Boston Terriers. Anyone who has owned one of the brachycephalic breeds can attest to the problems associated with such a short muzzle. Besides their loud breathing and snorting, these breeds can actually experience serious respiratory consequences. In addition, they do not tolerate high temperatures well.

The spinal column in dogs is composed of small, irregularly shaped bones called vertebrae. Between the vertebrae are intervertebral discs that serve as the connecting tissue and cushion for adjacent vertebrae. Just like people, dogs can suffer from disc and spinal problems. Some breeds, such as Dachshunds, with their long backs, are more susceptible to spinal problems than are other breeds, but any dog can develop back problems as he ages.

The vertebral column is divided into five groups: cervical, thoracic, lumbar, sacral, and caudal (or coccygeal). Different species have different numbers of each type of vertebrae. Dogs have the following spinal column formula: seven cervical vertebrae (C-7); thirteen thoracic vertebrae (T-13); seven lumbar vertebrae (L-7); three sacral vertebrae (S-3), which are actually fused in the adult as the sacrum; and six to 23 (average is 20) caudal vertebrae (Ca-20).

> Some breeds, such as Dachshunds, with their long backs, are more susceptible to spinal problems than are other breeds, but any dog can develop back problems as he ages.

The next area of the skeleton is the rib cage. Dogs have an average of 13 ribs. The first nine ribs connect to the sternum via sternal ribs (sternebrae). The next three ribs connect to costal cartilage to form what is called the costal arch. The thirteenth rib does not join to costal cartilage or the sternum and is thus referred to as a floating rib.

In people, the clavicle, or collarbone, is necessary to keep the shoulder in the proper position, but in dogs and most other domestic animals, the collarbone is only a rudimentary structure because of the different position of the front limbs in relation to the body.

The limbs correspond to those found in humans. In the front legs (arms), the upper part is composed of the humerus, with the lower aspect supported by the radius and ulna. The forepaw is made up of the carpus, metacarpus, and five digits (toes or phalanges). The rear legs are supported by the femur in the upper portion and the tibia and fibula in the lower part. The rear feet are composed of tarsus, metatarsus, and four digits.

The final bones to be discussed are associated with the pelvic girdle, which is made up of the two hip bones, the sacrum, and the first few caudal vertebrae. The hip is a ball-and-socket-type joint in which the head of the femur fits into the acetabulum of the hip bone. Hip dysplasia occurs when there's any abnormal development of the femoral head and acetabulum. It is also a major cause of secondary osteoarthritis. All dogs are born with normal hips, but genetic and environmental factors such as improper nutrition or obesity can cause irreversible changes to occur, which lead to degeneration of the joint.

Dogs have a lot more bones than the ones I've just described, but these are the ones of greatest interest.

Muscular System

The muscular system is composed of contractile tissue that enables dogs to run, jump, breathe, digest food, and much more. Muscles are classified into three groups according to the fibers they are composed of—smooth muscle, cardiac muscle, and skeletal muscle—and they're controlled by voluntary or involuntary nerve impulses. The skeletal muscles can attach directly to the bone or may be connected to the bone with a tendon.

One part of the dog's body that you might not have thought of as a muscle is the tongue, a muscular organ that is important for lapping water, handling food in the mouth, and swallowing. One crucial function of the dog's tongue is that it helps in temperature control through the heat loss that occurs with panting.

Organs

Dogs have organ systems just as humans do. I often let children listen to their dog's heart, and they are amazed to hear it beating—just like their own! Discovering and exploring the anatomical structures and functions of dogs and comparing them to humans' is amazing.

Digestive System

The dog's digestive system is similar to that of humans and includes all organs associated with eating, from intake to digestion to elimination. These are the stomach, and the small and large intestines. The accessory organs such as the teeth, tongue, salivary glands, liver, gallbladder, and pancreas are also part of the digestive system.

> One crucial function of the dog's tongue is that it helps in temperature control through the heat loss that occurs with panting.

Dogs have a simple stomach with only one compartment. After the stomach comes the small intestine. As in humans, the small intestine is divided into three sections: duodenum, jejunum, and ileum. The small intestine, the longest part of the entire digestive system, is where the body absorbs the majority of all nutrients. The last part of the digestive system is the large intestine. It has several divisions: cecum, colon, rectum, and anal canal. The primary function of the large intestine is to absorb water from the fecal contents.

Pearly Whites

When puppies are first born, they have no teeth until they're about three weeks old. Puppies are first equipped with 28 deciduous, or baby, teeth, which are all present and functioning by six to eight weeks of age. As the puppies mature, most of the deciduous teeth fall out and are replaced with the permanent teeth, which should be in place by six or seven months of age. Most dogs have 42 permanent teeth, but some brachycephalic breeds have fewer because of their shortened muzzles.

The liver is the largest gland in the body and is responsible for many complex functions associated with digestion and other vital aspects of maintaining life. For example, the liver is responsible for metabolizing carbohydrates, fats, and many drugs; and it's crucial in neutralizing toxic substances. The liver is also a storehouse for vitamins and iron and is necessary in the production of certain blood components.

The pancreas, another glandular organ, plays a role in the digestion of fats, proteins, and carbohydrates. The pancreas is where the hormones insulin and glucagon are secreted, which are key to maintaining the blood sugar concentrations at appropriate and constant levels.

Respiratory System

Among the structures of the respiratory system are the nostrils, the trachea, and the lungs. The function of this system is to transport and exchange oxygen and carbon dioxide into and out of the bloodstream. All cells for maintaining life require oxygen, and carbon dioxide is the resulting waste product of the body's cells.

The trachea, or windpipe, is a noncollapsible tube held open by rings of cartilage. Its job is to channel air to the lungs. Like people, dogs have two lungs, but canine lungs are fairly large in comparison to the rest of the body because dogs are animals that are adapted to running.

Urogenital System

The urogenital system is made up of the urinary organs and the reproductive organs. The urinary system includes the kidneys, ureters, bladder, and urethra. The function of the urinary system is to eliminate waste products and excess water. The kidneys filter the blood and excrete the body's waste products in the urine. Liquid waste products go from the kidneys to the ureters to the bladder to the urethra, from whence they are eliminated from the body.

The genital system includes all reproductive glands and organs. In male dogs this consists of the scrotum, the two testicles, the deferent ducts, the prostate, the penis, and the urethra, used for passage of urine and semen. The testicles of puppies generally descend into the scrotum shortly after birth. If one or both of the testicles fails to descend into the scrotum, this is referred to as monorchidism (one testicle fails to descend) or cryptorchidism (both testicles fail to descend). These conditions are hereditary, so male dogs that exhibit them should be neutered.

A female dog's reproductive system consists of the ovaries, the uterine tubes (fallopian tubes or oviduct), the uterus, the vagina, and the vulva. The uterine horns in the dog are quite long in comparison to the overall body to accommodate the carrying of a litter instead of just one offspring.

Circulatory System

The circulatory system includes the heart, blood vessels (arteries, veins, capillaries), and the lymphatics. The blood vascular system with its powerful pump, the heart, supplies the body with adequate oxygen and nutrition to meet all its metabolic requirements. Arteries carry oxygenated blood from the left side of the heart. They then branch into smaller vessels called capillaries, where the actual exchange of oxygen and nutrients occurs with the waste products of the body. From there, capillaries feed into veins that lead to the right side of the heart. The lymphatics remove waste and bacteria from the bloodstream. The dog's heart, which is similar to that of humans, is a four-chambered organ that acts as a muscular pump for the entire cardiovascular system. It constitutes only about one percent of the dog's total body weight.

Nervous System

The nervous system is the body's control center, allowing the dog to react appropriately to environmental stimuli and coordinating all of the organs and their responses. The nervous system has two parts: the central nervous system and the peripheral nervous system. The central nervous system is composed of the brain and the spinal cord. The peripheral nervous system consists of all nerves that connect to the central nervous system.

As far as function, the nervous system also has two divisions: the somatic nervous system and the autonomic nervous system. The somatic nervous system carries nerve impulses from the central nervous system to the skeletal

Did You Know?

Dogs see color less vividly than humans but are not actually color-blind.

muscles. This system is under voluntary control by the dog. The autonomic nervous system transmits involuntary impulses such as breathing. The primary function of this system is to regulate the internal functions of the dog's body.

Sensory Organs

Without these organs, dogs would lead dull lives indeed. Sensory organs include the skin, nose, eyes, and ears and are integral to the senses of touch, smell, sight, and hearing.

Compared to those of humans, many canine sensory organs are far superior. The dog's acute senses are yet another reason that we find dogs indispensable for a number of activities, from hunting to bomb and drug detection. When dogs are highly trained to use their senses, they are valuable companions in many lines of work.

The dog's sense of touch is relayed by the integument, which encompasses the skin, hair, skin glands, foot pads, and claws. The skin is the body's largest organ and is composed of connective tissue that contains muscles, blood vessels, lymphatics, and nerve endings.

In terms of function, the skin serves many important roles, including being the first line of defense against injury and the invasion of bacteria.

With its intricate nerve supply, the skin also acts as a major sensory organ. It is responsible for the perception of touch, pressure, heat, cold, and pain. Unlike a majority of mammals, dogs have few sweat glands in their skin, so the skin plays a limited role in heat regulation. Dogs rely more on their ability to control body temperature through panting. The glands within the skin aid in the processes of waterproofing, lubrication, and production of pheromones, chemicals which are important in recognition between dogs.

The many different breeds of dogs exhibit a variety of hair coats. Coats vary in length, color, and diameter of hair. Dogs come in six hair types: straight, bristle, wavy bristle, bristled wavy, large wavy, and fine wavy. All shed their coats on a timetable that is affected by both environmental factors, such as the amount of natural light the dog is exposed to, and genetic factors. For example, most dogs who live indoors shed small amounts year-round while dogs that live outdoors tend to shed seasonally. When and how much a dog sheds is also influenced by the type of hair coat it has. Breeds such as the Poodle are popular simply because they shed very little. Besides temperature, another environmental factor that affects the hair coat is the dog's diet. A poor, unbalanced diet results in a dull, dry coat.

> Because the foot pad is so thick and bears constant pressure from the dog's weight, it can often take a considerable amount of time to heal if it is injured.

In dogs, each hair follicle is associated with sebaceous glands and arrector pili muscles. It is the arrector pili muscles, which are more developed along the back of the neck, the back and the tail, that are responsible for the dog's ability to pull the associated hairs into a vertical position, which we call "raised hackles." This muscular action occurs during times of stress, fright, or cold. By placing the hairs in this position, the dog creates an intimidating appearance and gives a warning signal to an animal or even a person.

As stated previously, dogs have only a few "true" sweat glands, which are located only in the foot pads. Because of their small number and limited capacity to cool the dog, he relies heavily on his panting mechanism.

Ooh, That Smell!

The dog's acute sense of smell is due to the difference in the amount of space occupied by the olfactory mucous membrane. In dogs it covers 18 $\frac{1}{2}$ square inches versus only $\frac{3}{4}$ of a square inch in humans. Wow!

The pads of a dog's feet are the thickest and toughest of all areas on the skin. Because the foot pad is so thick and bears constant pressure from the dog's weight, it can often take a considerable amount of time to heal if it is injured.

A dog's claws (more commonly referred to as nails) grow fairly quickly when not kept trimmed to a short, comfortable length. This is especially true of the first digits on the front paws and the dewclaws on the rear paws, if present, because they don't bear any of the dog's weight. Trimming your dog's nails too short will cause pain and bleeding. See Chapter 7, Grooming, on how to avoid such painful mishaps.

A dog's sense of smell is its most acute sense of all. Different breeds have variable numbers of receptors (olfactory cells) in their nasal tissue; but in any dog, these receptors number in the millions versus only thousands in humans. This keen sense of smell enables dogs to hunt, find trapped or lost people, and detect a female dog in heat from miles away.

On the other hand, research has shown that structural differences in the retina mean that dogs have less developed vision than people. The retina is the inner part of the eye that functions in the formation of images. It contains photoreceptors called rods and cones. Rods are responsible for night vision and cones for color and sharpness of vision. In dogs, about 95 percent of the photoreceptors are rods, so it's believed that dogs have limited color vision.

Like many other animals, dogs are equipped with a third eyelid, called the nictitating membrane. This third eyelid is located at the lower inside corner of the eye and contains a small piece of cartilage for support as well as a lacrimal gland for tear production. The primary purpose of this eyelid, which is under involuntary control, is to protect the eyeball.

> A dog's extraordinary ability to detect sounds in the ultrasonic range allows trainers to use dog whistles that are undetectable to the human ear.

The dog's ear is the organ responsible for hearing and balance. The canine sense of hearing is more developed and sensitive to certain sounds than is that of humans. A dog's extraordinary ability to detect sounds in the ultrasonic range allows trainers to use dog whistles that are undetectable to the human ear.

Using Your Knowledge to Foster Your Dog's Health

Now that you understand the basics of how your dog is put together and how he functions, you'll be more likely to notice when something's not quite right. You'll also be able to describe his symptoms more accurately, and know what his veterinarian is talking about when he asks you questions or explains a diagnosis or treatment. Now you're ready to learn about a few of the more common health problems your dog could encounter.

Fleas, Ticks, and Worms

External and internal parasites are the bane of every dog and dog owner. Besides being irritating, fleas, ticks, and worms carry disease; cause physical problems such as bloody diarrhea and secondary bacterial infections; can help transmit other parasites, such as tapeworms; and may lead to allergic conditions. More than 50 percent of the skin problems seen by veterinarians are flea-related. Keeping your puppy or dog parasite-free is a tenet of good health.

What Every Owner Needs to Know

It's not uncommon for young puppies to have external and internal parasites. Parasites are organisms that rely on other life forms, such as your dog, for their existence. Internal parasites may make a cozy home inside your dog's gut; and external parasites may, like little vampires, feast on your dog's blood. These hardy devils can survive for long periods without food, sometimes even in extreme environments. Fortunately, most parasites aren't life-threatening, but they are a nuisance to animal and sometimes to human health. In the past, parasites were often difficult to get rid of, no matter how fastidious a housekeeper you might be; however, advances in parasite control have made the job much easier and more effective.

External Parasites

Among the external parasites that can affect your dog are fleas, ticks, and mites. If Scamp is scratching frequently or has bald spots or inflamed skin, there's a good chance that external parasites are the culprits. Fortunately, many highly effective and easy-to-use treatments are available that will kill these bugs dead.

Fleas

Dog owners often dread the warmer months for fear of a flea infestation. These annoying parasites plague dogs just about everywhere, and can become a serious problem in homes and yards if left untreated. The most common flea is *Ctenocephalides felis,* or the cat flea, although it certainly doesn't discriminate among the canine, feline, or human species. Fleas prefer to feed on dogs, but they'll gladly attack a person if no dogs are around.

Depending on where you live, flea season can be as short as four months or it can last all year. Fleas thrive in warm and moist climates, but not where the weather's too hot, too wet, or too cold. They can reproduce rapidly within the 65 degree to 85 degree Fahrenheit temperature range but require at least 70 percent humidity to survive. In the southern United States, flea control can be a year-round battle. Some fleas found in the Antarctic are even capable of surviving freezing temperatures. Given these facts, your dog is likely at some point to be scratching an itch caused by the bite of the pesky flea, which lurks outdoors in grass and piles of leafy debris and indoors in wall-to-wall carpeting, pet bedding, and upholstered furniture.

The cat flea is perfectly formed for its mission: to latch onto a warm body and suck its blood. The entomological equivalent of Superman, the flea is capable of jumping as high as 13 feet and consequently has no trouble leaping on to tall dogs in a single bound. Toy breeds are no challenge at all. The flea's six legs are fitted with claws that enable it to cling tenaciously to its prey. Attached to its large oval head is a beaky proboscis from which juts a drill-like feeding tube, which the flea drives into the body, injecting an anticoagulant that makes it easier to siphon out the blood (the anticoagulant, incidentally, is what causes that ferocious itching.) Some dogs are so sensitive to this substance that a single flea bite can result in a frenzy of biting and scratching. This agonizing condition, called flea allergy dermatitis, causes severe itching, crusty sores, thickened skin, and even bacterial skin infections. If

your dog is frantically chewing and scratching at his skin so much that he's losing hair, he probably has a flea allergy.

How does the flea know when and where to strike? It reacts to the vibrations caused by footfalls, changes in light caused by the shadow of an approaching body, and the scent of exhaled carbon dioxide. But even more pernicious than the flea's ability to find and attack its victim is its reproductive capability. In a typical life span of six to eight weeks, a single female flea will lay about 2,000 eggs, or even as many as 5,000. Assuming that your dog is hosting more than one female flea, the result could be a staggering number of flea eggs, all waiting for the optimum moment to hatch into larvae and begin the life cycle all over again.

> How does the flea know when and where to strike? It reacts to the vibrations caused by footfalls, changes in light caused by the shadow of an approaching body, and the scent of exhaled carbon dioxide.

Depending on conditions such as temperature and humidity, the flea's life cycle can be as short as 16 days or as long as 21 months. On average, though, fleas live six months to a year. The life cycle begins when female fleas lay their eggs on your dog. The eggs then fall off the dog and onto carpet or bedding. After incubating for two to 12 days, larvae hatch from the eggs and undergo a series of molts over a one- to two-week period. During the final molt, the larvae spin cocoons, inside which they transform into pupae. When conditions are right, they emerge from their cocoons as adult fleas, ready to feast on your dog. Newly emerged adult fleas must take a blood meal within two to three days of hatching, or they'll die.

To find out whether Scamp is hosting a colony of fleas, search his coat using a fine-toothed flea comb. Your mission will be easier if you have a short-haired or light-colored dog since the smooth terrain of its body offers the flea fewer hiding places. As few as one or two fleas can be evidence that an entire army of the pests is lying in wait throughout your home. Even if you don't see actual fleas on your dog, you may find more subtle evidence of an infestation: flea dirt, or excreted blood, on his skin. You can identify flea dirt by combing or brushing Scamp while he's standing on a white towel or piece of paper. If dark flecks fall onto the white area, moisten them to see if they turn red—a sure sign that Scamp will need to be treated for fleas.

Besides being a nuisance to a dog's skin and coat, fleas can also cause other health problems. They serve as the carrier for tapeworms, and a severe tapeworm infestation can lead to anemia.

Flea-Control Products

Fortunately, flea control is easier and safer than ever. The old-style, toxic products containing organophosphates, pyrethrins, and permethrins can still be found over the counter, but today's most effective products are topical treatments available from your veterinarian. These products are dangerous only to fleas, not to your dog. They are applied to the dog's coat on a monthly or quarterly basis and work by destroying the flea's nervous system.

But no matter how safe a product is promised to be, it's still important to read the directions carefully so you understand exactly what it does and how it should be used. For instance, some topical products require you to wear gloves when you apply them. Flea-control products are formulated for specific uses, which are spelled out in the directions. For in-

Did You Know?

The tallest dog on record was 42 inches tall at the shoulders and weighed 238 pounds.

stance, never use a premise (or area) spray directly on your dog. Most important, if you're mixing two or more products, be sure they aren't dangerous if used together. Ask your veterinarian if you have any doubts.

If your veterinarian recommends a treatment, ask how it works and why she thinks it's the best choice for your dog. In most cases, her recommendation will be based on the climate in your area, the status of your dog's health, and whether you are already experiencing an infestation.

Many owners still ask about flea collars and flea dips. Although flea collars have improved, they are less effective than the newer flea products so they are generally a waste of money. Dips can help if you need a quick kill for a severely infested dog, but they only kill the fleas on your dog at the time he's dipped. Also, dips are poisons and must be used with care. Because of the effort they require, their strong odor, and the short duration of their effectiveness, dips are less popular now than they were in the past.

Fighting a Flea Infestation

To ensure success, perform a thorough housecleaning at the same time you start your dog on the preventive treatment. To get rid of eggs, larvae, and pupae, vacuum every inch of carpeting, curtains, and upholstered furniture—especially under the cushions—and

throw away the bag when you're done. To really give fleas a one-two punch, have the carpet and furniture cleaned professionally and then treated with a nontoxic powder containing borax, which kills fleas by drying them out. This powder is available at pet stores, or you can have it professionally applied. Launder your own bedding and that of your dog in hot water. Don't forget to treat the inside of your car or any other place Scamp has been. If the fleas at your house are out of control, you may need to use a premise spray around baseboards or beneath furniture, or even a flea "bomb" that will permeate the entire living area. Naturally, you and your dog will need to vacate the house for several hours while the bomb does its work.

If Scamp spends much time outdoors, the yard must be treated as well. You can probably get by with spraying around the house, along the fence line, and under and around decks or patios. Keep the yard well raked so fleas won't have piles of debris in which to lay their eggs. If you hire an exterminator, be sure the products applied are safe for use around pets, and double-check the exterminator's information with your veterinarian before the yard is treated. The best flea control is prevention, so talk tactics with your veterinarian *before* a problem begins.

Ticks

Ticks belong to the arachnid family, which also includes spiders. They have eight legs attached to brown or black tear-shaped bodies and are about the size of a sesame seed or smaller, though some may be larger. Ticks aren't as widespread as fleas, but they can bring more serious problems in the form of diseases that can be transmitted to people as well as dogs. If a large number of ticks attach to a dog, they can cause severe anemia or tick paralysis.

North America is home to several tick species: the deer tick (*Ixodes dammini* and *Ixodes scapularis*), the western black-legged tick, the Lone Star tick, the Rocky Mountain wood tick (*Dermacentor andersoni*), and the American dog tick (*Dermacentor variabilis*). The deer tick, the American dog tick, and the western black-legged tick transmit Lyme disease, babesiosis, and ehrlichiosis. It has recently been found that the American dog tick can also spread ehrlichiosis to humans. Rocky Mountain wood ticks and American dog ticks transmit Rocky Mountain spotted fever and tularemia, while the Lone Star tick carries ehrlichiosis and tularemia. These diseases are unpleasant for both people and dogs, and serious cases can even be fatal, so don't take these bloodsuckers lightly.

Ticks operate by attaching themselves to the skin, and digging in with their sharp mouthpieces. They are most commonly found around the head, neck, ears, feet, and in the folds between the legs and body. When full, they appear bloated and round. Spring and summer are the tick's favorite seasons.

Examine your dog for ticks any time he's been outdoors, especially if you live in a tick-infested locale or have been playing in a heavily wooded area. Protect your hands with gloves, then part the fur and check all the way down to the skin. Ticks can be hard to spot unless they're already swollen with blood, especially if your dog has a dark coat.

If you find a tick, use tweezers to remove it. The spirochete that causes Lyme disease can enter through your skin, so never touch or crush a tick with your bare hands. Grasp it by the head and pull slowly yet firmly. Try not to leave any of it behind, but don't worry if you do. Just trim the hair around it and bathe the area for a few days with alcohol, hydrogen peroxide, or soap and water. Old wives' tales recommend burning ticks off or covering them with nail polish, petroleum jelly, kerosene, or gasoline, but these methods are all potentially harmful to your dog and should be avoided.

After the tick is removed, drop it in alcohol to kill it. If Lyme disease or some other tick-borne ailment is prevalent in your area, you may want to save the tick in alcohol, marking the date it was found. Knowing the type of tick can help your physician and veterinarian make an accurate diagnosis if you or your dog later develop signs of disease.

About Tick Paralysis

A dog suffering from tick paralysis may have many ticks or only one. It's not really understood how the ticks induce paralysis, but they probably produce some kind of neurotoxin that causes weakness, incoordination, and paralysis. Eventually, the dog is unable to sit or stand. Prompt treatment, which is as simple as removing the ticks, results in recovery in one to three days. Without treatment, the respiratory muscles will become paralyzed and the dog will die.

If ticks are a problem in your area, ask your veterinarian to recommend a spray, shampoo, dip, or other treatment against the little bloodsuckers. Spraying your yard and shrubbery can also help eliminate ticks.

Mites

Mites are microscopic members of the arachnid family. Dogs can become infested with any of four species of mites: *Demodex canis*, which causes canine demodicosis, also known as demodectic mange or red mange; *Sarcoptes scabei* var. *canis*, the cause of canine scabies, or sarcoptic mange; *Cheyletiella*, which causes a mild but itchy skin disease; and *Otodectes cynotis*, more commonly known as ear mites.

Demodex mites are characterized by their cigar shape. Low numbers of them usually coexist harmlessly with dogs, making their home inside the hair follicles of the skin and sometimes in the sebaceous glands. Demodicosis, also known as red mange, develops when the *Demodex* population rages out of control, often in response to stress or illness, and most commonly in puppies, although adults can also acquire it. Puppies that go to a new home at too early an age or that are underweight or ill are

What Is Lyme Disease?

This tick-borne ailment first made its appearance in 1975 in Lyme, Connecticut, from whence it takes its name. Since then, Lyme disease has been reported in 45 states, with 94 percent of the human cases occurring in California, Connecticut, Massachusetts, Minnesota, New Jersey, New York, Pennsylvania, and Wisconsin. New Mexico, on the other hand, has very few cases of Lyme disease.

The ticks that carry Lyme disease range from the size of the period at the end of this sentence to the size of a pinhead. They harbor *Borrelia burgdorferi*, a type of bacterium called a spirochete, which is spread to people and animals through the bite of the tick. The ticks are most active—and the risk of infection is greatest—from late spring to early fall, generally from May to September.

Because Lyme disease has a variety of symptoms, which may not develop until some time after the bite, it can be difficult to diagnose. People may develop a characteristic skin rash that resembles a bull's-eye, hives, flu-like symptoms, achy muscles and joints, swollen glands, fever, and headaches. Left undiagnosed or untreated, Lyme disease can eventually affect the central nervous system and cause joint damage, heart complications, and kidney problems.

Dogs are even more vulnerable to Lyme disease, and the disease in dogs is more difficult to pin down since they rarely develop the skin rash that's seen in people. Common canine signs of Lyme disease are high fever, lack of appetite, and sudden lameness for no apparent reason.

For both people and dogs, antibiotics are the treatment of choice, especially if the disease is caught in its early stages. A later diagnosis will take longer to respond to treatment.

Not every tick transmits Lyme disease, so you might ease your mind by finding out which types of ticks are common in your area. If you and your dog will be venturing through a tick-infested area, protect yourself by wearing clothing that covers your arms, legs, and feet. Tuck pants into socks so ticks won't have access to your skin. If Scamp is on foot, make sure he stays on the trail and away from tall grasses. Checking for and removing ticks promptly will reduce the chance of disease transmission.

especially prone. Dogs diagnosed with *Demodex* are considered to have some type of genetic immunodeficiency that allows the mite to proliferate in large numbers on their skin. Some breeds, such as Bulldogs, are more prone to *Demodex* than others, so before buying a puppy, ask the breeder if her dogs have a history of *Demodex*.

Reddened scaly skin and patchy hair loss are the classic signs of demodicosis and usually appear during the first year of life. In puppies, demodicosis is usually localized, occurring on the head—around the eyes and mouth—and on the front legs. Itchiness isn't common. Your veterinarian can confirm the presence of *Demodex* mites through skin scrapings or a skin biopsy.

Localized demodicosis rarely requires treatment. By the time the dog is about a year old, the condition usually disappears on its own, taken in hand by the immune system. Demodicosis is not contagious, but young dogs who develop it should be spayed or neutered, not only to prevent the stress associated with breeding but also to prevent the transmission of this inheritable genetic defect.

Demodicosis can become generalized, spreading over the entire body. Dogs with generalized demodicosis show the same signs that characterize the localized version, but the condition is more widespread and severe, especially on the feet, and chronic inflammation causes the skin to become darker and thicker. Generalized demodicosis is an extremely serious skin disease that often is never completely eradicated.

Generalized demodicosis requires drastic treatment involving frequent dips to kill the mites. In cases where the skin is infected, oral antibiotics are warranted. If the dog in question has long hair, it must be completely shaved or the dip won't be as effective. Since this disease develops in dogs considered to have an immunodeficiency, any conditions that can compromise their health—stress, poor nutrition, internal or external parasites, poor housing, trauma, immunosuppressive drugs such as steroids, or any other debilitating disease—must be eliminated. In addition, your veterinarian may recommend whirlpool soaks, regular baths with a shampoo containing Betadine or benzoyl-peroxide, a high-quality diet, and vitamins and supplements to boost the immune system. Fatty acid supplements may also be helpful.

Keep in mind that your dog will look worse during the first weeks of treatment before he starts to look better. Because the mites live in the hair follicles, treatment causes the affected follicles to shed their hair, so your dog may have a number of bald patches. Treatment must continue for a minimum of six weeks and often longer. Generalized demodicosis isn't fun for any dog, but it's especially debilitating to older dogs, who may not have a strong enough immune system to fight it off. Some dogs who suffer from the generalized form never fully recover even after intensive therapy; others may still require periodic treatments for the rest of their lives, especially in times of stress or illness.

Sarcoptic Mange

Also known as scabies, this skin disease develops when the *Sarcoptes* mite tunnels under your dog's skin. The result is intense itching, crusty sores, hair loss, and bloody self-inflicted wounds caused by the dog scratching and biting at the itchy spots. The most commonly affected areas are the face, elbows, hocks, underside of the body, and edges of the ears. These signs, plus skin scrapings or knowledge of exposure to other infested dogs, can help your veterinarian diagnose sarcoptic mange. In comparison to the *Demodex* mite, the *Sarcoptes* mite is much more difficult to find, even with multiple skin scrapings.

Scabies is highly contagious to other dogs, cats, and people. If you have a dog with scabies, separate her from other pets. Any animals that have been in contact with a scabies-infested dog should be treated at least once, even if they don't show signs of the condition, and all pet bedding should be washed in the dip. Be sure to check all family members for any skin rash, and consult your family physician if a rash develops.

Treatment requires a course of medicated baths or sprays, usually once every five days over a six-week period, using products prescribed by your veterinarian. A long-haired dog may need to be clipped. The shampoo needs to stay on your dog for at least 10 minutes. Once the shampoo is rinsed, apply the prescribed dip over the dog's entire body. It's important to soak the feet in the dip for at least 10 minutes. Then let the dog drip dry, without the help of a towel or blow dryer. Repeat this weekly as directed by your veterinarian. Short-term use of corticosteroids can help control the itching, and oral antibiotics may be necessary to fight secondary skin infections.

Cheyletiella

This mildly itchy skin disease occurs most often in puppies and adolescent dogs and is contagious to other animals and people. Fortunately, an infestation of *Cheyletiella* mites is uncommon, especially if you have a good flea-control program.

Cheyletiella mites look like small white specks, and if you have keen vision they're large enough to be seen with the naked eye on the skin or fur, especially of a dark-colored dog. The mites will

Did You Know?

Dogs have extremely sensitive hearing and a sense of smell up to 1000 times better than humans to compensate for their relatively poor eyesight.

An Unusual Diagnosis

Susie's eight Cocker Spaniels were all itchy. Her veterinarian wondered if they might have a food allergy but suggested an injection of a steroid first to see if that would relieve the problem. Susie pointed out that one of her dogs was new and had perhaps brought some unseen houseguests with him. She asked her veterinarian to do a skin scraping first. Much to his surprise, he found cheyletiella mites, an unusual diagnosis. Medicated baths and a thorough housecleaning soon had the Cockers well on their way to relief.

To keep the crawlies away, add a teaspoon of benzyl benzoate to the final rinse when you bathe your dog. A bonus is that your dog will smell great. Be careful not to add too much or the coat will become greasy and you'll have to shampoo all over again.

look like little white dots about the size of the sharp end of a pin. If you can't readily see them, examine your dog in the sunlight with the help of a magnifying glass. Under a microscope, they resemble crustaceans.

Mild itching and dandruff along the dog's back are indications of *Cheyletiella* infestation. The condition is sometimes called "walking dandruff." Your veterinarian can confirm the presence of the mites through a skin scraping or just by looking at the dandruff under a microscope. As with other mite infestations, a series of medicated baths and dips is the usual treatment. To rid your home of the mites, perform a thorough housecleaning and be sure other pets are treated if they were exposed to a mite-infested dog. Clean bedding and grooming tools thoroughly, as they can spread mites to you or other pets. People infested with cheyletiella often find bite marks at areas where clothing contacts skin, such as bra straps, waistbands, or elastic bands on underwear.

Ear Mites

When these mites house hunt, they look for the nice, warm moistness of an ear canal. Cats provide their preferred habitat, but they won't turn their noses up at a dog. Put ear mites on your list of suspects if Scamp has dry, reddish-brown or black earwax and frequently shakes his head or paws at his ears. If you carefully scrape out some of the wax with a Q-tip or a tissue wrapped around your finger and look closely at it, you might be able to see the white, pinpoint-size mites moving around.

Unless ears are checked and cleaned regularly, an ear mite infestation can reach the severe stage before it becomes noticeable. A bad case of ear mites can cause hair loss from scratching, bleeding sores around the ears, and can block the entire ear canal. Left untreated, an infestation can eventually lead to serious bacterial or yeast infections. Your veterinarian can confirm the presence of ear mites by swabbing out the ear canal and examining the material under a microscope. If mites are present, they are quickly and easily identified. Because ear mites are common in young puppies, your veterinarian will usually check for them each time you bring Scamp in for booster vaccinations.

Treatment is less drastic than for other mite infestations. Your veterinarian will flush the ear canals to rid them of the waxy buildup and prescribe eardrops to kill the mites. The drops must be administered for three weeks to a month to make sure all the mites are eliminated. In case any of them escape from the ear, a bath is also a good idea. Ear mites are highly contagious among pets; if one cat or dog has them, probably all of them do.

Ringworm

Unlike the previous external parasites, which all belong to the insect family, ringworm is caused by *Microsporum canis* and is a fungal infection. Often mistaken for other skin conditions, ringworm is characterized by dry, scaly skin, hair loss, and sometimes draining sores or itching. Discolored, ring-shaped patches on the skin give this parasite its name. Ringworm is common and contagious, spread through contact with an infected person or pet. It affects dogs, other domestic animals, and people. If a person contracts ringworm, it's not always the fault of the family dog, although physicians are usually quick to point in that direction.

The ringworm fungi, or dermatophytes, invade the outer layers of the skin, hair, and nails, where they find sustenance from keratin, a protein derived from dead skin cells. Warmth and high humidity are ideal growth conditions for this fungus. Typically, ringworm appears as a scaly, circular area of hair loss. Sometimes it takes other forms, though, and can only be ruled out through diagnostic tests.

Ringworm can be detected by using an ultraviolet light screening, or Wood's lamp exam. This light detects only one type of ringworm, however, and only 40 to 50 percent of detected ringworm tests positive. Skin scrapings and fungal cultures of hair are other methods of diagnosis.

Ringworm usually resolves on its own in one to three months, but because of the risk of cross-infestation, treatment is important. While your dog is being treated, limit your exposure to the affected areas as much as possible, and wash your hands well after handling the dog during the treatment period. If any family member develops a rash, consult your family doctor.

For minor cases, bathing affected areas with Betadine or applying Tinactin, available in drugstores without a prescription, can help soothe any itching. Resistant or extensive cases can require long-term treatment with ointments, shampoos, or oral antifungal agents to control or eliminate the infection. Topical antibiotic ointment may be needed to treat infected sores. The cost of these medications varies from reasonable to expensive.

For treatment to be most effective, affected areas should be clipped to prevent infected hairs from falling into the environment and increasing the likelihood of the fungus spreading to other pets or people. Even if it looks like the infestation has cleared up, continue treatment for another week or two. Pets and people that have been in contact with affected dogs should also be treated. To prevent a recurrence, disinfect household surfaces such as counters and bathtubs with a 1:10 solution of bleach and water. Also, because grooming equipment can be a persistent carrier, disinfect it with the bleach solution or throw it away. Vacuum thoroughly to remove any infected hairs.

Internal Parasites

Just as nasty as external parasites are internal parasites, which include roundworms, hookworms, tapeworms, whipworms, and heartworms, and the less commonly diagnosed parasitic protozoa such as coccidia and giardia. Other parasites exist, but as their occurrence is rare they aren't discussed here.

Through various methods, internal parasites make their way inside your dog, usually settling in its intestines, where they gorge on blood or tissues, robbing your pet of vital nutrients, and damaging or killing cells and tissues. Some reproduce inside the dog, eventually resulting in serious physical problems such as heart blockages (heartworms), or they hitch a ride out via the feces so they can infect other dogs.

Signs of internal parasites include lack of appetite, weight loss, coughing, bloody diarrhea, low energy, and anemia. Infected puppies

Collecting a Fecal Sample

When you take your dog out to eliminate, bring along a plastic sandwich bag and a container in which to store the sample. A clean plastic dish with a lid, such as an empty margarine tub, is ideal.

Place the plastic bag over your hand, pick up the sample, and put it in the container. It should be collected no more than 12 hours before being examined by the veterinarian. Refrigerate it (and mark the container to avoid surprising someone!) until you can get to the veterinary clinic.

If you aren't able or willing to collect a fecal sample, the veterinary technician can take one by passing a fecal loop into your puppy's rectum. This isn't a painful procedure, but some puppies do squirm or squeal, as you can imagine.

may appear potbellied, with rough, dull fur. Only roundworms and tapeworms can be seen in the feces without the aid of a microscope. Fortunately, internal parasites are easily diagnosed, treated, and prevented. Most heartworm preventives, which can be given on a monthly basis, also kill roundworms, hookworms, and whipworms. A good flea control program helps prevent tapeworm infection. There are new medications that control fleas, heartworms, roundworms, and other parasites—all in one topical dose that's absorbed into the bloodstream.

Intestinal parasites are most commonly diagnosed in young puppies, but they can attack a dog of any age. Puppies acquire intestinal parasites from several sources, including from the mother before birth or from ingesting eggs that are in the soil. When you take your new puppy to the clinic for the first time, your veterinarian will want a fecal sample to examine for parasites or their eggs, as well as follow-up fecal exams when you bring your puppy in for booster shots. It's also a good idea for your puppy to receive an appropriate dose of a broad-spectrum deworming medication at each of these visits. The reason for deworming the puppy as well as checking a stool sample is because the parasite may not yet be producing the eggs that are detected in the stool sample. An annual fecal exam will help make sure your dog stays worm-free.

If parasites are identified, your veterinarian will prescribe the appropriate medication. Each parasite requires a specific treatment. Your veterinarian can also suggest preventive medication so Scamp won't get reinfected. In some cases, you may need to disinfect your home as well. Several weeks after treatment, your veterinarian will want to recheck a stool sample to make sure all the parasites have been killed.

To prevent reinfection, start Scamp on preventive medication and keep him away from feces deposited by other animals. No sniffing allowed. Keep your own yard clean by picking up after him as soon as possible, especially if you have young children. Although it's rare, some internal parasites can be transmitted to people, and the most common occurrences involve children who come in contact with feces.

Roundworms

Toxocara canis, or roundworms, are the most common of the internal parasites. They are present in most dogs at birth, having been transmitted inside the womb or through the mother's milk. They can also ingest roundworm eggs from the soil or in rare instances by eating a rodent that's a carrier. Breeders can prevent roundworms by giving appropriate deworming medications to the dam during pregnancy and then to the puppies at two weeks of age.

Roundworms are rarely a problem for adult dogs, but a heavy load of them can make a puppy very sick or even kill it. A roundworm-ridden puppy has the potbelly of a seasoned beer drinker, but elsewhere his body looks thin and scrawny and is covered by a dull, rough coat. Other common signs of roundworm infection are vomiting and diarrhea, coughing, or even pneumonia. The long, thin worms can also be seen in the stool or sometimes in vomit. No matter how sorry you may feel for such a puppy, don't buy one with these signs. If you already have a puppy who appears to be infested, take it to your veterinarian for deworming. Dewormers available in pet stores are seldom as effective as those provided by your veterinarian.

It doesn't happen often, but roundworms can be transmitted to people. Dog-to-human transmission usually occurs when young children touch egg-laden feces or play in dirt or grassy areas where roundworm eggs have been deposited, and then put their hands in their mouths. Human infection is called visceral larval migrans and can be serious if left untreated. Prevent roundworm infection by keeping your yard feces-free and taking in a fecal sample annually so Scamp can be treated for any worms that may be present.

Hookworms

Hookworms (*Ancylostoma caninum*) are among the most harmful of the intestinal parasites found in young puppies and older dogs.

They favor a warm, humid climate, like that found in the southern United States, and hook up with your dog by penetrating the skin, usually through the feet, or by being transmitted to pups through the placenta or their mother's milk. Hookworms are a good reason not to raise puppies on dirt surfaces and to deworm the mother before you breed her. Young pups should be dewormed at two weeks of age.

Hookworms can also be ingested orally, if the dog eats some infected soil or an infected rodent or cockroach.

Once inside, hookworms travel through the body, where they attach to the wall of the small intestine and begin sucking out blood. A heavy load of hookworms can lead to severe anemia. Other signs of hookworm infestation include loose, bloody stools, weakness, weight loss, depression, and some degree of dehydration. Affected puppies may also have pale gums and skin lesions.

Hookworms are diagnosed through a stool sample and can be treated with medication when detected early. If the infection is severe, however, your dog may require hospitalization so he can receive fluid therapy, blood transfusions, and other supportive treatment. Hookworms are killers if left untreated.

Infection recurs quickly if feces aren't picked up daily. Just as with roundworms, many heartworm preventives kill hookworms as well, so you can ensure lifelong prevention.

Bear in mind that hookworms sometimes infect people as well, although this is less common today than in the past. The worms penetrate the intact skin, usually when people walk barefoot in infected areas. Suspect hookworm infection if you see a small lesion that becomes intensely itchy within a few days. The best way to prevent human infection is to not walk barefoot outdoors and to keep your dog's feces picked up on a regular basis.

Whipworms

These parasites (*Trichuris vulpis*) worm their way inside when your dog eats something that's been in contact with infective larvae or contaminated soil. They migrate to the large intestine and attach deeply and firmly to the lining of the intestinal wall where, like the hookworm, they feed on blood. Dogs can coexist with a small number of whipworms, but too many of these parasites can lead to anemia, bloody diarrhea, and weight loss. Whipworms don't pass eggs on a regular basis, so they are sometimes difficult to diagnose. Because of the whipworm's life cycle, evidence of infestation doesn't show up until puppies are at least three months old. Your veterinarian may need to run several fecal exams before hitting the jackpot. These buggers are difficult to eradicate, and treatment involves giving a specific deworming medication that is administered for three consecutive days, repeated in three weeks, and repeated again in three months.

Eggs can persist in soil for months or years, and it's impossible to completely rid the environment of them. To prevent reinfection, pick up feces regularly. If dogs are kept in runs, the area should be disinfected with bleach diluted in water.

Tapeworms

Tapeworms are one of the few internal parasites that can be identified with the naked eye. Segments of them look like cucumber seeds or small pieces of rice and are often seen clinging to the fur around your dog's rear end or crawling through his feces. If you notice either of these situations, take a stool sample in for examination to make sure other worms aren't involved as well. Tapeworms are treated with either an oral or injectable medication.

Fleas and tapeworms (*Dipylydium caninum*) work together in infecting your dog. Fleas carry tapeworm eggs, which remain in the flea's intestine until the flea is eaten by a dog. The tapeworm then continues its life cycle inside the dog. Thus, controlling fleas reduces Scamp's risk of acquiring tapeworms. Dog lice, rodents, and rabbits can also spread tapeworms, but this is a much less common route of transmission.

Heartworm

This parasite is perhaps the most deadly that can infect your dog. Like the tapeworm, the heartworm relies on a partner—the female mosquito—to complete its life cycle, which begins in the blood of a dog infected with microfilaria, or immature heartworms. When a mosquito bites an infected dog, it takes in the heartworm larvae, which spend several weeks developing inside the mosquito. The next time the mosquito bites a dog, the infective larvae are injected into the dog's body, where they migrate through the body tissues for several months, undergoing several stages of maturation. Eventually they enter the bloodstream and travel to the right side of the heart, where they will grow to adulthood. If both sexes are present in the heart, they'll reproduce, bringing forth more microfilariae to start the process all over again. The time frame from the moment the dog is bitten and infected by the mosquito to the establishment of mature adult heartworms in the right side of the heart is approximately six months.

Adult heartworms can reach a length of up to 14 inches, and dogs infected with heartworms can have more than 250 adults in severe infestations. Large numbers of heartworms will eventually block the heart, causing disease and death. If you live in an area where mosquitoes are common, your dog is at risk of heartworm disease, even if he never goes outside. As you know, mosquitoes can enter your house just as easily as any other insect can.

In the early stages of heartworm disease, dogs may show no signs at all. Later, depending on the number of worms present and the length of time since infection, the dog will lose weight, have a low level of energy, and cough after exertion. He may have difficulty breathing. If the disease has been present for some time, other signs can include coughing up blood, depression, lethargy, and fluid accumulation in the abdominal cavity. If the disease progresses far enough, the result is congestive heart failure.

A simple blood test can quickly confirm the presence of adult heartworms. Blood tests for microfilariae aren't as accurate because a dog can have adult worms in the heart without having microfilariae circulating in the blood. If a dog tests positive for heartworms, other diagnostic tests are performed to determine the severity of the disease. Radiographs, or x-rays, of the dog's chest will allow the veterinarian to check for enlargement of the heart and pulmonary artery as well as secondary lung disease. Blood work is done to gauge the dog's overall condition, including the status of kidney and liver enzymes and electrolytes. Other procedures that may be done are an electrocardiogram (ECG) to check for arrhythmias and ultrasonography to detect whether the heart is enlarged or if worms are present in the heart.

Treatment involves several intramuscular doses of a drug to kill the mature heartworms. Although the medication is extremely effective, the side effects can be quite severe. After the heartworms die, five to 10 days after the medication is given, they're absorbed by the body. During this time, the dog must be inactive or a clump of worms could dislodge and cause a pulmonary embolism, which could kill the dog. In severe cases, the worms must be removed surgically. Several weeks later, the dog receives medication to kill any immature heartworms. The dog should be tested again three months later to make sure all the adult heartworms are dead.

The good news is that heartworms are completely preventable

with medication. You'll want to get your puppy started on the preventive medication between 8-16 weeks old. This preventive medicine is prescribed only for dogs who are heartworm-free, so if your puppy does not begin taking it before six months of age, he must first be tested to ensure he hasn't been infected.

Heartworm Heartache

Harley, a little Miniature Pinscher fostered by a kind family since his former owners gave him up, had been diagnosed with heartworms and was now scheduled for treatment. Harley's former owners had previously stopped giving him heartworm medication because they said it was too expensive, and now Harley was paying the price.

The little black and tan dog would have to spend the next six weeks in a crate, unable to run, jump, and play in his usual energetic style. His foster family knew it would be a challenge to keep him quiet and were sad to see the happy little dog laid low by the painful treatment, which is especially uncomfortable for small dogs who have less muscle and fat to absorb the medication. The veterinarian recommended starting the first treatment when someone could stay home with the dog for a few days. His family gave him a bath first, since they didn't know how long it would be before he felt like having another one.

Four weeks later, little Harley would receive another shot to complete the treatment and would have to remain fairly inactive for up to four weeks. If Harley could talk, I'm sure he'd be the first to say that taking a preventive pill every month is far less painful than going through the ordeal of heartworm treatment, and his foster family can tell you that prevention is far less expensive.

Heartworm disease has been reported in every state, including Alaska. Depending on where you live, your veterinarian may recommend that heartworm preventive be given year-round or only during mosquito season. If your dog takes heartworm preventive only part of the year, he will need to be retested annually before going back on the medication. The medication can be given daily or monthly, depending on your preference. The monthly preventives come in the form of a chewable treat, so dogs love taking this medicine. Additionally, a new topical medication now prevents heartworms, intestinal parasites, fleas, and ticks. Treatment for heartworm infection is expensive, not to mention dangerous for your dog, so prevention is the way to go.

Coccidia

This protozoal parasite, which is uncommon in dogs, is most likely to affect those who come in contact with contaminated feces, usually under crowded conditions such as poorly run animal shelters, pet stores, or puppy mills. Dogs whose immune systems are compromised by ill health or malnutrition are also susceptible.

Coccidia comes in many forms, but the one that usually infects dogs is called *Isospora*. It's diagnosed through a fecal sample that contains the organism's eggs, or oocysts. Signs of coccidia are diarrhea, vomiting, depression, weight loss, and dehydration, but some dogs don't have any outward symptoms.

Coccidia can be treated with medication, which also helps prevent development of secondary bacterial infections. Some dogs may need supportive therapy for dehydration. Reinfection is unlikely as long as your dog doesn't live in crowded, unsanitary conditions or have the opportunity to chow down on rodents.

Giardia

Another protozoal parasite, *Giardia*, is also unlikely to infect your dog, unless he comes in contact with contaminated drinking water. If Scamp goes backpacking with you in the wilderness and drinks out of streams, however, you might have to worry about it.

This parasite affects the small intestine and most commonly results in mild stomach upset or intermittent diarrhea. Stools may be light-colored or covered in mucus. Your veterinarian will need a stool sample for a definite diagnosis and can then prescribe appropriate medication. To prevent *Giardia*, make sure Scamp shares your treated drinking water. Additionally, a Giardia vaccine is available for high-risk dogs.

First Aid

Being able to care for your dog in the event of an emergency could mean the difference between life and death. Of course, you'll want to get Scamp to the veterinarian as soon as possible, but if it's the middle of the night or the clinic is far away, you may need to take matters into your own hands until help is available. Knowing what to do for the following conditions and injuries can allow you to stabilize the situation and prevent further damage.

Insect Bites and Stings

Just like people, dogs can be sensitive to the bites and stings of insects such as bees, wasps, and mosquitoes. If your dog shows signs of a reaction, such as hives, itching, or swelling, use tweezers to remove the stinger (if it's a bee sting) and apply a soothing paste made with baking soda and water. An ice pack can reduce swelling, and calamine lotion will relieve itching. An antihistamine such as Benadryl is useful for treating hives. The amount given is determined by weight.

> Just like people, dogs can be sensitive to the bites and stings of insects such as bees, wasps, and mosquitoes.

Ask your veterinarian how much to give your dog in case of a reaction. For the next few days, watch the area for further swelling, discharge, or signs of an abscess.

Multiple stings, especially around the head, can cause more serious reactions, from the eyes swelling shut to swelling around the throat that inhibits breathing. Some dogs even go into shock. If this is the case, get Scamp to the veterinarian right away.

Vomiting

Throwing up is a common reaction in dogs, and it can be caused by something as simple as overeating or eating grass to something as serious as poisoning from spoiled food or a toxic substance. Your dog could even have a foreign object lodged in his intestines.

Occasional vomiting with no other signs generally indicates mild stomach upset and is usually not a problem, but if your dog vomits repeatedly or forcefully (projectile vomiting), or you see blood or fecal material in the vomit, it's time to make an immediate trip to the veterinarian. Sporadic vomiting combined with poor appetite and coat condition is also a sign of illness and should be checked out.

Diarrhea

Like vomiting, diarrhea can be a sign of a lot of different things, which may or may not be serious. Diarrhea often occurs when a dog's diet is changed too abruptly or he eats inappropriate food, when he's exposed to different drinking water—on a trip, for instance—or as a result of emotional upset or excitement. Usually, this is a mild form of diarrhea that can be treated by withholding food for a day, then giving a bland diet of boiled chicken and rice

for a couple of days to soothe the intestinal tract. If your dog is prone to hypoglycemia, check with your veterinarian before withholding food for any reason.

Diarrhea may signal something more serious if it lasts for more than a day, if there's blood in the stool, and or if it's accompanied by vomiting or fever. If any of these is the case,

Performing the Heimlich Maneuver

If your dog is choking and you can't grasp the object or are unable to see it clearly, try to dislodge it by placing your hands on both sides of your dog's rib cage and pressing firmly and quickly. With a small dog, you may find it easier to place the dog on its side and apply firm pressure over the rib cage. Repeat either above step until you're able to remove the object. If your dog was unable to breathe correctly for five minutes or more, take him to your veterinarian right away for a complete evaluation.

seek veterinary attention right away. With continual vomiting and diarrhea, it doesn't take long for a dog to become dehydrated.

Be prepared to tell your veterinarian the color of the diarrhea (yellow or greenish, black and tarry, light-colored, or bloody), its consistency (watery, foamy, greasy, or mucus-covered), how it smells (rancid, like food or sour milk, or just plain putrid), and its frequency (several times a day or several times an hour). The more you can tell your veterinarian about it, the more accurate his diagnosis and treatment will be.

Choking

Some dogs will eat anything, just on the off chance that it might be a treat. If Scamp chows down on something that gets stuck in his throat, you'll need to take quick action. Signs of choking include coughing, gagging, retching, and pawing at the mouth. This can be frightening to see, but try to stay calm and act quickly. Look inside Scamp's mouth, opening it by pressing your thumb and forefingers into the upper cheeks. If you can do so safely, try to remove the object by hooking it out with a finger or removing it with tweezers or needle-nose pliers, but take care not to push it in farther. Take the dog to the veterinarian right away if you're not successful.

Bleeding

If Scamp is bleeding, you need to get it under control—fast! Put pressure on the wound and keep it there, using your hand, a towel or whatever you have available. A sanitary napkin also works well. Maintain pressure until the bleeding stops or until you can get help. At least five minutes of pressure on the wounded area is needed to stop or slow down the bleeding. Don't constantly remove the pressure to check the wound, or you'll defeat the purpose and have to start all over again. Seek veterinary attention for all deep wounds or that won't stop bleeding profusely. Never apply a tourniquet, which can do more harm than good.

The ears, foot pads, and penis bleed more freely than other areas of the body. It may be awkward, but keep pressure on them just as you would any other part of the body. If the blood is coming from an artery—you can tell if it's spurting bright red—you may need to apply pressure over the artery in the groin to get the bleeding under control so a bandage can be applied. Ask your veterinarian to show you where to press.

If the bleeding is from a toenail you've trimmed too short, apply direct pressure with a gauze pad and then put a little styptic powder on the end of the nail until the bleeding stops. If you don't have styptic powder, you can use flour. It doesn't work as well, but is better than nothing.

Scratches and scrapes aren't life-threatening, but it's still a good idea to get the bleeding under control. Clean the wound

Quick Status Checks

If your dog is ill or has been injured, look at the color of his gums and tongue. Normally, they're moist and a healthy pink color. A dog who has lost a lot of blood or is showing signs of shock has pale pink or white gums.

To test your dog for dehydration, gently lift up the skin on the back of his neck. A well-hydrated dog has skin that returns quickly to its normal position. If the skin returns to place slowly or remains pinched up, your dog is dehydrated and needs immediate veterinary attention.

Monitoring your dog's heart rate or pulse is easily done as well. Simply place your hand on the inside of your dog's thigh close to where the leg joins the body. With light pressure you can feel the femoral pulse, which ranges from 70 to 150 beats per minute for dogs.

Observe his breathing as well. Heavy panting for no obvious reason can indicate pain. Shallow breathing can signal fluid in his chest, a collapsed lung, or other problems.

Knowing these health parameters will enable you to give your veterinarian a more accurate assessment of the situation before you even arrive. That way, clinic personnel can make preparations while you're enroute.

with 3 percent hydrogen peroxide, and apply antibiotic ointment after the bleeding stops. Later, you might want to have your veterinarian take a look at the wound to make sure there's no damage beneath the skin.

Fractures

Any time you suspect a broken bone, take your dog to the veterinarian immediately so he can examine it and take x-rays to determine whether there is a fracture and how serious it is. Be very careful when you're moving your dog. A fracture is painful, and poor Scamp may bite out of fear. Moving him the wrong way can also make the fracture worse by causing damage to the surrounding soft tissue. If you are able to do so, stabilize the fracture with a rolled newspaper or a small piece of wood and wrap it loosely. Shock is a very real danger, so keep Scamp as still and warm as possible until you can get to the veterinary clinic.

Shock

When the body sustains serious injury, its response is to shut down. There's not enough blood flow to meet the needs of all the organs, so they can't function properly. Situations that can induce shock include being hit by a car, blood loss from an injury, poisoning, or dehydration from severe vomiting and diarrhea. Signs of shock are a fast, weak pulse; dry gums; pale or gray lips; rapid, shallow breathing; low body temperature; weakness; and lethargy. If your dog is in shock, control any bleeding, keep him still and warm, and seek immediate veterinary help.

Car Accident

In the best of all worlds, dogs would never be hit by cars, but this happens often. You'd be amazed how many owners run over their own dogs! If your dog enjoys lounging near vehicles, always check before you back out of the driveway. This is especially important if you have an older dog who has lost her hearing and has little sense of what's going on around her.

Fortunately, some dogs are only hit by a bumper and thrown to the side. With a small dog, though, even a glancing blow can cause serious harm. As with any traumatic injury, your main concern will be shock. Gently place Scamp on a cookie sheet (if he's small) or a board, sturdy piece of cardboard, or blanket pulled taut as a stretcher.

Move slowly and talk to him quietly. (Again, beware of being bitten by a scared dog. Consider muzzling him to protect yourself.) Try not to move his head or neck in case there's spinal damage. Stop any bleeding, and make sure he's well wrapped up so he'll stay warm. Then get to the veterinary clinic on the double.

Heat Stroke/Exhaustion

When environmental temperatures rise to body level or higher, heatstroke or heat exhaustion are real possibilities. For a dog, whose normal body temperature is between 100 and 102.5, that means an outside temperature of 101 degrees Fahrenheit or more, which is common in the Midwest, South, and Southwest during the summer. Your dog should not be out in the heat of the day without adequate water, as well as shade, and shelter when temperatures are this high. Dogs cool themselves by panting, which simply isn't an efficient method when it's that hot outside. Nor should you leave your dog in the car on a sunny day, even if it doesn't seem particularly hot outside. Because the inside of a car heats up rapidly, many dogs die from overheating each summer, even though their owners left them in the car "for only a few minutes." If parking for a few minutes is unavoidable, choose a shady area and roll the windows down—don't just crack them.

A dog with heatstroke breathes loudly and rapidly, has a bright red tongue and mucous membranes, and drools thick saliva. He may vomit and will have a high rectal temperature, 105 degrees Fahrenheit or higher. Without quick treatment, bloody diarrhea, weakness, brain damage, and eventually death follow.

Heat exhaustion usually occurs when a dog overexerts himself on a hot day. Signs of heat exhaustion are collapse, muscle cramps, and vomiting; but his body temperature doesn't usually rise to dangerous levels, as it does with heatstroke.

How to Take Your Dog's Temperature

This is one of those indignities that your dog won't enjoy, but it doesn't take long and you can reward him with a treat afterward. You may find it helpful to have someone assist by holding the dog so he won't squirm. Lubricate a digital rectal thermometer using K-Y Jelly or vegetable oil. Gently insert it into the rectum, where it should remain for about 90 seconds. The normal canine temperature ranges from 100 degrees Fahrenheit to 102.5 degrees Fahrenheit. Call your veterinarian if Scamp's temperature is approaching 104 degrees Fahrenheit.

If Scamp appears to have heatstroke or heat exhaustion, it's imperative to cool him off. You can stop a mild case of heatstroke or heat exhaustion simply by moving the dog to a cooler area, such as an air-conditioned house or car. For a more advanced case, bathe the dog with cool, not cold, tap water to help bring his temperature down. Then take him to the veterinarian to make sure he's okay.

If you aren't able to get your dog's temperature down, rush him to the veterinarian, who can institute emergency therapy. Heatstroke and heat exhaustion are easy to prevent by making sure Scamp keeps cool in the dog days of summer. An easy way to do this is to provide him with a kiddie pool. Keep the pool in the shade and the water clean and fresh, and he'll love you for making his summer fun and safe.

Seizures

Some of the reasons a dog might suffer a seizure include heart problems, epilepsy, diabetes, hypoglycemia, distemper, a blow to the head, a bee sting, or a high level of anxiety. A seizure can also be brought on by poisoning, heatstroke, or kidney or liver failure.

A seizure is defined as a sudden uncontrolled burst of activity such as jerking legs, foaming at the mouth, making snapping motions, or collapse. The dog may also lose control of his bladder or bowels. A seizure may last only a few seconds or as long as a few minutes, gradually returning to normal.

This is a scary event to witness, but the best thing you can do is to make sure your dog doesn't injure himself by falling off the couch or down the stairs while the seizure is going on. If he's safe from injury, simply cover him with something and wait for the seizure to end. There's no danger of your dog swallowing his tongue, so don't try to stick your fingers in his mouth; you'll risk getting bitten. Call your veterinarian to report the seizure and ask what to do. She'll need to perform an exam and run some diagnostic tests to determine the cause. Some seizures, such as those caused by epilepsy, can be controlled with medication. Some young puppies can have mild seizures that are caused by stress from teething or traveling, and these shouldn't be confused with epilepsy.

Poisoning

Homes, garages, and yards are full of potential poisons. Even some of the products we use on our dogs, such as flea sprays and dips, are poisons. From antifreeze to aspirin, chocolate, and cigarettes, a number of items in every home can kill or seriously harm your dog. If Scamp shows any signs of poisoning, call your veterinarian or a poison control hotline immediately. If you know what your dog swallowed and can provide the packaging or a sample of the substance, this will help in making the diagnosis. A proper diagnosis is important because inducing vomiting is helpful for some types of poisons but can make matters worse with others. Don't induce vomiting in your dog unless your veterinarian tells you to. To get the job done, a small amount of syrup of ipecac or hydrogen peroxide orally will usually work.

Poisons that attack the neurological system include organophosphates and carbamates, which are found in some flea and tick products and lawn and garden pesticides. You may also know them by such names as diazinon, fenthion, malathion, carbaryl, or carbofuran. A dog who has gotten into this type of poison seems apprehensive and exhibits high levels of drooling, urination, defecation, vomiting, and diarrhea. His pupils are the size of pinpoints.

Other neurological poisons include pyrethrins and pyrethroids, also found in flea control products. They are less toxic than organophosphates and carbamates, but the situation is still serious. Excessive salivation, vomiting, diarrhea, and tremors are signs of this type of poisoning, as are extreme excitability or depression.

Rat and mouse poisons prevent the blood from clotting. If you even think your dog has eaten any of this kind of poison, rush him to the veterinarian. Today's rodentcides are extremely dangerous, even in small amounts, and in fact it takes less rat poison to kill your dog than it does a rat. Labored breathing, refusal to eat, nosebleeds, bloody urine or feces, and tiny hemorrhages on

the gums are all indications of this type of poisoning, but you shouldn't wait until you see these symptoms to get to the veterinarian. It may be too late.

Your dog may not be a smoker, but chomping on cigarettes, cigars, chewing tobacco, or marijuana can still be the death of him. Signs of tobacco poisoning are excitement, drooling, vomiting, and muscle weakness, all of which develop in minutes. Large amounts may lead to coma or death.

Pain relievers such as aspirin, acetaminophen, and ibuprofen aren't safe for your dog either. Although a veterinarian may prescribe a small amount of aspirin for pain relief, too much can cause anemia and gastric hemorrhage. And a single 200 mg tablet of ibuprofen is toxic to a small dog, causing painful stomach ulcers. Acetaminophen will severely depress your dog as well as cause abdominal pain. If treatment isn't provided, your dog could be dead within 24 hours, just from ingesting two extra-strength tablets. Other medications that can be harmful to your dog include cold pills, antidepressants, and vitamins.

Don't forget cleaning agents and automotive products. If swallowed, cleaning products can cause problems ranging from mild stomach upset to severe burns of the tongue, mouth, and stomach. As little as one teaspoon of antifreeze (ethylene glycol) can be fatal to a seven-pound dog. Other common household items that can cause poisoning include mothballs, pennies, potpourri oils, fabric softener sheets, batteries, homemade salt dough, and alcoholic drinks.

Contaminated food foraged from the trash can cause problems, too. If your dog suddenly starts vomiting or has bloody diarrhea, a painful and distended abdomen, or shows signs of shock, consider food poisoning as a possible cause. Get him to the veterinarian right away.

To prevent poisoning, keep a tight lid on anything potentially dangerous and store it well out of your dog's reach. Whenever possible, don't use or keep anything in your home that you

> ## Did You Know?
>
> The average gestation period for a dog is 63 days.

The Canine First-Aid Kit

You shouldn't leave home without a first-aid kit for your pooch. What follows are items that you should always have on hand should the unexpected occur. The kit will be valuable for you, too, since many of the items are useful for human emergency care, as well.

- ○ Your veterinarian's phone number
- ○ An after-hours emergency clinic's phone number
- ○ The National Animal Poison Control Center's hotline number: (888) 426-4435 or
- ○ Muzzle
- ○ Canine first-aid book
- ○ Sterile gauze bandaging, rolls and pads of various sizes and lengths
- ○ Nonstick wound pads, gauze squares, and roll cotton to control bleeding
- ○ Elastic bandage
- ○ Adhesive bandaging tape
- ○ Cotton balls and swabs
- ○ Antiseptic ointment
- ○ Antibiotic cream or ointment
- ○ Hydrogen peroxide

- ○ Rubbing alcohol (handy, too, for removing tree sap from the coat)
- ○ Eye dropper
- ○ Saline eye drops
- ○ Tweezers
- ○ Needlenose pliers
- ○ Snakebite kit
- ○ Clean towels
- ○ Clean socks (for foot injuries)
- ○ Scissors
- ○ Large blanket (for stretcher)
- ○ Tincture of iodine
- ○ Rectal thermometer
- ○ Penlight flashlight
- ○ Syrup of ipecac and activated charcoal liquid or tablets (poisoning antidotes)
- ○ Styptic powder (in case nails are cut too short)

wouldn't want your dog to eat, such as rat poison or snail bait. Graduate to the use of humane traps and release the pests where they won't bother anyone. Use natural deterrents for snails and other garden annoyances, and keep compost heaps enclosed so your dog can't get to them. Wash your dog's feet with mild soap and water if he walks on a yard that's been treated with pesticides. Never give your dog any medication meant for people unless your veterinarian specifically advises it and recommends an appropriate amount.

Fish Hooks

Your dog might be a great catch, but he certainly doesn't need to be caught on a hook. Many times curious dogs get fish hooks lodged in their lips or muzzle area. Naturally, this is painful and causes the dog to paw furiously at the area, which only results in more damage. Swelling at the site is rapid and adds to the dog's discomfort. If your dog tangles with one of these sharp objects and you can't get to a veterinarian quickly for its removal, figure out which way the barb is pointing. Then grit your teeth and push it on through the soft tissue. When swelling is severe, this can be difficult, especially if the dog is wriggling in pain. Once it's through, though, you can use wire cutters to cut the shank next to the barb and remove each piece separately. Your veterinarian may recommend antibiotics to ward off any infection.

Burns

Bathe a burn caused by flame with cool water or cover the area with a cool compress. Avoid treating burns with butter, ointment, or ice. Butter and ointment hold the heat in, and ice damages the skin. If the burn covers a large area of the body, use a thick layer of gauze or cloth to bandage it. Don't use cotton balls or

cotton batting; they'll stick to the damaged skin. Keep the dog warm to prevent shock, and get him to a veterinarian right away.

Treat chemical burns caused by substances such as battery acid or toilet bowl cleaners the same way, but be sure to protect your hands with rubber gloves before touching the burned area. Chemical burns require veterinary treatment.

Dogs can get sunburned as well. If your light-skinned dog has turned pink or red from sun exposure, take him to your veterinarian for treatment. Until you can get there, bathing him with a cool compress may offer temporary relief.

Allergic Reactions

Frantic scratching and biting at the skin is a sure sign that your dog is suffering from an allergy of some sort. Allergies can also manifest themselves in other ways, from skin problems such as rashes and hot spots to sneezing, coughing, face-rubbing, and foot-licking. When no other cause is present, suspect allergies if your dog develops ear infections, vomiting, loose stools, or gas.

Allergies can develop in response to inhaled substances, such as pollen; to particular types of food, most commonly corn, wheat, soy, beef, or dairy products; or to materials with which the animal comes in contact, such as wool or carpet or even cats. Dogs can also suffer allergic reactions to vaccinations, antibiotics, and insect bites or stings.

Scratching, biting, licking, and rubbing at that ever-persistent itch lead to infection characterized by red bumps and pimples. In severe cases, your dog may be lethargic or have difficulty breathing. If you've ever had allergies, you know how uncomfortable they can be, so get veterinary advice as soon as possible.

Inhalant allergies, also known as atopy or allergic inhalant dermatitis, are usually diagnosed after fleas or other possible causes have been eliminated; but sometimes skin tests are necessary. Treatment can range from dietary supplements and medicated shampoos to drugs such as antihistamines and steroids to regular allergy shots. This can be a very frustrating condition to treat, and rarely is there a quick cure.

In the same vein, food allergies are usually diagnosed after other possible conditions are ruled out. Again, treatment is long term, beginning with feeding a hypoallergenic diet for six weeks. This type of diet contains ingredients to which the dog has never been exposed. Because the variety of proteins used in dog foods has greatly increased over the years, today's hypoallergenic diets often contain unusual ingredients such as catfish or herring. If signs of the allergy disappear, ingredients are added back to the dog's diet, one at a time, until it's discovered which one causes the reaction. Then that substance is eliminated from the dog's menu.

The diagnosis of contact allergies, or irritant contact dermatitis, is based on owner observations or sometimes skin tests. Washing the exposed areas to remove the irritant is helpful, but the main thrust of treatment is to prevent re-exposure.

> ## Did You Know?
>
> An average of 800 dogs and cats are euthanized every hour in the United States.

Eye Problems and Injuries

When we wake up, one of the first things we do is rub our eyes to get the "sleepies" out. That dried, crusty stuff accumulates in the corners of our eyes while we sleep, but it's not harmful and is easy to get rid of. Goopy eyes are a common affliction of dogs as well.

Like people, dogs produce tears—a combination of mucus and water—as a way of cleansing and lubricating the eye. As the tears drain, the result is a watery or mucus-like discharge that can be clear, whitish, cloudy, light yellow, brownish, or reddish. This type of discharge is normal and can simply be wiped away with a dampened tissue, paper towel, or soft washcloth (use warm water but no soap). Carefully trimming the hair around the eyes can help prevent eye-goop buildup.

Some eye discharge, though, can be a sign of serious injury or disease. Thick, greenish gunk or heavy amounts of normal discharge are a clue that a visit to the veterinarian is in order. It's especially important if the dog's eye is red or swollen or he's squinting or pawing at his eye. A normal eye is bright and shiny. Your dog should look out of it at you without pain. If squinting is persistent and painful, or associated with redness, cloudiness, or discharge, your veterinarian needs to have a look right away. Early diagnosis and treatment could save your dog's vision.

Dogs with large protruding eyes are more susceptible to eye problems. These can run the gamut from irritation or injuries to allergies, inflammation or infection, and dry eye.

A scratch from a cranky cat or a brush with sharp-edged foliage can scratch the cornea. Eyes can also be injured by blowing dust, dirt, or debris when a dog hangs its head out the car window. Grass seeds or particles can enter the eye when a dog runs

through tall grass. During the pollen season, many dogs have mild allergies, which are manifested in red, itchy, watery eyes.

Conjunctivitis, also known as pinkeye, occurs when the eye's normal population of bacteria and fungi get out of control. The viruses that case distemper and canine hepatitis can also cause conjunctivitis. Both forms of con-

Clearing Up Eye Stains

One of the most frustrating aspects of eye discharge is the staining that's often left beneath the eyes, especially in Poodles, Spaniels, Shih Tzu, Lhasa Apsos, or any light-colored dog. This staining is caused by pigments in the tear called porphyrins. These pigments are clear when secreted in the tear, but they turn reddish or brownish when dried on the hair and left to oxidize. Porphyrins are harmless, but they're unattractive and difficult to remove safely because you don't want to use chemicals near the eye. Oral tetracyclines prevent stains if the eye is being treated for a problem, but the long-term effects of constant administration of antibiotics is riskier than the purely cosmetic gain of eliminating eye stains. To prevent buildup, wipe away staining daily with a damp tissue or soft cloth. If you have a long-haired dog, keep the fur around the eyes trimmed so the tears don't clump up in it. You can find commercial stain removers at a pet store or grooming shop.

junctivitis are highly contagious between dogs. Keratitis, or inflammation of the cornea, results from injury or infection.

A thick, sticky discharge is often a sign of a condition called keratoconjunctivitis sicca, more commonly called dry eye. The eyes become dry and irritated, because the dog isn't producing enough tears. Dry eye usually affects older dogs.

When irritation occurs from a speck of dust or dirt, blinking usually produces tears that clean the eye. You can also bathe the eyes with preservative-free saline solution, such as that used for cleaning contact lenses. Never use any ointments or eye drops without checking first with your veterinarian. Drops containing any type of steroid that are put on an eye with a scratch or puncture can permanently damage the eye.

If an irritated eye doesn't improve within a day, take your dog in for a veterinary exam. Be sure you don't clean the eyes before the visit. The veterinarian needs to see the discharge to establish the cause and an appropriate treatment course. If you treated the eye with saline solution or some other mixture, be sure to tell the vet what you used. Any information you can provide is helpful. Once the problem is diagnosed, your vet will prescribe eyedrops or ointments containing antibiotics or anti-inflammatories.

Electric Shock

All young dogs are explorers at heart, and lacking hands they use their mouths to discover the world around them. Chomping down on an electrical cord is a dangerous method of discovery, though. It can lead to electrical burns on the corners of the mouth or on the tongue and palate, or even electrical shock.

Signs of electrical shock are convulsions, loss of consciousness, and slow respiration. Severe shock can cause the heart to stop beating. Before you touch a dog who has suffered electrical shock, switch off the electrical source. Next, make sure your dog is breathing. Then scoop him up and get to the veterinarian right away. If the heart has stopped, you may need to perform cardiopulmonary resuscitation first. Ask your veterinarian to show you how so you'll be prepared.

Frostbite

Prolonged exposure to cold temperatures can cause frostbite or hypothermia. Frostbite is most common in dogs who are young, old, or ill, especially those who have short hair. It usually affects the feet, tail, and ear tips. Signs of frostbite are pale skin that later reddens and becomes hot and painful to the touch, swelling, and peeling. Don't cause further damage by massaging the skin or applying hot compresses; instead, thaw the areas slowly with

Skin Disease

The skin is the body's largest external organ, and it's a good overall indicator of your dog's health. Nice pink skin that's odor-free, unblemished, and covered with shiny fur is a mark of great health. When your dog isn't doing too well, though, the signs are often mirrored in his coat: You may notice rough, dull fur; hair loss; or a bad smell. Once begun, skin problems can be difficult to treat, especially if the underlying problem isn't identified. Besides parasites and allergies, some of the problems that can cause poor skin condition are bacterial infections, hypothyroidism and autoimmune diseases.

Bacterial infections rarely occur on their own. They usually attack once an allergy or other underlying disease has made the first penetration. That's why veterinarians often prescribe antibiotics in addition to other treatments—to stop bacteria in their tracks. Hot spots and pyodermas are other forms of infections, which are usually treated with shampoos and topical antibiotics. Keeping the dog from biting or scratching at the area is also important and may require the use of an Elizabethan collar to prevent contact.

Hypothyroidism is a deficiency of thyroid hormone, which often manifests itself in symmetrical hair loss; a dull, dry coat; hair that falls out easily; and scaly skin. It usually occurs in middle-aged or older dogs.

Autoimmune disease occurs when the body mistakenly attacks itself. There are several autoimmune skin diseases, which are usually diagnosed through biopsy. Diet, immune-mediating drugs, and the judicious use of steroids all play a role in treatment.

warm, moist towels that you change frequently. Stop warming the skin as soon as it regains its normal color. A dog in shock needs immediate treatment from a veterinarian.

The above medical scenarios are just a few of the emergencies dog owners can face and give you an idea of what you should look for and what you can do before reaching the veterinarian. You should at least contact your veterinarian in all cases of illness or injury. Never hesitate to seek medical advice or attention for your dog. He's counting solely on you to provide the best care. If you always consult your veterinarian, either via phone or in person, you will have the peace of mind that your dog was treated appropriately, no matter what the outcome.

6

Basic Training

In This Chapter

○ The Importance of Early Training
○ The Teaching Process
○ What Every Good Dog Needs to Know

Training a dog will launch one of the most rewarding relationships you can ever experience. A well-trained dog is a tremendous source of pride and joy to his owner, and training opens a door for your dog to enter a wider world. Your well-trained dog can go just about anywhere with you, fulfilling his job of companion to the utmost. His good manners and instant obedience will make him a popular caller at the veterinary clinic, grooming salon, local businesses, hotels, and almost anywhere you choose to take him.

Besides being able to go places with you, a well-trained dog is just nicer to live with. Whatever his size, he'll willingly permit you to groom him as needed, give him medication, and take things out of his mouth that shouldn't be there. That polite behavior carries over to examinations by the veterinarian and bathing and clipping by a groomer. Training class is an opportunity for your dog to interact with other dogs so he learns not to growl or bark at them when he meets them on the street, vocalizations that other dogs might view as a challenge. A trained dog is less likely to have behavior problems such as barking, biting, chewing or digging. He's able to control himself in the face of distractions that would have an untrained dog barking his head off and lunging at the end of his leash.

A well-trained dog will accept your guidance even when he would rather be doing something else.

The number one reason dogs land in shelters is "uncontrollable behavior," but that simply doesn't have to be. Dogs of any age can learn good manners—if you're willing to put in the training time. Training takes time and patience, but the result is well worth the effort. You'll be rewarded many times over by a dog who's dedicated and responsive, a trusting and loyal friend who's easy to understand and get along with. The satisfaction you'll feel and the respect you and your dog will have for each other is worth all the dog biscuits in China.

The Importance of Early Training

Puppies have often been likened to sponges, soaking up everything around them. Your little Bear will learn rapidly at a very young age.

Contrary to the old wives' tale that training should begin at six months, Bear should begin his lessons the first day he comes home. He'll be watching you closely—studying you, in fact—to make sense of his new environment. You can take this opportunity to start him off on the right paw by presenting him with consistent behaviors on your part and a consistent schedule for him to follow. With kindness and guidance, he'll learn quickly what pleases you and what doesn't.

The critical learning period for puppies is between the ages of six and 16 weeks. Puppies can certainly learn during other periods of their development, but this is the time when you can really make an impression—positive or negative—about what's right and what's wrong in your puppy's world. Ideally, of course, you'll want as many of your pup's experiences as possible to be positive. We all learn more when we're happy and having a good time, and puppies are no exception.

Start training early so that your puppy learns good behavior instead of bad habits.

Much of a puppy's personality is formed during this early period, so it's a good time for your puppy to learn to look to you for guidance and discipline. You are his leader, top dog in the pack, and he'll respect and listen to you if you establish yourself as firm and consistent, yet caring.

If you set some rules and boundaries for the puppy before you brought him home, good for you! The hard part, though, is sticking to them. It's not easy to put a cute puppy back on the floor when he jumps up on the sofa and looks at you with his baby browns, but if you've decided not to let your Great Dane on the furniture, now is the time to teach him that rule. Puppies learn through repetition, so if you want to teach Bear that something is right or wrong, you must be consistent. Wrench your glance away from his beseeching eyes, and kindly put him back down on the floor—every time he gets on a couch that's off-limits. This same tactic applies to anything else you don't want the puppy to do, such as jumping up on people. Make sure other family members enforce the rules as well. It takes only one person to bend the rules "just this once" to set back all the previous training. When Bear is in obedience class, the trainer can help you teach him the difference between being invited up on a piece of furniture and choosing to go there on his own. For now, though, consistency and simplicity will help your puppy learn quickly with little confusion.

The commands sit, down, come, stay, and heel are the foundation of good manners for a well-trained dog. Your dog should know and respond readily to these directives by the time he's six months old. Additionally, he can be expected to learn where to relieve himself and how to let you know that he needs to go out; how to greet people politely, without barking or jumping on them; and to discriminate between his own toys and your belongings, playing with and chewing only what's appropriate. The command "leave it," useful in numerous situations from investigating dead birds to raiding garbage cans, is an easy lesson to teach, as is the realization that begging won't get him anywhere but in the corner. The polite dog waits for permission to go through doorways or get in the car, and he wouldn't dream of touching food that's not his (unless he's a hound—then your best bet is to keep all food well out of his reach). Anything you teach him beyond that is gravy on the dog food.

> The polite dog waits for permission to go through doorways or get in the car, and he wouldn't dream of touching food that's not his.

The Teaching Process

At 10 to 12 weeks of age, after he's had two full sets of vaccinations, your pup is ready for the informal fun and socialization of a puppy kindergarten class with other vaccinated puppies of his own age and size. In puppy kindergarten, Bear will learn to be handled by other people, will get practice getting along with other dogs, and (with the lure of a treat or toy) will learn the basics of behaviors such as sit, down, come, and stay, and how to walk nicely on a leash. What you'll learn, though, is even more important. A good trainer will teach you the psychological foundation of understanding and motivating your dog, along with positive ways to reward good behavior and tricks for heading off unwanted behavior.

At four to six months, Bear has all the basics he needs to enter an obedience class. Don't wait too long after puppy kindergarten to begin basic obedience class, or your dog will lose the advantage of his early training. If your dog never went to puppy kindergarten and is over four months old, you can start his formal training with basic obedience class. You'll continue to focus on several commands: sit, down, stay, come, and heel. The emphasis will be more on accuracy and speed. In this class, the trainer is also likely to discuss problem behaviors and how to counteract them and even prevent them from starting in the first place. Training methods should always be positive. Avoid any class where the trainer spends a lot of time yelling at students—canine or human—or advocates cruel methods such as "hanging" a dog by its choke chain. There's nothing wrong with the proper use of a choke or prong collar, but in the wrong hands or with the wrong methods, they can ruin your dog.

Choosing a Trainer

Word of mouth is the best way to start looking for a trainer. Ask friends or neighbors who have nice dogs if they can recommend someone. Your veterinarian might refer you to a trainer or even offer classes through his or her clinic. Some trainers advertise in the Yellow Pages or offer classes through community colleges.

When interviewing trainers, sit in on a class so you can get an idea of their teaching style and training techniques. If you own a particular breed, ask whether the trainer has experience with members of that breed. Trainers who are successful with easily trained breeds such as Golden Retrievers and Shetland Sheepdogs often don't have the right experience or attitude to work with more difficult dogs. It's a good sign when the trainer belongs to an organization such as American Pet Dog Trainers (APDT) or the National Association of Dog Obedience Instructors (NADOI). These professional associations have requirements that trainers must meet before they can join. Contact the APDT and NADOI at the addresses listed in the appendix and ask for referrals to qualified trainers in your area.

Should I Attend Classes or Train On My Own?

Whether you decide to attend an obedience class or do the training yourself, you will be spending a fair amount of one-on-one time with your puppy, either to teach him or to practice what you've learned in class. If you have little experience training dogs, it's probably best to participate in a class taught by a professional. Even if you do have a fair amount of knowledge about training, a class may help you make sure Bear gets plenty of socialization with other people and dogs. Early socialization can make all the difference between your dog tucking his tail when others approach or making friends wherever he goes.

Instead of a class, you may choose to use the services of a private, in-home trainer. This can be beneficial if class times or locations don't suit you or if your dog has behavior problems that require intensive personal attention and an individually tailored program. Private training can be quite expensive, up to $75 an hour or more, so before you contract with a trainer for his services, be sure you like his manner with you and your dog as well as his training philosophy.

If you want to train Bear yourself, the following suggestions will help you get started. All family members should participate in training. Everyone should understand what is being taught and the theory behind rewards and corrections, as well as how to administer them.

It's been said that consistency is the hobgoblin of little minds; but when dealing with puppies, consistency is a must. Teach specific commands for each action you want Bear to learn. For instance, he might become confused if you say "Down" when you want him to "lie down" and use "Get down" when you want him to stop jumping on you. Substitute the command "Off" for "Get down," and he'll quickly understand the difference.

Puppies, like young children, have the attention span of a gnat, so limit those first training sessions to about 10 minutes. By keeping them short, you can have two or three training sessions of this length each day. Train every day at the same time, in a quiet area with few distractions. Later, when Bear has learned his lessons well, test him in a more distracting environment that includes people, other dogs, and traffic, to make sure he pays attention to you no matter what. This is called proofing.

End all training sessions on a high note. Don't give up in disgust if Bear isn't picking up what you're trying to teach. Step back and give him a command to do something you know he likes doing. When he complies, give him lots of praise and end the

Nan Makes Good

If Nan were a soccer player, she'd be Mia Hamm. If she were a basketball player, she'd be Sheryl Swoopes. But she's a Border Collie, and when Alasdair Macrae acquired her, his intent was to train her for herding trials so she could follow in the pawprints of her grandsire Mirk, who won the Scottish championship. After two years, though, Macrae was ready to give up on the dog, who simply did not seem to understand her purpose in life. Nan was put up for sale, but before a buyer came along, she tore the ligaments in her knee and required surgery and six months of rest—no walking. When Nan was back on her feet, Macrae discovered she had a new attitude. She seemed to have absorbed everything he had been teaching her for the past two years and ran with it— straight to the international championship, which she won handily. Today Nan is nine years old and still competing. She has probably earned more championships and set more records than she can count on four paws.

session there. You can always try the new command later. Sometimes dogs just need a little quiet time to assimilate what they've learned, even if you don't think they got it at all.

Most important of all, be patient with your puppy. He's young and full of energy so his antics, including some you may not find desirable, are only natural. A significant concept to grasp is that you're bringing an animal into your human environment and expecting him to follow your rules and boundaries. This doesn't come naturally to your puppy, so give him the time and patience he needs to become a well-behaved family member. Another concept to keep in mind is that just as people are different, each puppy has a distinct personality and a different learning pace. Some puppies learn faster than others, but don't be frustrated with a "slow" learner. Often these dogs learn their lessons best of all. If you've had a puppy in the past, don't compare one to the other. What any puppy wants most is to receive a lot of love and attention. Give it!

By four months of age, your puppy should know the basic commands sit, stay, and come, and should walk on a leash without thrashing around or pulling. The manners he's learned not only allow you to continue with more advanced training but help keep him safe wherever he goes. Even if you're pleased with what he's learned so far, enroll him in an obedience class if one is available. These classes reinforce your training in a more structured environment, test your pup's ability to respond in the midst of distractions, and give him the all-important socialization he needs to become an upstanding canine citizen.

> A significant concept to grasp is that you're bringing an animal into your human environment and expecting him to follow your rules and boundaries.

Training Tools

The only supplies your puppy needs for kindergarten are his own flat leather or nylon collar and a lightweight leash that's four to six feet long. There's no need for a choke collar at this stage, and you should avoid working with a trainer who advocates using one on a young pup.

In a regular obedience class, the trainer may or may not recommend the use of a training, or choke, collar. Some trainers have various canine students using different collars, depending on the dog's size and personality. With proper use, a choke collar is harmless yet effective. The same is true of a prong collar, which may look like a torture device but can actually be less negative than a choke chain.

The most important thing to know about a choke collar is how to put it on so it releases correctly. Ask the trainer to demonstrate, and practice until you're sure you can do it. To give a correction, simply snap and release the collar, using a quick motion. You want to get your dog's attention, not choke him.

Safety Tip

Remove a training collar and replace it with the dog's regular collar immediately after every training session. Training collars can get caught on crates, gates, or even shrubbery and choke the dog.

If you own a dog who likes to pull, a head collar may be just the ticket. This collar, which resembles a horse halter, operates on the principle that by controlling the head, you control the rest of the body. Used correctly, it's a safe, gentle way to keep your puppy or dog under control. Avoid using a harness, which only encourages the dog to pull more.

Seeking Professional Help

It's usually pretty easy to teach a puppy the basics. If you have difficulty, it's wise to seek advice from a professional trainer or behaviorist (see Appendix C) who can help you understand the causes behind undesirable behavior and take steps to prevent it. If you can't find a good trainer, you can consult any of numerous books on behavior and training. Some good ones to read, even before you get a puppy, are *Culture Clash* by Jean Donaldson; *Good Owners, Great Dogs* by Brian Kilcommons; and *Dogperfect* by Sarah Hodgson. For a humorous yet understanding look at dog behaviors, see *Why Do Dogs Do That?* by Kim Thornton.

Is It Ever Too Late?

Contrary to a popular adage, even an old dog can learn new tricks. It's never too late to train a dog. The sooner you start, however, the better the results and the easier training your dog will be. As your dog gets older, more of your time and patience are required. So do things right from the beginning: train your puppy early.

Housebreaking Your Dog

Potty training is most effective when you take your puppy on a leash to the same location each time. By keeping him on leash, you reinforce the idea that he's on a mission and prevent him from wandering and becoming distracted from doing his business. Use the same command each time, such as "go potty," "do your business," or another short command that you choose. As the puppy eliminates, praise him so that he knows exactly what he's done that pleases you. Then go back inside. Playtime should be differentiated from potty time. Besides going to the same spot every time, which helps the puppy to understand why you're both there, limit the time as well. Allow five to ten minutes at the most. This helps your puppy to "potty" quickly, which is important, especially in times of inclement weather. If your puppy doesn't perform during the allotted time, go back inside and try again in thirty minutes. Be sure he's crated during that time so he doesn't have an accident in the house.

Hints and Guidelines

A regular schedule and consistency are crucial to good results. Take a weekend or part of a vacation to devote to setting the routine firmly in your puppy's mind. If he knows when he can expect to go out, he'll be less likely to make a mess in the house. Take him out first thing in the morning, before you get your coffee. If he takes a nap later in the day, take him out as soon as he awakens. Before crating your puppy and going to bed yourself, take him out to relieve himself. Besides these times, take the puppy to "potty" every two hours throughout the day when you're home.

A regular feeding schedule helps, too. Most puppies eat two to three meals per day. Take the puppy out before and after each meal. Limit the length of meals so you'll have a better idea of when your puppy needs to go out. If you leave food out all the time, you won't know when he's eaten.

Constant supervision and limiting the puppy to a single area of the house will prevent accidents as well. Any time you're unable to watch the puppy, put him in the crate. He shouldn't have free run of the house until he's proven himself completely house-trained for at least several weeks and you're sure he won't be destructive in other ways. Many dogs aren't fully reliable in the house until they're a year old or more.

When Accidents Happen

If you catch your puppy eliminating inside the house, loudly say "stop" or "no" and quickly pick him up and go to the designated spot outside. If you don't catch him in the act, don't scold him. Dogs don't have the same sense of time we do, and your puppy won't understand that you're scolding him for something that happened in the past. Rubbing his nose in the mess may make you feel

better, but it's worthless as a training tool and will only make your puppy fear you. Instead, put him away while you clean up the mess. Make sure the odor is completely removed or your puppy will be drawn to the spot again. Try using a mixture of one part

Safety Tip

For safety's sake, always remove your puppy's collar before placing her into the crate. It may seem unlikely or impossible, but collars have been known to get caught on crates, with the unhappy result that the dog chokes to death.

white vinegar to three parts water, or purchase a commercial odor neutralizer.

How A Crate Can Help

If your dog will be spending most of his time indoors, you may dread housetraining, which encompasses not only perfecting potty protocol but also refraining from destructive behavior. House-training does not have to be frustrating. A tool that will simplify the process is the dog crate. A dog crate will not only aid in housetraining your puppy, but will prove to be one of the most beneficial pieces of training equipment you can buy. Although no puppy is housetrained overnight, you'll be surprised how easy this process can be when you use a crate and exercise a little patience and consistency.

If you believe crating a dog is cruel and plan to skip this section, let me emphasize that it's not inhumane in any way. A correctly used dog crate is among the most effective ways to train your puppy to become

A crate is your puppy's special place and helps her become a happy, well-adjusted family member.

a happy and well-adjusted family member. That's why I crate-train my puppies and highly recommend this method to all my clients, as do numerous trainers and behaviorists known for their sensitivity and positive training techniques. Remember that dogs are pack animals whose ancestors lived in dens for security. Your puppy will view the crate not as a cage but as a safe haven where he can rest, away from noisy kids and blaring televisions. Crate training makes life easier for you and your puppy.

Crate Benefits

Most trainers, veterinarians, and dog owners who have experience with crates recommend using them for every puppy regardless of size or breed. The first reason is that a crate will restrict your puppy's movement and activity when you aren't around to supervise. Not only will you have peace of mind, knowing your puppy will not chew the house down while you are away, but your puppy will be safe from electrocution, from downing the contents of a Tylenol bottle, and from the wrath that would descend upon him if he were to leave a big stinky pile on your expensive Oriental rug. A puppy safely confined to a crate doesn't learn the destructive habits that result from boredom and lack of supervision. Your puppy will never learn to chew furniture, clothing, shoes, walls (yes, flat walls), or other items. The cost of any good dog crate pales in comparison to replacing furniture, flooring, clothing, or other valuables.

Besides preventing access to electrical cords, toxic materials, and other hazards in the home, a crate offers your puppy security should bad weather arise while you are away. Experiencing his first thunderstorm alone and exposed can send your puppy into a tizzy, but he'll feel safe from the frightening noise and flashes of lightning if he's in his crate.

Car travel, whether to the veterinarian or across the country, is another instance in which a crate is useful. Your crated dog can't cause an accident by getting underfoot or jumping in your lap. In the event of a wreck, his crate would help prevent him from being injured or thrown from the car. For extra security, run a seatbelt through the crate's carrying handle or bars and buckle it in. By becoming accustomed to a dog crate early in life, your puppy will have no trouble traveling in a crate by car or airplane, or even being boarded in a kennel.

As far as potty training a puppy, no other method even comes close to the effectiveness of using a crate. To see the value of the crate, look again at the world from your dog's point of view. A puppy's natural instinct is not to soil his den. By confining your puppy to this limited area when you're unable to supervise him, you ensure that he doesn't have any accidents in the house or in his den.

Your part of the bargain is to make sure that he's never in the crate long enough to have an accident. Until they're about four months old, puppies aren't physiologically capable of controlling their bowel and bladder movements for any great length of time. Your puppy shouldn't be crated for more than four hours without being taken out to relieve himself. If you take him out to potty first thing in the morning, immediately after every meal, immediately after playtime, and just before bed, and crate him when he's not being watched with an eagle eye, he'll quickly learn where and when it's okay to relieve himself.

The Crate Is Your Puppy's Friend

Never use the crate for punishment. For your puppy to trust you and feel safe in her crate, her experience with it must always be positive. If you catch your little Gretchen chewing your $300

Coach bag and stuff her in the crate while shouting "Bad dog!" Gretchen (who has impeccable taste, by the way) will not think of her "den" as a happy, secure place.

Place the crate in an area such as the family room where your family spends most of their time. This allows the puppy to feel part of the family even while resting in the crate. Although even the nicest dog crate does not complement the décor of any home, temporarily including a crate in your furniture collection is well worth the effort.

> Never use the crate for punishment. For your puppy to trust you and feel safe in her crate, her experience with it must always be positive.

Line the bottom of the crate with an old towel or bedding that can be easily washed if soiled. Make sure there are no frayed ends for your puppy to chew on.

When you first introduce your puppy to the crate, simply put it down and leave the door open so she can investigate. Encourage her to go inside by placing her bedding and bowls in the crate. You can even place some treats or a toy inside to reinforce the positive message. The first several times the puppy goes into the crate, praise her but don't close the door. When you're ready to leave her in it for a trial run, use a simple command such as "kennel up" or "get in bed" while placing the puppy in the crate. Hand her a small treat and close the door. The only other items in the crate should be a toy that can't be swallowed and a small non-spill bowl containing a little water. Once the door is closed, praise the puppy in a happy, reassuring tone of voice, but don't fuss or let her out if she whines. Leave the puppy for short periods, such as 10 minutes, gradually extending the time you're gone. When you return, the puppy will probably be excited to see you. Greet her calmly, open the door, and take her straight outside to go potty. She may have accidents in the beginning, but be patient, especially if she's less than 12 weeks old. Remember that training your puppy will take a lot less time and effort than potty-training a child.

Even while you're at home, leave the crate door open so the puppy can retreat to her special place whenever she desires. This reinforces the idea that the crate is a good, safe haven. A puppy or dog who needs time away from small children to rest peacefully will find his crate an especially satisfying retreat. All family members, whatever their ages, should learn to respect the crate as the puppy's special place where she can't be disturbed.

Choosing a Crate

A variety of crates are available. The type you purchase depends primarily on your puppy's future lifestyle and your preference.
If house-training will be your primary use for the crate, choose one that's not much larger than the dog itself. Your dog should be able to stand up, turn around, and lie down comfortably, but shouldn't have so much space that he can eliminate in one corner of the crate and still have room to move away from the mess. This is especially important for puppies, who will never learn not to have "accidents" if the crate is too large.

If your puppy is small now but will grow much larger, select a full-size crate that comes with a divider. As the puppy grows, you can move the divider to give the pup the space he needs. This is a less expensive option than buying a puppy-size crate and then an adult-size crate.

If you plan to show your dog or otherwise travel frequently with him, look for such features as portability, sturdiness, and ease of use and cleaning. The way you plan to travel will also affect your decision. Air travel requires the purchase of a high-quality plastic airline crate, but if you'll be traveling by car, van, or motor home, you may prefer wire or plastic crates that stack easily, offer easy access to the dog, and fold up when not in use.

Each type of crate has advantages and disadvantages. Plastic crates are made of heavyweight material that's sturdy and easy to clean. They have a door in front but otherwise offer limited viewing. Some dogs like this, while others prefer to be able to see everything that's going on. A plastic crate offers protection from the elements if the dog is outdoors, but it can also get hot. Remove the top and a plastic crate becomes a nearly indestructible bed, although there will always be dogs who can destroy anything into which they sink their teeth. Usually the doors of a plastic crate are removable to give the dog easier access. Most plastic crates are easily disassembled for storage or cleaning.

Wire, or cage-style, crates are lightweight. Some of them offer the convenience of folding up so they're easily portable and storable. Wire crates with epoxy coating resist rust, scratches, and staining, and are easy to clean. A top that lifts off gives easy access to your dog while still keeping him confined. Wire crates provide better ventilation and allow the dog to see out. Some wire crates are specially designed for use in cars or vans. They come with doors on the side rather than the front, allowing owners to pack around them yet still remove the dog easily. Some crates have both side and end doors. This type of frequent or heavy use means a crate must be well built, made with heavy-gauge wire that's strongly welded. This is especially important in foldable crates, which tend to be more lightweight. If you choose to let your dog ride in the car restrained by a canine seatbelt but wish to have access to a crate, one that folds flat may be your best choice, especially if space is at a premium. Look for one with an easy-carry handle.

A new crate option is a lightweight container made of 420 or 600 denier nylon with a PVC backing and quarter-inch aluminum rods to give it shape. The advantages of this type of crate are that it's lightweight and easy to transport, repels dirt, and cleans easily. It doesn't heat up in the sun, blocks UV rays, and allows a breeze to flow through. If the crate is outdoors, at a dog show, for instance, loops at the lower corners allow the crate to be staked down so it won't tip over or blow away if the dog's not in it. Collars and tags can't get caught on the fabric, so there's no need to remove the collar before putting the dog inside. If you're traveling, this crate is easy to carry and set up in a hotel room. One version—for small dogs only—can be used as an under-seat carrier on airlines. On the downside, a determined or destructive dog could chew through the crate. It's not suitable for young puppies that aren't yet reliable when it comes to chewing. This type of crate comes in five sizes: mini, small, medium, large, and maxi. It's sold through vendors at dog shows, or you can order from the web site at www.homestretchcrate.com, or call Stopgap Enterprises in Alpine, California, at (619) 445-8856.

No matter which type you choose, high-quality construction is a must. Avoid any crate or pan with sharp edges on which a dog could injure himself. Crates with smooth edges are also easier to clean. Bars should be narrowly spaced to prevent puppies and small dogs from sticking their muzzles through and suffocating. Make sure latches fasten and unfasten easily, yet are strong enough so they don't come undone if the crate falls, drops, or is ejected from a vehicle. For additional safety, always use rust-resistant brass clips on all the latch sites to make sure they don't come open.

You can purchase a crate from many retail pet stores, discount stores, dog show booths, or directly from crate manufacturers. Always check local newspapers and garage sales for used crates that are often in great condition. If you buy a used crate, wash it thoroughly and bleach it prior to introducing your puppy to it. Remember that even an expensive, well-made dog crate is a bargain compared to the cost of replacing expensive items such as carpeting and furniture.

Basic Dog Psychology

Just as parents often use "psychology" to get a child to behave, dog owners can similarly steer their pet's behavior in a positive direction. By becoming more aware of how your dog thinks and feels, you can anticipate his instinctual behavior and more effectively teach the lessons that will make him a compatible companion. As with children, if you stay consistent in daily interactions with your dog, you'll be amazed how well your dog can anticipate proper behavior.

What Does It Mean to Be Top Dog?

Dogs are pack animals, so playing "follow the leader" is natural for them. If they don't see a leader, they'll take over the role themselves. Your goal is to present yourself as top dog, so your puppy knows you're in charge; you're the one to whom he owes respect and loyalty. Once you've established yourself as leader, your puppy will not only listen to your commands but will allow you to restrain him for ear cleaning, nail clipping, or whatever you need to do.

Dogs, and their close relatives the wolves, operate on a strict hierarchical system. Every dog knows his place and behaves appropriately toward higher ranking members of the pack. The two main elements of top doghood include controlling the food supply and determining any course of action. Ways you can reinforce your position as "top dog" include requiring your dog to sit before receiving his meals or a treat and teaching him to let you take up his food—even if he's not finished eating yet. When you take up a puppy's food, return it right away if he doesn't offer any protest but correct growls with a stern "No!" Don't give the food back until he's behaving politely. If you start this during early puppyhood, your dog should learn quickly that you are the source of all good things. If you try it with an older dog and he growls, get help from a trainer or behaviorist. It's not something you should try to handle on your own.

Other ways to let your dog know you're in charge are to practice training regularly so he's used to taking instruction from you, and encouraging him at least once a day to roll over for a tummy rub. His willingness to place himself in a vulnerable position—on his back—is a good sign that he trusts and respects you. Teach your dog not to jump up on you, and avoid rough games such as tug of war that could encourage him to challenge your position of authority. Most important, never let your dog get away with snapping, growling or biting. Give him a swift verbal correction, and consult a trainer to make sure the problem doesn't get worse.

Correction Versus Punishment

Puppies thrive on the attention they receive during training, so it's important to

Don't let your dog use her body language to show dominance. Your dog should recognize all humans as above her in the family pack.

make this time fun and rewarding. Positive reinforcement is the basis of all successful puppy training. By rewarding your dog with praise or treats, you'll earn respect and loyalty that can never be gained by harsh punishment.

A well-known dog trainer produces a T-shirt that reads, "The 11th commandment: Never hit your dog." He's right. Physical punishment does nothing but create a fearful and mistrustful puppy. Often, a simple change in voice inflection is enough to let your puppy know that he's done wrong or, conversely, that he's done right.

In fact, catching your puppy doing something right is one secret of successful dog training. He's smart so will quickly catch on that he must be doing something that pleases you when you praise him. Instead of expecting Buster to make mistakes, seek out opportunities to let him know when you like what he's doing. When you catch him in the act, whether he's chewing one of his toys or ringing a bell to let you know he needs to go outside, offer lavish praise in a happy tone of voice. If you want to get his attention to correct undesirable behavior, simply switch to a sharp or deeper tone. (Give commands in a normal tone of voice.) Always respond immediately to Buster's actions with praise or correction. This will help the puppy associate certain behaviors with specific responses from his leader. It's important that you're consistent, perhaps using the words "good boy" for praise, and "shame" for correction.

Another good bit of advice is to use short commands and short words for praise and correction. This helps keep things simple. Also, if you have to correct your puppy, use a word such as "shame" instead of "no," which becomes ineffective with overuse. Another option is to make an unpleasant sound, such as "aaaaght"—which sounds a bit like a game show buzzer when contestants give wrong answers. Also, use your puppy's name in association with commands or praise. For example, say "Good Murphy" or "Murphy, sit." By using the puppy's name, you teach him to pay attention when his name is being used.

Teaching Your Dog to Be Handled

As part of your daily teaching of proper puppy behavior, handle your puppy all over so she learns that being held or restrained is okay when necessary. The easiest and most pleasant way is to hold her in your arms for three to five minutes while talking calmly. If she struggles, hold her closer to your body, but don't give in by putting her down. This will enforce the idea that you are the boss and being restrained is okay. Do this every day until your puppy responds readily by relaxing into your arms.

Next, open the puppy's mouth, look in the ears, and pass your hands over her body, again reinforcing that no harm will be done. It's also important that all young puppies become accustomed to having their feet handled. Pick up each paw and examine each individual toe. Don't let the puppy resist you. If these actions become second nature, your puppy will be a joy for her groomer and veterinarian to work with, and you'll find you can give medications and deal with other situations easily. It's a pitiful situation when a simple nail trim turns into a battle because the dog hates being restrained or having her feet handled and howls as though the veterinarian or groomer were performing an amputation without anesthetic. Later in your puppy's life, you'll be glad you spent a little time getting her used to being handled.

Teaching your puppy to let you handle her is also important in the bonding process and helps build her trust in you. You'll never be frustrated by being unable to brush your dog's coat, let alone clean her ears, and you may even save money you'd otherwise spend at the veterinary clinic or grooming salon since you're more likely to perform these services yourself. In some cases, an animal's coat, skin, ears, and nails are so neglected that she must be heavily sedated before even simple procedures can be performed. Neither veterinarians nor groomers have a magic wand they can wave to make the dog willing to be cared for.

The Importance of Good Socialization

Teaching your puppy to be comfortable in all kinds of situations and around all kinds of people is indeed an invaluable lesson for her to learn. Exposing your puppy to different people and animals builds a foundation of trust instead of fear. Ideally, your breeder has begun your puppy's socialization process, but you'll need to continue after your puppy comes to your home.

All puppies need to become accustomed to unusual sights and sounds, other animals (especially other dogs), and people from all walks of life—those wearing uniforms; those using walkers or wheelchairs; and those riding bicycles, skateboards, or inline skates. By encountering different people, environments, and situations at an early age, a puppy will be comfortable with these throughout life instead of feeling threatened. For example, every puppy needs to be exposed to young children, whether or not your immediate family includes children. Puppies not exposed to children won't learn to trust them and may be afraid of them. Fear can be expressed

Introduce your pup to other friendly, well-behaved, healthy dogs. Avoid rowdy, poorly behaved, agressive dogs; they could scare your dog and ruin the socialization you've done so far.

through aggression or shyness, neither of which is an acceptable trait. A fearful dog is unpredictable and unsafe, especially around children, whose quick movements and loud noises can startle a dog.

Start socializing your puppy on day one. Invite the neighbors over, one or two at a time, to meet her, and let them pet and hold her. Just make sure she's not overwhelmed by a crowd of people standing around her.

When her immunizations have kicked in, take her with you on errands to places where she's likely to be permitted inside, such as the dry cleaners or video store. Until you're sure of her potty manners, carry her inside so you don't run the risk of an accident. At four months, some breeds are already too big to be carried, so give them an opportunity to eliminate before you leave the house. Have breakfast or lunch at an outdoor café, where your pup can sit by the table with you. Playgrounds, parks, strip malls, and outdoor shopping areas are also great places for socialization. Besides being a cornerstone of basic puppy training, socialization is one of the easiest and most fun lessons to teach your dog. After all, who doesn't want to show off a new puppy?

Play Biting, Growling, and Other Games to Avoid

Most puppies are playful and can become aggressive or challenging during play. While much of the biting or growling play seems innocent, neither behavior should be allowed or encouraged. A quick way to teach aggression is to tease or play roughly with a puppy's face. Tug-of-war games have the same effect. Don't let your kids or Uncle Joe or Cousin Jim encourage the puppy in rough play. You'll regret it when the dog challenges you or becomes aggressive to other people or dogs.

A daily tummy rub can help relax your dog and teach him that you are in charge.

One of the easiest and best ways to teach a young puppy to submit to your authority is to encourage him to roll on his back for tummy rubs. If he doesn't roll over on his own, gently place him on his back and hold him down in this position with just enough pressure to prevent him from getting up. He will probably struggle and fuss, but hold him still and talk calmly until he gives in and stops fighting. Usually this will take about a minute, but may take longer if you have an overly dominant puppy.

What Every Good Dog Needs to Know

To ensure both their safety and social acceptance, dogs should learn to obey the basic commands sit, down, stay, and come, and to behave politely on a leash. Before you begin training, be sure you understand these simple techniques. They'll help you get your point across quickly and effectively.

1. Associate the command with the action. Say the command—sit—as the dog is moving into position. Practice this several times so that he learns to connect the word with the action.
2. Mary Poppins was right: a spoonful of sugar helps the medicine go down. Use a treat or toy as a lure to move your dog into the desired position or to elicit the desired action.

Things to Avoid When Playing with Your Puppy

○ Never play tug-of-war—it encourages the puppy to challenge you.

○ Never play roughly with a puppy's head.

○ Don't encourage growling, even in play.

○ Never wrestle with your puppy—it teaches him to fight you.

3. Timing is everything. Offer praise or reward with a treat immediately when the dog complies with the command.

4. Don't correct mistakes until you're sure the dog understands what he's supposed to do.

5. End training sessions on a happy note, after your dog has performed correctly and been rewarded. Neither of you should go away mad.

Sit

Every well-behaved dog should know this command, as it's probably one of the easiest to teach and among the most useful. Take a treat and hold it directly above your dog's head. As he looks up at it, he should naturally move into a sit position. If he doesn't, you can guide him by placing your hand on his rear and gently pushing down. He'll proba-

A treat can be a wonderful tool to help your dog pay attention and cooperate with training.

bly be so intent on the treat that he won't even notice. As he moves into position, say "Sit" and reward him with the treat once he's completed the move. Repeat this several times. It won't be long before your puppy sits on command without any hands-on help. Once he's responding successfully to your voice command, teach him to obey a hand signal simply by moving your hand up, as you do when it's holding a treat, and saying "Sit." Soon the hand signal alone will be enough to get him in position. During the early stages of this training, reward your puppy every time he's successful, but as he gets better at it, cut back the treats and give them only if he sits especially quickly or does it in response to a hand signal.

Down

Once your dog knows the sit command, you can use it to teach down and stay. Again using a treat as a lure, hold it in front of your sitting puppy's nose and move it forward and down. He should crouch to follow its path, then you can keep encouraging him until he's all the way down. Tell him "Good down" and give him the treat. Repeat as you did for the sit command, rewarding him each time. Many dogs don't like performing the down command because it puts them in a submissive position, so make the proposition pleasant for them with plenty of praise for a job well done. Just as with the sit, you can teach a hand signal—a down and outward motion—after your dog responds well to the verbal down.

Hold a treat in your hand and let your dog sniff it, then move the treat up and over his head. As his head goes up, his hips should go down.

Stay

Along with the word come, the word stay is another important word your dog should know. Both commands can save his life—if he responds to them.

To teach Fritz to stay, put him in a sit or a down. Then say "Stay," holding your hand in front of his face. Slowly back up, still facing him. In the beginning your puppy will want to come with you. If he gets up and follows, don't yell;

Shape your dog into a sitting position if he doesn't respond to the treat.

just put him back in position, give the hand signal and tell him again to stay. Once he holds the stay for 10 or 15 seconds, praise

him and tell him what a good dog he is. As he becomes more comfortable with this command, you can back away farther and expect him to stay for greater lengths of time. When he fully understands the verbal command, start working with the hand signal only. As with all the other commands, repetition and rewards are the keys to learning.

Have your dog sit and then show him a treat. Tell him to lie down as you move the treat forward and down.

Come

Because you want him to respond instantly, make learning the come command the most fun of all for your dog. To start, take a box of dog biscuits and shake it loudly, saying "Fritz, come." When your puppy comes running, reward him with a treat. Repeat this exercise

When your dog lies down, praise him and give him the treat.

The signal for stay is an open-palmed hand in front your dog's face.

several times over the next couple of days. Once he knows you're the source of good things, place Fritz on a long line—the length of a clothesline, for instance—and feed out the line as you walk away. While the line is still loose, say "Fritz, come." Always speak in a happy, excited tone. As he runs toward you, keep backing away, still encouraging him to come. Your dog will enjoy this fun game of chase. When he reaches you, give him a treat and lots of praise. By practicing with the dog on a line, you are always able to enforce the come command by giving a slight tug on the leash as a signal. Until you're sure your dog will respond immediately, keep him on his leash or on the long line whenever you practice.

Leash Training

Exercising your puppy on a leash is the safest method unless you have access to a fenced park where dogs are permitted to run free. Teaching a puppy to walk on a leash can be challenging, but these tips will help you be successful.

Before you go for a walk around the block, let your puppy wear the leash around the house for a few days. Just attach the leash to his collar and let him drag it. Your puppy will be curious about his extra "tail" and will probably spend a lot of time looking backward or trying to shake it off. That's natural and isn't anything to worry about. When he seems to accept the leash, call him and give him a treat for coming to you. If you repeat this exercise a few times, he'll get the idea that wearing the leash isn't so bad after all.

Make sure you dog will respond immediately before trying the come command outdoors without a leash.

Once you've established that the leash means good times are coming, practice walking in the house. Hold the leash loosely and encourage the puppy to follow you by calling him as you walk forward. As always, give him a treat and lots of praise when he obeys. Practice this step for a few minutes three or four times each day, and keep things lighthearted. If your puppy gets bored or frustrated, stop and try again later.

When you're ready to hit the sidewalk, the first lesson to teach your puppy is not to pull. Especially if he'll grow up to be a big bruiser, you'll want to make sure he's polite on leash before he's too big to control. The first step, says trainer Brian Kilcommons, is to let your puppy "ask questions" about the leash. Hold it loosely so he can find out himself what the limits are. When he walks nicely, praise him, but if he pulls, give a correction, either physical, such as a snap and release of the leash, or verbal, "Aaagh!"

In puppy kindergarten, your dog will get more practice walking on a leash.

Behaviors to Discourage

There are certain behaviors you will want to train your dog not to do.

Normal Dog Behavior

Owners need to know what behaviors are normal in puppies. Even though behavior isn't directly related to the health of a puppy, it can be a matter of the animal's life or death if you're unprepared for the normal behaviors of a young dog, such as his desire to mark his territory. At Canyon Animal Hospital in Laguna Beach, California, veterinarians and technicians make a special effort to tell their clients what to expect with a new pup. "Especially in the case of dogs," says veterinary technician Susan Hamil, "we strongly believe that owners should understand dog behavior, particularly behaviors likely to lead to housebreaking problems. If owners avoid such problems during the first two or three months they have the puppy, the puppy is more likely to stay in the home for his lifetime. When owners get off on the wrong foot, don't go to puppy class, drop off their veterinary visits, that dog is much more likely to end up in another home or in an animal shelter where it's euthanized. Sometimes people just aren't aware of normal behaviors in dogs, and when they get the puppy, they think the chewing and digging and biting behaviors are abnormal when they're really normal for that particular animal. They just need to be channeled properly through play, training, and exercise."

Jumping Up

Puppies can quickly acquire the habit of jumping up on you and others as a greeting or for attention. Owners often encourage this when puppies are small because it's cute or fun. As the puppy grows, however, jumping on people can become a serious and even dangerous problem.

For example, your puppy will be excited and want to welcome you home by jumping up on you. To teach her not to do this, greet her calmly when you enter the house (if she's loose) or when you let her out of the crate. If she tries to jump on you, step aside so she misses, then tell her "Sit." When she sits, give her lots of praise so she knows that this is what you want her to do.

Instruct visitors to do the same thing so she learns not to jump on them, either. If your puppy tends to jump on people she meets during a walk, correct this habit with a quick snap of the leash. Reinforce at all times that jumping up is not acceptable behavior.

Nuisance Barking

Barking is a dog's natural response to a number of different situations. It's his way of warning you that people are passing by or approaching your house, and it serves as a joyous greeting. Excessive barking, however, can become a real annoyance. I often hear new puppy owners complain that their puppy has yet to bark, despite their encouragement. Do not fear! Some pups are naturally quiet, but most will bark when they're ready, probably much more than you ever desired. As a puppy matures and becomes aware of his territory (your home and yard), he will often become protective and bark in warning to anyone who approaches. Then he just needs to learn when it's okay to bark and how much to bark.

There's nothing wrong with a dog barking when someone comes to the door, but he needs to learn not to bark continuously. To get this lesson across, wrap your hand around his muzzle and say "No bark" or "Quiet." Whenever he barks appropriately—for instance, barking once or twice and then stopping when someone comes to the door—heap on the praise. It's the only way your dog will know when he's doing something right. Enlist the kids or neighbors in this training exercise by asking them to come over and ring the doorbell. Let the dog bark once

> Barking is a dog's natural response to a number of different situations. It's his way of warning you that people are passing by or approaching your house, and it serves as a joyous greeting.

or twice, but correct him if he continues. When he stops, praise him for being quiet.

One way to cut down on excessive barking is to make sure your puppy is familiar with all the neighbors. He may learn that there's no need for alarm or barking when friends approach, but will still bark at strangers.

If you've been unable to correct your dog's barking habit and the neighbors are starting to complain, you may want to consider using an anti-bark collar that administers a correction (an unpleasant noise, a static shock, or a spray of citronella scent) every time the dog barks longer than a pre-set time. When the barking stops, so does the correction. Anti-bark collars work best in conjunction with rewards for quiet behavior and getting the dog used to sounds that elicit barking (a knock on the door, for instance) so that they don't set him off unnecessarily. You also need to understand why the dog is barking before you can use the collar effectively.

Enlist the help of a trainer or behaviorist when choosing a collar. Most trainers prefer the corrections of sound or citronella over static shock. Be sure to choose a collar with safety features such as adjustable levels of correction or automatic shutoff. The trainer can also help you make sure that the level of correction is appropriate and that the collar isn't used improperly. It can backfire with dogs that are extremely sensitive, shy or fearful.

Biting

Many puppies, especially when they're teething, enjoy participating in what is referred to as "play-biting." When they're young, though, their needle-sharp baby teeth can do harm, especially to children or elderly people, so this should never be permitted. If you encourage play-biting in your young pup, he'll learn that biting is okay.

To Chew or Not to Chew

Some breeds are more prone to chewing than others. Among them are the scent hounds, whose powerful noses provide strong incentive to either chew to find out more about their surroundings or to escape so they can follow an intriguing scent. Melvin's owners, for example, came home one day to discover that their bloodhound puppy had eaten their lawn furniture. Snoopy, a Beagle, ate through his owners' drywall. Any breed can be destructive, though. One owner of Cavalier King Charles Spaniel puppies discovered that her little darlings had made some real progress gnawing on her new hardwood floor.

The best way to stop your puppy's play-biting is to grasp the upper part of his muzzle and roll the upper lip down over his teeth. In a stern tone of voice, say "no bite" or "easy." Most puppies quickly learn that they should stop doing this. Some more rambunctious puppies view this as a game and snap back harder. If this is the case, your "no" may have to be more stern. Reinforce it by walking away from the puppy. Remember, you control all activity, and the puppy needs to learn that if he doesn't play by your rules, the game is over.

Destructive Chewing

Chewing is a natural behavior for dogs. Puppies chew when they're teething and as a means of investigating their environment. Dogs chew because they're bored, lack exercise, or feel separation anxiety. There's nothing wrong with chewing, but dogs need to learn what's okay to chew and what's not. Teaching your puppy early can prevent costly damage to your home and furnishings.

As your puppy begins the teething process, he will seek out anything to relieve his aching gums. His pain is best soothed by gnawing on chewable toys to his heart's content. Although the image of a puppy chewing on an old shoe is classic, that outdated idea can seriously hurt your wallet. You can't expect your puppy to know the difference between your ratty old Keds and your Gucci loafers. Puppies just know they're both nice to chew on (and that Gucci leather smells especially appealing!). Your puppy needs such items as hard rubber toys or rope bones, which are easy to differentiate from expensive shoes. When you see him chewing on his toys, tell him what a good dog he is. If you see him gnawing on something other than a toy, quietly take it away and replace it with a Kong or rope bone. Then praise him for chewing on it.

Once again the dog crate is indispensable for preventing your puppy from learning to chew on inappropriate items. When you leave your puppy in his crate, supply several safe chew toys to soothe his aching gums and to satisfy his need for activity. It's only when left to their own devices that many puppies take up the hobby of destructive chewing.

The perfect chew toy is too large for your dog to swallow and sturdy enough to last a while without being eaten. Keep a supply of chew toys on hand and rotate them so your dog doesn't get bored and look for something new to sink his teeth into. Chewing should diminish after your puppy's permanent teeth come in, at around six months of age, but some dogs always find chewing enjoyable and relaxing.

Digging

Like chewing, digging is natural canine behavior. Dogs dig to relieve boredom, to find a cool spot to lie, to bury a prized possession, to find a mate, or to excavate your favorite shrubs for the pure fun of it.

Using a crate is one way to prevent digging, but your dog can't stay in it all the time, nor should you want him to. If your puppy has a favorite excavation site, place cayenne pepper in that area. The forceful sneezing it causes may help your puppy decide that digging there isn't such a great idea. For puppies or dogs seeking a cool spot for a nap, be sure to provide plenty of fresh, clean water, and a shady place to rest. For large dogs, a baby pool is a great way to offer relief from the heat.

If your dog is trying to dig out of your yard to seek a mate, have him or her spayed or neutered. This will remove your dog's urge to breed.

Plenty of exercise is a deterrent to not only digging but also to chewing and other destructive behaviors caused by boredom. Exercise can involve anything from relatively sedentary pursuits such as playing fetch or taking a walk to fast-paced activities such as jogging, bicycling, or agility training. It takes little effort to get a puppy excited about any type of exercise. Exercise relieves tension or stress for puppies, just as it does for people. Exercise can also serve as a reward for good behavior.

If you've tried all these distractions and the digging continues, seek the help of a professional. Meanwhile, limit the time your puppy spends alone in the yard or your lawn may become a minefield and you'll have a serious digging problem that can be difficult to correct.

No Begging

Begging is cute during puppyhood, and it's certainly difficult to resist those big brown eyes, but that cute behavior can quickly escalate to an annoying habit, with your dog constantly underfoot hoping for a tidbit to fall or even nudging and pawing you in an aggressive demand for a treat. Once your dog is on the slippery slope of begging behavior, it won't be long before he's sneaking food off the table or grabbing it from the kids. Stop begging before it starts by making it a family rule not to reward this behavior. If you like to have the dog in the kitchen while you're preparing meals, put him

A well-behaved dog is a joy to own and a pleasure to spend time with.

in a down/stay in an out-of-the-way spot. Give him his own meal or a treat after the family has finished eating. He should never expect to be fed from the table. If you're consistent in your expectations, your dog will learn that treats come when you decide to give them, never when he begs for or demands them.

Without a doubt, effective puppy training takes time and thought, but you will be rewarded with an obedient dog. If you experience problems, seek professional advice. The money you spend can sav e your possessions from destruction and rescue your dog from the possibility of ending up homeless in the pound. A well-trained dog enjoys the confidence that comes from being with a loving, approving, and reliable owner.

7

Grooming

Proper hygiene and grooming have a number of benefits and are important aspects of your dog's overall health. A dog who's groomed regularly is more likely to be comfortable being handled by a veterinarian, professional groomer, dog judge, or trainer. A grooming session can be relaxing—as good as a massage—for a dog who enjoys it. And dogs just feel better when they're clean and tangle-free. Many pet owners notice that their dogs are livelier and seem younger after being groomed. The earlier you begin exposing your puppy to the pleasures of being combed and brushed, the easier it will be to keep her clean and well groomed.

Routine Care Every Dog Needs

The amount and frequency of grooming your dog depends on its hair coat and lifestyle. Short-haired dogs can usually get by with a weekly brushing, but if they have an undercoat you may need to brush a little more frequently, especially during shedding season. A long-haired dog may need to be brushed and combed two or three times a week, or even daily. Dogs that enjoy getting down and dirty in the great outdoors may also need to be brushed more often.

The bond between you and your dog will be strengthened in many ways, from mealtime to playtime, but one step in the bonding process you shouldn't overlook is grooming, since it can be the most important in terms of getting to know a dog. Your dog's body is a topographical map to her well-being, and by becoming familiar with its terrain—through regular brushing, combing, and eye, ear, and dental care—you will find that the road to good health will be smoother and have fewer detours.

Grooming is a good way to keep tabs on what's going on with a dog's body. By establishing a grooming routine early in her puppyhood, you will quickly learn what's normal for your dog. Anything unusual will stand out, often allowing you to catch problems such as ear infections, skin disease, parasite infestations, and tumors before they become serious. Symptoms you might notice during grooming sessions include itchiness, hair loss, redness, tenderness, or lumps—all of which you should report to your veterinarian.

Whether your dog proves fearful of or enjoys grooming depends on her early experiences. She will come to look forward to her sessions if grooming is introduced properly. Keep your sessions short at first, and fun. Teach your puppy to open her mouth so you can look at her teeth, and offer plenty of praise when she complies. Avoid scaring her in any way. For extra practice, fondle her ears and paws while the two of you watch television. Dogs are especially sensitive around the ears, so they need to learn that having their ears handled can be pleasurable. Grooming is not only a great way for you to spend time with your dog and develop a level of trust, but early at-home grooming experiences also help prepare your puppy to accept veterinary exams, professional grooming, and show judging.

Establish a weekly routine so your puppy comes to expect grooming at a certain time, grooming her the same way each time. Plan your sessions when you won't be interrupted, and assemble your grooming tools in advance so you don't have to leave the pup to find something. Grooming is best done before a pup has eaten, so her tummy isn't full, and after she has relieved herself. Groom the dog on an elevated, nonskid surface, such as a picnic table, washer/dryer with a rubber mat placed over it, or a professional grooming table. Be sure you keep one hand on the pup at all times. If you have to walk away for any reason, put the dog on the floor. Don't take the chance, especially with a toy breed, that she will jump or fall off. Praise your puppy when she sits still for grooming to help make the experience as pleasant as possible.

> Grooming is not only a great way for you to spend time with your dog and develop a level of trust, but early at-home grooming experiences also help prepare your puppy to accept veterinary exams, professional grooming, and show judging.

Coat and Skin Care

Brushing is the foundation of good grooming. It loosens and removes dirt, dead hair, and skin cells; distributes the skin's natural oils through the coat; and prevents tangles in long-coated dogs.

The type of brush you'll use depends on your dog's coat. A hound mitt that fits over your hand or a brush with short, natural bristles is a good choice for dogs with short coats. Such brushes remove loose hair quickly and easily. A small, gentle wire-slicker brush or a rubber-tipped pin brush helps prevent mats from forming and is ideal for long-haired dogs. A pin brush is softer than a slicker and prevents hair breakage, something to consider if you plan to show your dog. Some dogs just prefer the feel of the pin brush. Whichever you choose, be sure the brush fits your hand well and is suited to your dog's size and shape.

A fine-toothed flea comb made of metal should last your dog's lifetime. Use the comb not only to search for fleas but also to re-move loose, dead hair.

Be sure you brush down to the skin, not just over the surface of the coat. If your dog has long hair, brush in layers from the skin outward, working in the direction the coat lays. Then brush in the opposite direction and finish by again brushing in the di-rection the hair lays. Brush the stomach area, even if your dog re-sists, by having her lie on her side or back. Firmly insist that she submit politely to being groomed everywhere. Don't miss the legs, rear end, and the areas behind the ears, which tangle if they're not brushed regularly. Tangles often cause the dog pain when they're removed, so avoid letting the hair get tangled. The coats of some terriers must be hand stripped to retain the proper texture. Clippering will make the coat soft. Hand stripping is only necessary for show dogs. The dog's breeder can show you how to do this properly.

Shedding

Most dogs shed twice a year. In the fall, the dog loses hair so its winter coat can start to come in, and in spring it sheds the winter coat for a lighter summer look. During shedding season, you can help keep hair under control by bathing the dog, grooming her thoroughly, and brushing her daily. A double-coated dog will lose the topcoat and the fuzzy, insulating undercoat, which often comes out in clumps.

Fleas and Ticks

While you brush, examine your dog for evidence of fleas and ticks. Although you may not find fleas on your dog, she may have flea dirt, or excreted blood, on her skin. You can identify flea dirt by brushing the dog over a white towel or piece of paper. If dark flecks fall onto the white area, moisten them; if they turn red, that's flea dirt, which means you need to treat your dog for fleas, even if you didn't find any on her body. Your veterinarian can advise you on the best method of flea control for your climate and lifestyle. If you find a tick, remove it carefully with tweezers, grasping it at the head and pulling firmly until the tick comes off. Never try to remove a tick by burning it or applying substances such as kerosene or gasoline. Be careful not to touch the tick with your bare hands, and disinfect the bite area after the tick is removed. (See Chapter 5 for more information on ticks.)

Did You Know?

Human bites are usually more dangerous than dog bites because a dog's mouth has fewer germs and bacteria.

Neatening Up

Use blunt-tipped scissors to trim stray hairs in and around the ears, on the legs, between the toes, and around the feet. To prevent dripping after your furry wonder urinates, you might want to trim the hair around the penis. Using scissors or a clipper to trim the hair beneath the tail will keep feces from clinging to the area. If you're squeamish, a groomer can take care of these areas for you.

Ear Care

After you've brushed the coat, move on to the ears. Your dog's ears need to be cleaned about once a week, as well as after every bath. If his ears build up with wax quickly or if he swims a lot, you'll need to do it more often. After swimming, apply a cleaning/drying agent to remove any debris or trapped water.

Look inside the ears to check for dirt, scratches, foxtails, parasites, or discharge. Then give the ears a good sniff. There shouldn't be any unpleasant odor. Moisten a cotton ball or cosmetic pad with mineral oil or a liquid ear cleaner recommended by your veterinarian, and gently wipe the ears out to remove any wax or debris. If necessary, place a small amount of ear-cleaning solution into the canal and gently massage the base of the ear for about a minute. This will break up any wax or debris that can be trapped deep in the ear canal and flush it to the external opening. Then you can wipe out the ear canal with a cotton ball. You can use cotton swabs to clean the tight crevices of the outer ear flap, but don't put them inside the ear. They can push wax farther into the ear, and if your dog moves suddenly, you run the risk of rupturing his eardrum.

The ear canal is a sensitive area, so don't use alcohol as a cleaning agent. The ear solutions made for dogs' ears are gentle and often contain a mild drying agent to prevent the ear from staying moist for an extended time. Avoid using drying agents such as alcohol or hydrogen peroxide because they can dry out the ear too much. If the ear is oozing, drying it up without discovering and treating the underlying cause simply begins a cycle of ear problems.

Some dogs' ears contain hair, which must be plucked to prevent hair and wax from clogging the ear and causing an infection. Poodles and many terrier breeds must have this done. You can pluck the hair by hand or with a pair of tweezers. Grasp only a small amount of hair each time and pluck it out. This isn't comfortable for the dog by any means, but it's no more painful than plucking your eyebrows. Be sure you actually pluck the hair out. Simply trimming it with scissors won't do the job.

The shape of many dogs' ears predisposes them to problems. For instance, the long, floppy ears of Cocker Spaniels and Basset Hounds hang over the opening to the ear canal, providing a dark, warm environment, the perfect place for bacteria and yeast to multiply rapidly. Typically, breeds whose ears stand erect have far fewer problems with ear infection than those with floppy ears. If your dog develops an ear infection, clean the ears thoroughly before applying the prescribed topical medication. If there's too much buildup in the ears, the medication won't be as effective.

Eyes

Check the eyes for redness or other signs of irritation. Healthy eyes are bright and clear, and the eyeball is white.

Many dogs suffer from runny eyes, which can cause unattractive stains beneath the eyes. Tearing has a number of possible causes, from low-grade infections that scar the lacrimal duct to the corner of the eye being too small to permit tears to collect.

Did You Know?

Nose prints can be used to identify dogs just as fingerprints are used to identify humans.

Homemade Eye Stain Remover

Professional dog handlers have had success with this recipe for getting rid of eye stains. You'll need a new, clean hair-coloring bottle (not the color, just the bottle, which you can find at a beauty supply store) and hydrogen peroxide, milk of magnesia, and cornstarch. Mix equal parts of the three ingredients and put the solution in the bottle. Squeeze the mixture directly onto the tear stains, being careful not to get any in your dog's eyes. The solution separates easily, so keep shaking it as needed. Apply daily until the stain lightens, and let the solution flake off on its own. To keep the stain from returning, put mayonnaise—not salad dressing—on the area.

Because hydrogen peroxide can be drying to skin and fur, you may want to try another method. Soak a cotton ball with Visine or preservative-free saline solution and rub beneath the eye where the stain is. Do this every day for a week, then once or twice weekly thereafter to keep the stain from returning.

You can help prevent or reduce staining by keeping the eye area clean. Wipe away discharge in the corners of the eyes with a cotton ball or soft washcloth moistened with warm water. Avoid rubbing the cotton ball directly over the eye, since the fibers can irritate it. If tearing is caused by an infection, a course of antibiotics may help solve the problem, but this isn't something that should be repeated frequently. You can also buy commercial products that will help lighten or remove stains.

Tooth Care

Dental care is an aspect of grooming that many pet owners ignore, but it can pay off in fresh breath and better health. Gum disease is a common problem in dogs, but regular brushing will help keep it at bay. The American Animal Hospital Association recommends brushing a dog's teeth at least three times a week. If you do this from puppyhood, your dog will never develop that foul "doggy breath" that signifies a professional cleaning is in order.

Gum disease begins when food particles and saliva accumulate on the teeth, forming a soft plaque that later hardens into tartar. The bacteria trapped in the plaque contributes to bad breath and to the development of gingivitis (inflammation of the gums) and periodontal disease (inflammation of the lining of the tooth socket). Remember that canned and semi-moist foods adhere more to the teeth than dry foods do. (Think what your mouth would be like if you ate peanut butter every day and didn't brush your teeth!) Dry foods, especially the specially formulated abrasive diets, don't play as big a role in plaque formation and can even help reduce plaque.

Signs of periodontal disease are a brownish buildup on teeth; gums that are swollen, red, or bleeding; bad breath; loose or broken teeth; lost teeth; pus between the gums and teeth; and any unusual growth in the mouth. Your dog may also have gum disease if she's reluctant to eat, frequently drops bits of food, doesn't want to drink cold water or doesn't want to chew on her favorite toy.

Untreated teeth can also cause serious problems in your dog's overall health. Abscessed teeth or periodontal disease can lead to heart and kidney disease in dogs. By brushing your dog's teeth on a regular basis, you can prevent or decrease the need for expensive veterinary cleanings, which require anesthetizing the dog.

Begin during puppyhood by gently scrubbing the teeth with a soft gauze pad. Puppy mouths are sensitive during teething, so you don't want to hurt them and make them mouth-shy. Wrap some gauze or a soft washcloth around your finger and wipe all the teeth, front and back, with strokes from the gum-line to the tip of the tooth. This will familiarize your dog with having her gums and teeth rubbed. It will also help you make sure your puppies' permanent teeth are coming in correctly. Sometimes puppies don't lose all their baby teeth, even after the permanent teeth have emerged. If this is the case, your veterinarian will remove them, usually at the same time your pup is spayed or neutered.

After the permanent teeth come in, you can graduate to a finger brush or a toothbrush and toothpaste. Be sure to use a brush and toothpaste made for dogs; toothbrushes should be soft, and toothpaste needs to be formulated for the dog's system. Toothpaste made for people can cause an upset stomach if your dog swallows it. Teeth can also be cleaned with a paste made of baking soda and water.

Start by brushing the front teeth, then move to the upper and lower teeth in the back. Hold the brush so that the bristles are at a 45-degree angle to the tooth surface, and move it in an oval motion. Be sure you get down into the crevices where teeth and gums meet, because this is where odor and infection begin. In between brushings, feeding your dog dry kibble or hard biscuits can help reduce tartar buildup.

Veterinary teeth cleaning includes use of a short-lasting anesthetic that allows for gum-line probes, removal of tartar, and tooth polishing. If your dog's teeth don't have too much tartar built up and you are concerned about the risks of anesthesia, ask if your veterinarian offers ultrasonic cleaning. This is a simple procedure that shouldn't involve anesthetizing the dog.

Foot Care

Your dog's nails will grow quickly, so regular trimming is a must. Puppies, especially, have sharp, fast-growing nails, so keep them trimmed regularly, both to accustom the dog to trimming and to prevent painful gouges in your skin. Overgrown nails also snag easily on carpets, upholstery, and bed coverings. If they get too long, nails can grow right into the footpad, which is extremely uncomfortable and can even impair the dog's ability to walk. Most house dogs don't wear down their nails as quickly as do dogs who are more active. If you hear your dog's nails clicking on the floor, it's time for a trim.

Nail trimming often involves much howling on the part of the dog and flinching on the part of the owner. With care and early training, you can accomplish this task without trauma for either your dog or yourself. If Rosie puts up a struggle, recruit your spouse or one of the kids to hold her. Your assistant can best immobilize the dog by placing her between his knees, facing outward, and supporting her chest with his left hand.

Once the dog is settled, you're ready to trim. Firmly grip one of her legs at the elbow so she can't pull it back. The same technique works on the hind legs. As you clip, praise Rosie if she's behaving well, and give a firm verbal correction to put a stop to her squirming.

Clip only the tip of the nail; avoid clipping past the curve, or you risk hitting the quick, a blood vessel inside the nail. Being "quicked" is painful and will cause bleeding. It's easier to avoid the quick in dogs with light-colored or clear nails, because you can see the vein. In case you clip too far, though, have some styptic powder on hand to stop the bleeding. Flour or corn meal will work in a pinch.

Did You Know?

The pom-pom cut used on Poodles was originally developed to increase the breed's swimming abilitites as a retriever. The short haircut allowed for faster swimming but the pom-poms were left to keep the joints warm.

You can purchase nail clippers at pet supply stores. Choose a high-quality guillotine-style clipper to make the job easier. For some toy breeds, you can use nail trimmers made for cats, or even those used for people. A smaller nail trimmer is easier to fit between a toy dog's little toes. Smooth the nails with a small metal file after trimming.

> If you can't stand the fuss your dog puts up—and if your budget allows—simply take the dog to a groomer or veterinarian to have nail clipping done. You'll both be happier.

If you can't stand the fuss your dog puts up—and if your budget allows—simply take the dog to a groomer or veterinarian to have nail clipping done. You'll both be happier.

Part of the grooming process should include examining the foot pads for foreign objects or injuries. In winter, clean your dog's feet after she's gone outdoors; this removes de-icing chemicals, salt, snow, and ice, which can injure the feet or make the dog sick if she licks her paws.

Anal Glands

Probably the most unpleasant part of grooming a dog is checking—and if need be, expressing—the anal glands. These glands are located on each side of the anus. If you imagine the anal area as a clock, the anal glands would be found at about the 5:00 and 7:00 positions. These scent glands produce a fluid that plays a role in territorial marking. This fluid is usually excreted when the dog defecates, but sometimes the glands become clogged, which is usually indicated by the dog's scooting its rear on the floor or biting and licking at its anal area. If clogging isn't relieved, the glands can become impacted or infected, a situation that usually requires a course of antibiotics and hy-

Preparing Your Pup for Nail Trimming

When your puppy is young, handle her feet daily to accustom her to the process. Look at and touch each toe. If she starts to struggle, give her a firm verbal correction. Let her know you're not going to give up, so she might as well sit still for the exam. By demonstrating daily to your puppy that you won't harm her when you touch her feet, she'll learn to trust you and let you handle her for any grooming procedure.

drotherapy to remedy. Sometimes a high-fiber diet can help solve the problem. Clogged anal glands are most common in small breeds.

If you notice your dog scooting or biting, you can ask your veterinarian or a groomer to empty, or express, the glands; but if it occurs frequently, you may want to learn to do it yourself. The veterinarian or groomer can show you how. Check the glands regularly—monthly or at bath-time is a good way to schedule this grooming chore. Most likely, though, you'll prefer to leave this stinky task to someone else.

Bathing

It was once believed that dogs should be bathed only when dirty, but that was back when shampoos for dogs were more harsh than they are today. If a gentle shampoo is used, a dog can be bathed weekly without drying out its coat. Most dog owners find that their dogs do well on a bath schedule of every four to eight weeks, or whenever they start developing doggy odor or a dull coat. Regular bathing can improve coat condition and simply make a dog more pleasant to be around.

Use a shampoo that's specially formulated for dogs. Their skin has a different pH level than ours, so a human shampoo could strip away beneficial skin oils. Choose a gentle shampoo that doesn't contain flea- or tick-fighting insecticides (the fewer chemicals to which your dog is exposed, the better). You'll find shampoos available for oily skin, dry skin, and other dermatological conditions, as well as shampoos that will brighten or deepen coat colors. For a dog with sensitive skin, you can purchase a medicated shampoo from your veterinarian.

Brush the dog thoroughly before bathing to remove dead hair and mats that will otherwise tangle when they get wet. The room temperature in the bath (and drying) area should be at least 70 degrees Fahrenheit. Gather everything you need for the bath—shampoo, towels, mineral oil or petroleum jelly, cotton balls—then get the dog. Small dogs can easily be bathed in the kitchen or bathroom sink, but larger dogs will have to go in the tub. Plan everything in advance, or before you know it, you'll be coping with a wet dog shaking herself all over you or dragging her sopping body along your walls, carpets, and furniture.

Before you begin, put some mineral oil or petroleum jelly around the dog's eyes to keep water from running into them, and pack cotton balls into the ears so the insides won't get wet. Place the dog in the sink or tub, with a rubber mat beneath her to pre-

vent slipping. Wet her to the skin with warm water, using a gentle spray. Lather with a gentle dog shampoo, then rinse her thoroughly with warm water. Repeat.

If you're using a medicated shampoo, follow the directions carefully. The treatment won't be effective if the shampoo doesn't stay on the skin for a long enough period.

Thorough rinsing is a must if you don't want your dog to have dry, flaky skin. A 50/50 mixture of cider vinegar or lemon juice and water is a good final rinse that will help remove shampoo residue.

Apply a light conditioner and rinse again. (Leave-in conditioners can be sprayed on after the bath.) Conditioners help remove tangles and leave the coat shiny. Again, use a product that's formulated for dogs.

Then squeeze as much water as you can out of the coat and absorb more with a towel. If you have a short-haired dog, that's all there is to it. Simply keep the dog in a warm, draft-free place until she's completely dry. If you want to speed the process, follow the procedure for using a blow-dryer described below. Blow-drying is a good idea for puppies because they are more susceptible to chills.

For a long-haired dog, you may prefer to use a blow-dryer to prevent the coat from matting as it dries. As you blow her dry, start to brush the dog out, moving the brush in the same direction as the coat grows. Be sure to use a low, gentle setting. Hold the dryer at least a foot away from the dog so you don't burn her skin. If your dog has long, thick, or fluffy hair, simply combing the hair out and letting it dry naturally will keep her from looking as if she stuck her paw in a light socket.

Did You Know?

The bloodhound is the only animal whose evidence is admissible in an American court.

If your dog's fur tends to develop a greasy feel between baths, rub in some dry oatmeal or cornmeal to absorb the oil. Then brush it all out, using the same brushing technique discussed earlier. A bristle brush is the best tool for this dry bath.

Sweet Dreams

If you allow your dog to sleep on the bed, you may notice a slight doggy odor developing between baths. The solution of one dog owner is to sprinkle a citrus-scented silk-based powder on her sheets every morning when she makes the bed. The lovely, aromatic scent doesn't bother dogs or people with allergies, and the room always smells fresh.

A Happy Ending

End each grooming session with a soothing massage and a treat. Clean equipment thoroughly after each use so that it's ready to go for the next time. And if you're ever tempted to skip a grooming, remember that we brush our hair and wash our faces every day, and should do no less for our dogs.

The Professional Grooming Option

Most pet owners are capable of providing the basics—brushing, nail trimming, and so forth—but when it comes to styling, clipping, stripping, or other complicated techniques, it's often best to leave the job to a professional. And if you're the busy owner of one or more dogs, you may simply find professional grooming more convenient. By leaving the job to professionals, you can better spend your time juggling your own job, school, kids, and dog care.

Groomers not only save time for busy professionals but enable many senior citizens who may be unable to do the grooming themselves to provide proper care for their dogs. In fact, some areas have mobile groomers, which are especially convenient.

Home Grooming: A Cautionary Tale

My family once owned a white miniature Poodle, François. Naturally, François required regular grooming. Since money was tight, my dad decided he could be a good barber. After a few practice attempts on the bangs of the girls in our family and my little brother's crewcut, he decided he was ready to tackle dog grooming. Using the same scissors and electric clippers he used on my brother, he proceeded to clip François' coat. Unfortunately, he hadn't brushed out all the matted areas first. He slipped the point of the scissors beneath a thick mat near the dog's knee and snipped. He cut right through the skin, exposing her bone. While he did indeed save the $15 grooming fee, he incurred a $45 veterinary bill for the suturing of poor François' wound. Dad no longer enjoyed her confidence, even with respect to baths.

Dog owners in general benefit by being able to spend more time with a pet who looks nice and smells good, free from worries about hair or odors getting on furniture and clothing.

People who have their pets professionally groomed usually bring them in every six to eight weeks. The interval varies, though, depending on your dog's breed and on your ability and willingness to do home maintenance between professional groomings. Owners with good maintenance skills may only take their dogs to the groomer every three months. Coated breeds—such as Poodles, Cocker Spaniels, Bichons Frise, Miniature Schnauzers, Lhasa Apsos, Yorkshire Terriers, and Shih Tzu—usually visit the groomer as frequently as once or twice a month.

If you opt to have your pretty Bella professionally groomed, begin during puppyhood. It's much easier for groomers to teach a youngster to accept the professional process than to persuade an older dog that grooming is fun. An early introduction will give the groomer an opportunity to develop a good relationship with Bella that will last into her golden years.

What to Look For in a Groomer

Should you decide to have your dog professionally groomed, you'll want to choose your groomer as carefully as you choose your veterinarian or other pet-care professional. Top-notch groomers not only treat their canine clients with love and respect; they can spot potential health problems early on. Before you select a shop from the Yellow Pages or simply plop Bella on the counter of the shop down the street, interview the groomer carefully to make sure you're willing to entrust your dog to him or her.

> Top-notch groomers not only treat their canine clients with love and respect; they can spot potential health problems early on.

Start your search through that old standby—word of mouth. Ask your veterinarian if he or she recommends a particular groomer. Some veterinarians even have groomers on staff. Grooming brings pets in on a regular basis, and veterinary technicians who are trained as groomers (or groomers who are trained as veterinary technicians) can be the first line of defense against disease. They are often able to identify looming skin or health problems you might not notice.

Your dog's breeder and pet-owning friends and neighbors are good sources of recommendations as well. Ask how long they've taken their pets to the groomer and whether they're satisfied with the service they receive. Boarding kennel operators and pet-store managers may also point you in the direction of a good groomer.

You can also contact professional grooming organizations for the names of members in your area. To find members of the National Dog Groomers Association of America in your area, call (412) 962-2711. Or contact the American Grooming Shop Association at (719) 570-7788 for their recommendations.

Once you have a list of names, call each groomer for information about the services offered, types of products used, pricing, and whether they offer pickup and delivery. Ask how long they've been in business and which breeds they usually work with. Some groomers specialize in a particular breed or do a better job of grooming certain breeds. Besides a breed's standard clip, groomers can also suggest other, more practical cuts for each breed.

Educational credentials are important as well. Groomers may learn on the job—by apprenticing with another groomer—or they may attend a grooming school. Following that, a groomer can further her education by becoming certified by one of the national organizations, a voluntary process that requires a groomer to be evaluated by her peers. Although certification is not required by law (and there are good groomers who are not certified), certification is a clue that the groomer is dedicated to improving her own skills

If your dog is a senior citizen or has a health problem, find out what steps the groomer takes to ensure the dog's comfort and safety. A shop that's associated with a boarding kennel may require proof that your dog's vaccinations are up to date or that she has received a bordetella vaccine within the past six months.

Once you're satisfied with the groomer's responses, visit the shops of those you're interested in. Before you walk in the door, note how long it took you to drive there and whether parking is easily available. Inside, the shop should be clean, neat, and well lit. Watch how the groomers

Did You Know?

The Dog Museum in St. Louis, Missouri, contains paintings, sculpture, and other works of art about or featuring dogs.

handle the dogs in their care. Are they firm but gentle, or do they seem uninterested or hurried?

A good groomer will greet you with a smile and take the time to explain procedures, answer questions, and show you the kinds of brushes and combs you need to use at home to maintain your dog between grooming appointments. If you like what you see, make an appointment to bring Bella in for a bath and blow-dry. Always discuss with the groomer beforehand how you want your dog to look, since the groomer may have something else in mind. The grooming session should include care of the ears, nails, and anal glands.

Of course, you hope Bella's good manners will permit the groomer to handle her without difficulty. The socialization you've done should ensure that she doesn't growl or shy away when a stranger touches her. If you foresee a potential problem, warn the groomer ahead of time so he won't be bitten. Training classes and regular handling by other people will help Bella learn that being touched can feel good, especially when she feels clean afterward.

If Bella's coat is severely tangled, don't expect the groomer to work miracles on the first visit. Your dog may need several repeat trips or even a complete shaving to get her coat back in good condition. Regular brushing and combing between visits to the groomer will help keep tangles to a minimum.

In extreme circumstances, your dog may need to be tranquilized before grooming. A tranquilizer can help relax a dog who has a heart

condition, seizures, arthritis, or heavy matting, or a dog who's simply too fearful to permit grooming without it. If your dog needs a tranquilizer, you may find it best to work with a groomer associated with a veterinary clinic, since most groomers are not authorized to administer medications.

Groomers are trained, skilled professionals. By choosing carefully, you're sure to be pleased with your dog's appearance and the care she receives.

8

Family Life

Dogs love to be with their people. Whether that companionship involves exercise, play, or travel, your dog will be ready, willing, and able to participate. He can learn to do just about anything his size permits. And, of course, there's almost no limit to the places you can take him, given that he's been exposed to early socialization and has learned good manners. With plenty of activity and companionship, your dog can't help but be a fine family friend.

Exercise

No matter what their size, all dogs need exercise to keep them physically and mentally healthy. An inactive dog is generally a fat dog, with the accompanying likelihood of joint strain or torn ligaments. Inactive dogs are also prone to mischief—anything to relieve their boredom. This often leads to behavior problems such as chewing or barking. Daily exercise will help keep your dog slim, trim, and happy.

Like people, dogs can tend toward laziness as they age. You can't count on your dog exercising himself, so be sure you provide him with plenty of opportunities for fun activity. Exercise can be as simple as chasing a ball in the backyard or going for a walk, or as demanding as participation in dog sports such as agility, obedience trials, and tracking.

The American Animal Hospital Association recommends walking a younger or middle-aged dog for 10 to 15 minutes once or twice each day. This can begin when your dog is about four months old. As your dog's stamina builds, you can increase the length of his walks to whatever he finds comfortable. On cold or rainy days, a good game of indoor fetch will suffice for toy breeds; other breeds, such as the Labrador Retriever or the Siberian Husky, will revel in the rain or snow.

If your dog is older or overweight, consult your veterinarian about how much and what type of exercise to give. Usually, a 10- to 15-minute walk once a day is a good start. As the ounces drop off, your dog's energy level will rise, and you can increase the amount of daily exercise.

Play Time

Dog sports are not only fun; they double as exercise. Dare your dog to go for the gusto by intro-

Road Safety Tips

○ Walk your dog on leash. The leash should be short enough to offer easy control.
○ Walk toward traffic with the dog on your left.
○ Wear light-colored clothing if you're walking after dark. Put a reflective collar or tag on your dog.

ducing him to activities such as agility, carting, herding, obedience trials, and tracking. Size is no barrier when it comes to success in canine sports, so don't think your toy breed can't participate.

Agility

J.R. is a Jack Russell Terrier with lots of brains and energy. His owner decided to channel J.R.'s energy and tendency to mischief by enrolling him in a beginning agility class. J.R. was so good at it, and they both had such a good time, that they soon moved on to the intermediate class. J.R.'s trainer now says he is ready for competition.

Phoebe, a two-year-old chocolate Labrador Retriever, also needed a way to run off her abundant energy. Her owners turned to agility as well. The ball-loving Lab is fast and agile, just the characteristics needed to be successful at this game.

The fast-paced sport of agility is a race against time. Dogs, with their people running alongside, must maneuver through a series of obstacles such as A-frames, hoops, weave poles, and tunnels. Scores are based on accuracy as well as speed. Although agility is dominated by medium-size and large dogs, nothing prevents a confident, enthusiastic dog of any size from competing successfully. Californian Cindy Luke owns Peppy, a six-pound male Chihuahua known to other competitors as the Brown Bullet. Peppy has earned several agility titles. Nigel, a Cavalier King Charles Spaniel, earned his agility title in 18 months and loves the sport.

Agility is wonderful for building a dog's confidence; but as with any sport, you must consider some safety precautions. A dog could fall from an A-frame or sustain an injury completing a jump. An agility dog should be sturdy, and should respond to the sit, down, stay, and come commands. He should also be reliable off leash.

To see if your dog might be interested in this fun sport, take him to a local agility event or class. If he's raring to go, sign him up for a class and let him rip.

Carting

Back before the days of motorized vehicles, dogs pulled carts for butchers, dairy farmers, and other small-business owners. Nordic breeds pulled sleds in the snow-covered north. Among the breeds used as draft and freighting dogs were Bernese Mountain Dogs, Greater Swiss Mountain Dogs, Rottweilers, Siberian Huskies, and Alaskan Malamutes. Today, these dogs and others can relive their heritage by learning to pull a small wagon or cart. Even breeds as small as Papillons and Chihuahuas can participate, pulling carts to match their size. Like agility, carting builds a dog's confidence and enables your dog to participate in parades or make therapy rounds at a nursing home or children's hospital.

To take up carting, your dog should know the commands sit, down, stay, and come. In class, he'll also learn directional commands such as left, right, and forward. Of course, you'll need a small, well-fitting harness as well as an appropriate-size vehicle. The trainer you're working with can recommend something that's the right size.

Flyball

This exciting team sport is a thrill a minute for dogs and their people. Flyball is a relay race in which each of the four dogs on a team must scramble over four hurdles, step on a lever that triggers the release of a tennis ball, and take the ball back over the hurdles to where the next dog is anxiously awaiting his turn. The first team to run without errors—such as skipping one or more hurdles—wins the heat. Tournament play may be organized in double-elimination or round-robin style. Because several teams race at once—with dogs barking, handlers shouting instructions, and spectators cheering on their favorites—it's not surprising that flyball is an extremely noisy sport.

A potential flyball dog should be a team player and not aggressive toward other dogs, especially smaller ones. The hurdles are set four inches below the shoulder height of the smallest dog, with eight inches being the minimum height. It's not unusual for a team to recruit a toy dog such as a Papillon or Chihuahua to keep jump heights low. A successful flyball dog should enjoy running, jumping, and playing with balls, and needs to be physically fit and under your control. As the trainer, you need to take things slowly and patiently so your dog will learn accuracy as well as speed.

Did You Know?

The Beatles song "Martha My Dear" was written by Paul McCartney about his sheepdog, Martha.

Titles your dog can earn are based on the number of points he earns in competition. They are Flyball Dog, Flyball Dog Excellent, Flyball Dog Champion, Flyball Master, Flyball Master Excellent, Flyball Master Champion, Onyx Award, and Flyball Grand Champion. For more information about flyball rules, equipment, or teams in your area, contact the North American Flyball Association, 1002 E. Samuel Ave., Peoria Heights, IL 61614. The rules are available for $10; all other information is free.

Freestyle

A fusion of traditional obedience exercises and the equine sport of dressage, freestyle is a routine set to music that shows dog and handler working in harmony and expressing their creativity through costume and movement. Think of it as dancing with the dog. Using heeling routines and other elements of obedience training, owner and dog present a uniquely choreographed display. This event calls for a dog who is athletic, attentive, flexible, and trainable.

For more information about freestyle competitions, which take place across the United States, contact Pup-Peroni Canine Freestylers at P.O. Box 350122, Brooklyn, NY 11235; (718) 332-8336; (718) 646-2686 (fax); or pupfreesty@aol.com.

Herding

One of the earliest uses of dogs was to herd and guard flocks, a talent people molded by redirecting the dog's prey drive. Naturally, the dogs that take best to this sport are those in the Herding Group—such as Border Collies, Collies, Shelties, and German Shepherds—but other breeds take it up as well. Rottweilers, for instance, who once drove cattle to and from the market, also perform well in herding.

To develop your dog's confidence, a trainer will probably start him herding ducks. Besides being a good starter flock, ducks are more accessible for those who live in urban environments. More experienced dogs can work sheep and even cattle. A herding dog should be able to move quickly and trot for long distances, so your dog should be in good shape to take up this activity.

The AKC permits certain breeds to earn the following herding titles: Herding Started, Herding Intermediate, Herding Excellent, and Herding Championship. For a list of clubs approved to hold herding events, contact AKC Customer Service at 5580 Centerview Dr., Raleigh, NC 27606, or visit the AKC Web site at http://www.akc.org.

Obedience Trials

Again, every dog should learn basic obedience commands: sit, down, stay, heel, and come. But learning doesn't have to end there. Your dog can build on those commands to earn beginning and advanced obedience titles. Mixed-breeds can participate as well in obedience trials sponsored by the American Mixed Breed Registry. As with any performance event, success breeds self-confidence.

> Some people believe Terriers and Hounds are too independent-minded and stubborn to make good obedience dogs; but the secret, trainers say, is persuading these willful dogs that competing is fun.

Breeds that traditionally take home high scores in obedience trials are Golden Retrievers, Shetland Sheepdogs, and Border Collies, but any dog can be competitive in the obedience ring. Some people believe Terriers and Hounds are too independent-minded and stubborn to make good obedience dogs; but the secret, trainers say, is persuading these willful dogs that competing is fun. The key is positive reinforcement rather than harsh correction. In the ring, though, your dog will have to perform solely for love of the sport, because treats and coaxing aren't allowed.

Obedience titles dogs can earn are Companion Dog (CD), Companion Dog Excellent (CDX), Utility Dog (UD), and Utility Dog Excellent (UDX). Overachievers can go for the title of Obedience Trial Champion.

To earn a novice, or CD, title, your dog will be expected to readily heel on- and off-leash at an appropriate pace, sitting nicely whenever you stop; stand politely for the judge's examination; perform a proper sit-stay and down-stay; and come when called. The dogs with the highest scores respond to these commands with alacrity and precision. A title is earned when a dog achieves passing scores (170 or more out of a possible 200 points) at three obedience trials. More advanced titles require the dogs to perform off leash and for longer periods, as well as to complete jumping and retrieving exercises. Utility dogs must be proficient at scent discrimination.

If your dog seems to enjoy the work and you decide to take up obedience trials, be sure to work with a trainer who enjoys and has successfully trained your breed.

Canine Good Citizen

If obedience work sounds too regimented but you'd still like your dog to have a title, prepare him for the Canine Good Citizen test. This program is sponsored by the American Kennel Club, with tests administered by local dog clubs, private trainers, and 4-H clubs.

To earn a CGC title, your dog must be well groomed and demonstrate the manners that all good dogs should exhibit. The CGC test requires a dog to perform the sit, down, stay, and come commands; react appropriately to other dogs and distractions; allow a stranger to approach him; sit politely for petting; walk nicely on a loose lead; move through a crowd without going wild; calm down after play or praise; and sit still for examination by the judge.

Tracking

Tracking isn't just for scent hounds. All dogs have powerful noses. If you've ever seen your dog sniffing out a treat, then you know he's probably capable of earning a tracking title. Tracking is a fun way for the two of you to get some outdoor exercise, and you just might show those Bloodhounds and Beagles a thing or two. A stubborn dog who never gives up is ideal for this pursuit.

A tracking trial is simply a test of whether a dog can follow a trail by scent. There's no competition, either against the clock or against other dogs. Of course, you can't just show up at a field trial and give it a go; your dog will need to learn the elements of tracking first. An obedience instructor or a tracking club can help you train for one of the following titles: Tracking Dog (TD), Tracking Dog Excellent (TDX) and Variable Surface Tracking (VST). A dog who earns all three titles is awarded the status of Champion Tracker (CT).

Did You Know?

According to the American Animal Hospital Association, more than 40% of pet owners talk to their pets on the phone or through the answering machine.

To pass a TD test, your dog must be able to follow a track 440 to 500 yards long, with at least two right-angle turns. The track is laid by someone unknown to the dog and is one or two hours old. The goal is for your dog to find the scented article dropped at the end of the track.

Things get a little tougher with the TDX test. The track is 800 to 1,000 yards long and three to five hours old. It may take the dog through tall grass or ditches, and the track-layer will try to trick him with dummy scent articles (an article that looks like the item the dog is supposed to find, but doesn't bear the correct scent).

Urban dogs with street smarts can learn to follow a trail on such surfaces as asphalt, concrete, and linoleum, for a VST title. The VST track takes a dog over at least three types of surfaces for a distance of 600 to 800 yards. The track is three or four hours old with up to eight turns.

Conformation Showing

We often think of dog shows as the Miss America pageants of the dog world, but their underlying purpose is to select the dogs most suited for breeding. With that in mind, each dog's structure (or "conformation"), movement, and attitude are

judged against the breed standard, which purports to describe the perfect dog of a particular breed. The dogs who most closely meet the standard earn championships and are considered good breeding prospects. If your dog has what it takes to compete in this arena, you may enjoy conformation showing. It's an opportunity to travel, get together with other dog lovers, and see other nice dogs in the breed.

Your breeder can give you good advice about whether your dog is suited to the show ring, not only conformationally but temperamentally. Besides good looks, a winning show dog has pizzazz. She sparkles as she shows her stuff, practically ordering the judge to give her a win. If you don't plan to use a professional handler, ring craft classes offered by a local dog club will teach you how to present your Princess to best advantage.

All-breed dog shows offer your dog opportunity to earn points toward a championship. Each win brings one to five points, depending on the number of dogs defeated, and a three-, four-, or five-point win is called a major. To earn a championship, your dog needs 15 points won under three different judges. Two of the wins must be majors, each won under a different judge.

Therapy Work

Daily walks and dog sports are not the only activities that you and your dog can enjoy together. If your dog is gregarious enough, the two of you can bring pleasure and laughter to people confined to hospitals and nursing homes. Therapy-dog visits are a wonderful way for you to share the joy of dog ownership with others. Petting Buster can ease the loneliness of a widower in a nursing home, lower the blood pressure of a hospital patient, and bring big smiles and shouts of laughter from children in a cancer ward.

> Therapy-dog visits are a wonderful way for you to share the joy of dog ownership with others.

Your therapy dog will need to be clean and flea-free with good manners (no food stealing or potty accidents!). He must pass a temperament test to ensure that he's suited to this type of work. A sweet, tolerant, fearless disposition is ideal since therapy

Fun Things Kids Can Do with a Dog

Teaching Tricks

Dogs can learn to do all sorts of tricks. Amaze your friends by teaching your dog to sit, beg, dance on its hind legs, speak on command, and play dead (roll over). Other tricks include the dog playing a toy piano, giving the high five, talking on a toy phone, and pulling a toy by a string. A good book for learning how to teach tricks is *The Trick Is in the Training: 25 Fun Tricks to Teach Your Dog* by Stephanie J. Taunton and Cheryl S. Smith.

Bobbing for Biscuits

You can play this game any time of year, not just at Halloween. It's great fun at birthday parties—yours *or* the dog's! You'll need a small bowl, four biscuits per dog, and a watch with a second hand.

To get started, put some water in the bowl (not too much since some dogs may try to drink their way to the biscuits) and drop in four dog biscuits. One at a time, let the dogs try to get the biscuits. The object is for the dog to eat as many biscuits as he can within the time limit—30 to 60 seconds. No help from the audience, please, but cheering and clapping are okay. The dog who eats the most biscuits in the least amount of time is the winner.

Junior Showmanship

If you'd like see what dog shows are all about, junior showmanship is a great way to learn about dogs and develop good sportsmanship and dog handling skills. It doesn't matter whether your dog is show quality, although he must be purebred. You'll be judged on your ability to present and handle your dog, not on your dog's appearance. There are also junior handler programs for agility and obedience. For more information on junior showmanship, contact the AKC.

4-H

These nationwide clubs offer a chance to learn about all kinds of activities, including dog care. The 4-H dog program teaches grooming, training, and other aspects of responsible dog ownership. At the beginner level, 4-H members learn how to choose a dog, feed him, keep him healthy, teach him good manners, and show him. Intermediate and advanced members learn how to train a dog for obedience or other activities.

work involves encounters with new or unusual places, people, and equipment. Both of you will attend training classes before visits begin. Be sure to take normal precautions against a fall to the floor from aged, shaky hands or run-ins with wheelchairs or walkers. A short leash attached to a harness will help you keep control.

Playing Nicely with Children

If it's put to them the right way, young children can learn how to treat dogs properly, but any interaction between children and dogs needs to be grounded in close parental guidance. It's simply not smart to bring home a dog unless you're willing to supervise, set rules, and teach your child how to behave with the dog. When any of those elements are absent, the likely result is an injured dog or a bitten child. On the other hand, children and dogs who are brought up to respect each other can form lasting, loving bonds that will forever be special to them.

Even if you don't have children in your home, your dog is still likely to encounter them. Be aware of approaching children and take steps to control the interaction. Toddlers, especially, tend to

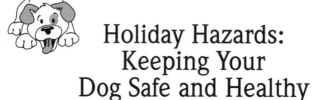

Holiday Hazards: Keeping Your Dog Safe and Healthy

Naturally, you'll want to include Buster and Bella in your holiday celebrations. After all, they're special family members. But the holidays hold a few hazards that you'll want to be aware of so you can make these times fun and safe for the whole family.

New Year's is a loud and raucous time of parties, fireworks, and noisemakers, all of which can be stressful to dogs who aren't used to this. Spend some time with your dog before you have a party or go out. If you're having people over, confine him to a quiet room where he won't be disturbed. On the other hand, if your dog is a party animal, let him join the fun. One couple says their Mastiff makes the rounds at all their parties, contributing his bit to the conversations. Just make sure he's kept well away from chocolate, champagne, paté, and other rich goodies. You don't want him to start the new year with an upset tummy or a hangover.

For most people, Valentine's Day means chocolate—lots of it. But as you know, chocolate, even in small amounts, can be hazardous to your dog's health. Keep chocolate out of Buster's reach to prevent his nibbling.

Marching bands, cookouts, and fireworks mark Independence Day. If your dog goes to the parade with you, carry him in a backpack or keep him on a tight lead to protect him from being stepped on. At the picnic, your dog will no doubt want to taste all the goodies, from deviled eggs to hot dogs. Ignore his pleading eyes and ply him with healthy treats, such as carrots or bits of dog biscuit. At night, sparks fly and the sky is filled with the colorful flash and whizzing sounds of fireworks. The combination can frighten even the most self-possessed dogs, so be sure your dog is indoors or securely restrained during the show. This is the holiday when dogs, fearful of the strange noises, are most likely to run away.

Wee ghosties and goblins roam the streets in search of sweet treats at Halloween. The costumed visitors may alarm your dog, who will sound a long, loud warning whenever they come to the door. If the stress of these unearthly visitors sets your dog to trembling, confine him to a room in which he can rest in peace rather than go to pieces. Some dogs enjoy the fun, though, and will even get in the Halloween spirit by allowing themselves to be dressed in costume. As with Valentine's Day, keep the candy well out of reach.

The most famous feast of all is Thanksgiving. The smells of turkey and dressing wafting from the kitchen will set your dog to drooling, but such rich foods aren't good for his digestive system and can lead to vomiting or diarrhea. If you can't resist giving a bite, limit it to no more than a tablespoon of breast meat (dark meat is higher in fat) and forgo the gravy and dressing. Neither you nor your dog will be very thankful if he ends up at the emergency clinic with a case of pancreatitis, a serious inflammation of the pancreas, usually brought on by consumption of fatty table scraps or garbage, or by obesity.

Trees, ornaments, and decorative plants are holiday traditions, but all can be dangerous to your dog. For instance, chemicals you may put in the water to keep your tree fresh aren't good for your dog to drink. Make sure Buster doesn't have access to the tree stand. Consider putting the tree in a room that you can close off when you aren't around to supervise, or setting up a decorative but effective barrier around the tree. Tinsel is hazardous if swallowed, and electrical cords will attract dogs who like to chew. Wrap them up and put them out of the way to avoid a shocking experience. Mistletoe, holly, Jerusalem cherry, amaryllis, and other flowering bulbs can be toxic to dogs, so place these plants out of reach. A chewed poinsettia can irritate the lining of the mouth and intestines. By taking these precautions, you can ensure that your dog will enjoy the holidays along with the rest of the family.

be unafraid of animals and will run right up to Buster and try to pet him. Intercept the approach so you can control any interaction. Explain that Buster needs to be touched very gently, and hold the child's hand while she strokes him.

Making Your Dog a Good Neighbor

At one time or another, we've all known an obnoxious neighbor who never seemed to stop talking, expressing opinions in a voice you could heard three houses down. Perhaps this neighbor also scattered trash everywhere—cigarette butts, empty fast-food containers, and plastic wrap from picnics.

To ensure that your dog doesn't gain the reputation of neighborhood nuisance, introduce him to your neighbors so he'll know it's okay for them to come around. You'll want to ensure that his barking doesn't reach an annoying level and that you always pick up after him when you go on walks. Keep him confined to your yard so he doesn't eliminate in the neighbors' yard, overturn their trash, or dig up their gardens. When he interacts with neighbors, make sure he sits nicely instead of jumping up on them, biting their ankles, or tangling his leash around their legs. With good manners, Buster will be the most popular neighbor on the block.

Traveling with and Boarding Your Dog

Dogs are loving and convenient travel companions. They never complain about the length of the trip, and the amount of luggage they require is minimal. Some hotels, even luxury ones, cater to pet owners and welcome canine companions with open arms. Wherever you're going, you couldn't ask for a better comrade.

Making the Decision

Most dogs love outings, short or long, especially if they've been conditioned to trips during their puppyhood. When deciding whether to take your dog along, consider his previous experiences, his personality, and the purpose of your trip.

An outgoing dog who's used to running every errand with you will adore the experience of a long car trip or a stay in a hotel. This dog is open to adventures of all kinds, as long as she's with you. A dog who's more a stay-at-home type can find the same experience unnerving. What you'll be doing on the trip is another consideration. If you're traveling

> An outgoing dog who's used to running every errand with you will adore the experience of a long car trip or a stay in a hotel.

on business, your dog won't have much fun staying alone in the hotel room all day. He'd much prefer staying home this time and going with you for a relaxing vacation where you'll have plenty of time to devote to him.

Pros and Cons of Traveling and Boarding

Traveling with a small dog is much easier than with a larger dog. Most airlines permit small pets to travel in the cabin, and most hotels welcome small, well-behaved pets. While it can be difficult in a big city to find a grassy area for a large dog to eliminate, a small dog can make do with paper on the bathroom floor or a small patch of concrete or greenery.

On the other hand, unless you're traveling in France or another dog-loving European country, dogs are generally not welcome in shops, restaurants, museums, or on public transportation. You can sneak small, quiet dogs into many places, but be prepared to leave if you're discovered.

Consider leaving your dog in a boarding kennel or at home with a pet sitter if the trip you're taking won't allow you to spend much time with him, or if your destination would be unsafe for your dog or requires that he be quarantined for a long period, such as in England or Hawaii. Many boarding kennels provide daily play time and petting sessions, or even offer dog camp activities such as agility or other games. A live-in pet sitter allows your dog to stay in familiar territory, without the stress of encountering strange dogs and people.

Traveling with Your Dog

If you decide Buster will enjoy the trip you're taking, all you need to do is make the arrangements. He'll need his own plane reservation if you're flying, and you'll need to pack a bag that includes an appropriate food and treat supply, bottled water to prevent tummy upset, grooming supplies, medications such as heartworm preventive, a first-aid kit, and a favorite toy.

Your veterinarian can provide you with a health certificate, which you may be required to present at the airport or at any state or international border crossings. Even if you're traveling by car across state lines, it's a good idea to bring along a health certificate stating that your dog is current on his vaccinations, including rabies, and is free of any infectious disease.

Check international requirements far in advance to make sure pets are permitted entry. Some countries require quarantines of up to six months, and even the state of Hawaii has a four-month quarantine. If you plan to travel outside the

United States, either permanently or on vacation, your veterinarian can assist you in this process by contacting the United States Department of Agriculture at (310) 734-7517 to determine the requirements of a particular country or by accessing their Web site at www.aphis.usda.gov/oa/imex.html.

Before You Leave

If you are moving or traveling with your dog, obtain a temporary write-on tag with your new phone number or the phone number of a friend. Temporary tags are available at pet stores or from veterinarians or animal shelters. Should you move, provide your dog with an engraved ID tag that lists not only your new address and phone number but also a contact name and number for your previous neighborhood, in case your dog returns there. If your dog gets lost along the way, rescuers may not be able to reach you immediately at your new address. It is important to remember, if your dog does get away from you, to always check at your home (previous home, if moving) no matter how great the distance may be. There are many documented cases of dogs travelling hundreds of miles to get back "home."

Traveling by Air

A small dog can travel in comfort and style in a soft-sided carrier. Choose one that permits the dog to stand up and turn around inside it and will fit beneath the airplane seat, where it must be stowed during flight. Most airlines permit these soft-sided carriers, some of which come with such amenities as wheels, pockets in which to store documentation, and side flaps that can be rolled up or down to give your dog a view or privacy.

Not just any old tote bag will do; the bag must be approved by airlines for

Did You Know?

Chinese royalty considered their Pekingese dogs to be sacred and provided them with human wet nurses, servants, and guards to protect them from other dogs.

carry-on use. These bags are available at pet supply stores or through catalogs. Look for such features as mesh panels with roll-up flaps, top and front zippers for easy placement and removal of the dog, a zippered end pocket, an adjustable shoulder strap that doubles as a leash, and a coordinating accessory bag to carry such items as medication or plastic bags for scooping poop. The bag should wipe clean in case your dog has an accident inside it.

Another compact carry-on crate is made of plastic with a wire top and sliding door. The wire top makes it easy for owner and dog to make eye contact during the flight, which can be frightening for a dog making his first plane trip.

Larger dogs are required to travel in the cargo bay, which is stressful given the noise, turbulence, and possibility of other luggage falling on the crate. High-quality plastic airline crates are the only kind in which dogs can be shipped. Most airlines do not carry dogs when temperatures exceed or fall below certain limits, so plan your trip carefully. Try to schedule your dog on a nonstop flight so the chance of loss or misdirection is minimized.

The American Humane Society recommends against tranquilizing pets for flights. Sedation alters an animal's natural ability to balance and maintain equilibrium, and increased altitude can create respiratory and cardiovascular problems for sedated animals.

Limit food and water intake for several hours before the flight to lessen the chance your dog will become airsick. Let your dog lick an ice cube or two in flight to alleviate his thirst, and give him a few bites of kibble if he seems to be calm and enjoying the trip.

The American Humane Society recommends against tranquilizing pets for flights. Sedation alters an animal's natural ability to balance and maintain equilibrium, and increased altitude can create respiratory and cardiovascular problems for sedated animals. If your dog is so nervous that you believe sedation is necessary, it may be best for him not to fly at all.

Traveling by Car

The image of a dog with his head sticking out the car window, ears flapping in the wind and tongue hanging out, is irresistible; but a moving car is not a safe place for a free-roaming dog. Your dog should ride in a crate, which will keep him in snug comfort and prevent him from getting underfoot, jumping in the driver's lap, or being tossed out of the car in the event of a wreck. If a crate isn't practical, restrain Buster with a specially made dog seatbelt or a carseat that will give him a view while still keeping him in one place.

Before embarking on any long trip, exercise your dog well and allow him sufficient time to eliminate. Even if your dog doesn't usually get carsick, it's a good idea to withhold food for two to three hours before leaving. You can offer small amounts of water each time you make a rest stop. Schedule a break every couple of hours so both of you can stretch your legs and use the facilities. Some rest stops have designated potty areas for dogs, which you should be sure to use. Pick up waste with a plastic bag or poop scoop and dispose of it in a trash can.

Keep your dog on leash at rest stops, for his own safety and for the peace of mind of others around you. Just because you love your dog doesn't mean other people do. Conversely, don't run the risk of theft by leaving him unattended in an unlocked car. Wherever you go, Buster should be wearing a collar and identification tags. You'd be surprised at the number of dogs who get away from their owners for one reason or another and are lost forever because they lacked identification.

Hotels and Campgrounds

The number-one piece of advice about staying at a hotel or camp-ground is to call ahead to make sure dogs are permitted. If the answer is no, offer to pay a deposit—the usual amount is $25 or $50—or to provide proof of Buster's good behavior, such as his CGC or CD certificates.

If the answer is yes, be sure you and Buster are on your best behavior. Don't permit barking, put a cover on hotel bedspreads to protect them from dog hair, and pick up after him wherever he eliminates.

Most hotels prefer that you not leave your dog alone in the room. If you must, however, confine Buster to a crate so he won't have an accident or escape when the cleaning people come in.

At campgrounds, the same rules of good behavior apply. Keep Buster quiet, don't let him foul the grounds or eliminate near streams or other bodies of water, and keep him on leash to pro-tect him from wildlife—and vice versa.

Boarding Your Dog

You'll want to choose a boarding kennel just as carefully as you would a veterinarian. Ask for referrals from friends or your vet-erinarian. If the breeder from whom you bought Buster lives nearby, ask if she offers boarding services. Many breeders do, and it's ideal if you can leave Buster with people and dogs who are fa-miliar to him.

Before You Board   If leaving Buster with his breeder isn't feasi-ble, start checking out places other people suggest. You'll want to inspect them in person to satisfy yourself as to cleanliness, handling of dogs, and the competency of the staff. You won't want to leave Buster in any but the most loving and trustworthy of hands. By making an appropriate choice, you can help make the time the two of you are apart less stressful.

Look for easy-clean concrete floors, large runs—even a toy Poodle needs space to play—and clean grounds. Some odor is natural, given the presence of many dogs, but feces should be picked up unless they've only been recently "delivered." If you do see stools, check to see if they're well formed—an indication that the dogs staying there are eating a high-quality food and aren't unduly stressed.

Key Considerations in Boarding   See whether the kennel has a grassy play area where dogs can exercise. Ask how many dogs are let out at a time and whether an effort is made to segregate them by size. Many kennels offer camp-style games or will provide your dog with a set amount of one-on-one attention and petting each day. These services may or may not be included in the daily boarding cost. Be sure you understand what's covered and what's not.

Find out whether the kennel is an accredited member of the American Boarding Kennel Association. Accreditation ensures that a kennel meets certain standards for operation and cleanliness. This doesn't mean that an unaccredited kennel will never be a worthy place to leave your dog, but accreditation is a factor that will help you make an informed decision.

Did You Know?

In Homer's <u>The Odyssey</u>, the only one to recognize Odysseus when he arrived home disguised as a beggar after a 20-year absence was his dog Argos, who wagged his tail at his master and then died.

Ask how the boarding facility handles illnesses or emergencies. Do they have a veterinarian on staff, or one on call? Always leave an emergency number where you can be reached, the number of your own veterinarian, and the number of a trusted friend to whom you have given permission to make decisions about your dog's health and well-being.

Does the kennel offer pickup and delivery service? This can be a great convenience and a crucial time saver when you're in the process of packing up, getting your car ready, and doing the many other tasks necessary to leave town on a trip. As helpful as a pickup service can be when you're preparing to leave, it's even more wonderful to have your dog delivered when you return from a tiring trip.

Find out what diet the kennel operators feed. You may prefer to bring your own food supply so as not to disrupt Buster's eating habits. Provide written instructions on how much Buster should eat and what types of treats—and how many—he's permitted.

Does the boarding facility provide a climate-controlled environment? This is especially important for small breeds or inside dogs who are used to the comforts of home such as air-conditioning.

Note the design of the dog runs. Raised runs are easier to clean and drain. Some kennels have runs of different sizes to accommodate the needs of different-size dogs.

If you have more than one dog, you may want them to be boarded together in the same kennel. Make sure this is allowed before you schedule your dogs for a stay.

Ask how often dogs are exercised and for how long. Being able to get out of the run to eliminate and to  stretch his legs is in the dog's best interest. This is especially important for indoor dogs who will "hold it" for hours if necessary rather than soil their living quarters.

Expect to be asked to provide up-to-date vaccination records. Any kennel worth its salt will require proof that Buster has been inoculated for rabies, distemper, and parvo within the past year, and they may require a bordetella vaccination within the past six months. The kennel operator will also check to see whether Buster is flea-free and may require him to have a bath—at extra expense—if he's not.

Ask whether the kennel provides grooming services. Even in the cleanest boarding facilities, dogs can acquire a "kennel" odor, especially after an extended stay. Some kennels provide a complimentary bath if the dog stays for a certain number of nights. If a complimentary bath isn't offered, you may choose to have your dog bathed before picking him up. If grooming services are provided, just before he returns home is often a wonderful and convenient time to have this taken care of.

If the boarding facility is associated with a veterinarian's office, make sure sick and hospitalized dogs are kept separately from those who are simply boarding. This is a vital consideration in the prevention and spread of contagious diseases.

If your dog is on medication, make sure the medication can and will be administered at the proper times. This is especially important for dogs with diabetes, heart conditions, and seizures. Be sure to bring enough medication for the entire stay. Some kennels have an additional charge for administering medication.

Make sure the kennel is staffed 24 hours a day, seven days a week. This is a must for Buster's safety. In case of fire or other emergency, someone needs to be there to handle the situation. Nevertheless, don't expect to be able to drop Buster off or pick him up at any time of the day or night. Just like any other business, kennels have specific hours during which they do business. Ideally, weekend or Sunday pickups are available, potentially saving you the cost of an additional night's stay.

Expect the kennel manager to answer your questions openly and readily. A surly attitude or an unwillingness to answer questions is a red flag. Turn right around and leave. There are bound to be better options for your dog.

When you find the right place, be sure to make boarding reservations early, especially during the holidays and summertime, when boarding kennels fill up weeks and sometimes months in advance.

Hiring a Pet Sitter

The advantages of a live-in pet sitter are many. Buster gets to stay in his own familiar home, with all its comforting scents and toys, plus he'll have someone to keep him company while you're gone. A pet sitter eliminates the stress of staying in a strange place and limits your dog's exposure to parasites or disease carried by other dogs. A live-in pet sitter is an especially good option for older or smaller, nervous dogs who are easily upset by a lot of noise and activity, which is commonplace at boarding kennels. (Many pet sitters also bring in mail and newspapers and water plants!)

> A live-in pet sitter is an especially good option for older or smaller, nervous dogs who are easily upset by a lot of noise and activity, which is commonplace at boarding kennels.

Think carefully before asking a friend or neighbor to take on pet-sitting duties. (Nice people who mean well are not necessarily capable sitters!) Proper care takes time, planning, and some expertise and experience. Often friends agree to take on the responsibility but have no idea what's actually required. Unless you have a fenced yard, your dog must be walked on leash and fed and taken out to potty on a regular schedule. It's not unusual for friends or neighbors to have problems attempting to care for a dog, so instead consider getting the services of a professional, who is trained to administer oral or injectable medications, better equipped to notice signs of illness, and accustomed to handling dogs.

As with any service, word of mouth is a good way to start the search for a pet sitter. Ask friends for recommendations. Your veterinarian may have veterinary technicians on staff who moonlight as pet sitters. Once you have some names, schedule personal interviews in your home so you can see how well they get along with Buster and what he thinks of them.

Ask the following questions when you're interviewing the pet sitter:

○ *Are you bonded? Do you carry commercial liability insurance?* A positive answer to these questions indicates that the pet sitter takes the job seriously. Expect the pet sitter to show you proof of bonding and insurance.

○ *Are you a member of a professional organization, such as the National Association of Professional Pet Sitters?* Like bonding and insurance, professional membership indicates that a pet sitter isn't just an animal lover hoping to make a little extra money; he or she has met exacting professional standards.

○ *What is your background in pet care?* Some pet sitters are veterinary technicians, while others are experienced pet owners. If your dog has a medical problem, you may prefer someone who's trained to spot health problems or who is experienced at giving medication or insulin injections.

○ *Can you provide references?* A good pet sitter should be more than willing to give you the names of other satisfied clients. Don't be afraid to call them and ask about their experience with the pet sitter.

Leaving a List for the Dog Sitter or Boarding Kennel

Even though you are satisfied with the pet sitter's or boarding kennel's credentials and have explained everything thoroughly, leaving behind written instructions will help set your mind at ease. In them, you can detail feeding and medication instructions, exercise and elimination requirements, and favorite pastimes. Consider including some or all of the following information:

- ○ Feeding/medication times
- ○ Amount of medication
- ○ Amount of food
- ○ Favorite toys/games
- ○ Commands dog knows
- ○ "Secret" passwords to get the dog to eat or potty
- ○ Favorite hiding places
- ○ Name and phone number of where you'll be
- ○ Airline, flight numbers, and departure/arrival times
- ○ Who to contact in case of emergency
- ○ Veterinarian's name, address, and phone number
- ○ Directions to nearest animal emergency hospital
- ○ Permission for the pet sitter to authorize treatment and guarantee of payment
- ○ Pet's guardians in case something happens to you

○ *What are your prices?* The pet sitter should give you a brochure or other written material that details prices and services. He or she may ask you to sign a contract that spells out exactly what will be done. This protects both of you from misunderstanding.

○ *Who will take care of my pet if something happens to you?* The pet sitter should have a partner or some sort of contingency plan in the event of a personal emergency.

If you're satisfied with the pet sitter's replies, set up an appointment a few days before your trip so you can explain Buster's routine and show him or her where food, toys, and other necessities are kept.

By making your dog an integral part of your family life, through training, exercise, play, and travel, you will build a special bond with him. With a strong bond you create a companion that will be loyal to you and a joy to live and travel with.

Did You Know?

The saying "three dog night" is attributed to Australian Aborigines, who would sleep with three dogs (dingos, actually) to keep from freezing on cold nights

9

A Lifetime of Love and Good Health

In This Chapter

❍ Your Aging Dog—What to Expect
❍ How to Keep Your Older Dog Comfortable
❍ Saying Goodbye

A dog's life is never long enough for those of us who love him, but barring disease or trauma, you can usually expect your dog to live to 10 or 12 years of age. Giant breeds generally have shorter life spans—a brief seven or eight years—while toy breeds have been known to live well into their teens. Older dogs have different veterinary and nutritional needs and can benefit from specialized care, health testing and dietary planning. The following tips will help you keep your senior dog in good shape over the years. If your dog has good genes and excellent care, you can be sure that his life will be a long and happy one.

Dogs start entering their golden years at about age seven, earlier for giant breeds. Your dog will probably start to slow down, and the aches and pains of age are unavoidable. His joints may be a bit creakier, and he probably won't tear through the house at his old rate of speed, moving instead at a more dignified pace. Dental problems may surface or become worse. The questions below will help you recognize the signs of aging and take appropriate steps. Diseases associated with aging are more easily identified if you report small changes in appearance and behavior to your veterinarian or if you take your dog in for checkups more than once a year. Remember that dogs age five to seven years for every chronological year, so problems can develop more quickly.

> Dogs start entering their golden years at about age seven, earlier for giant breeds.

Your Aging Dog—What to Expect

To determine whether your dog is beginning to show signs of age, ask yourself these questions:

○ *Has your dog gained or lost weight recently?* Weight control is extremely important in dogs, especially as they age. A fat dog is more prone to disease, especially diabetes, arthritis, or congestive heart failure. To keep your dog's weight at a normal range, limit the number of calories he consumes by switching him to a lower-calorie food, feeding him several small meals each day instead of one big meal, or increasing the amount of exercise he gets. If weight gain or loss is enough for you to notice, there may be something wrong. If your dog is eating well but losing weight, he may have developed diabetes. Weight loss can also be an early warning sign of cancer.

○ *Is your dog drinking more water than usual?* Excessive thirst can be a sign of diabetes or kidney disease.

○ *Has your dog's appetite changed?* Is he picky or does he act hungry all the time? If your dog is picking at his food, his teeth may hurt. You may need to moisten his dry food or switch to a canned food. Lack of appetite or an excessive appetite can also be a sign of disease.

○ *Has your dog's stool changed in any way?* Is the stool dry, soft, or bloody? Is the color different? Does your dog strain to defecate? Straining to defecate or producing a hard, dry stool may mean your dog is constipated. The opposite condition—a loose or liquid stool—can be a sign of intestinal disease.

○ *Does your dog have bleeding gums, loose or broken teeth, or bad breath?* Just like people, dogs can get periodontal disease, which can affect their ability to eat as well as lead to serious infections of the heart or other organs.

○ *Has the condition of your dog's skin changed?* Is it dry, dull, or flaky? Has it developed bald patches? Poor skin condition can indicate nutritional deficiencies, hormonal diseases, allergies, or parasites.

○ *Do you notice a change in your dog's energy level?* Lack of energy can signify problems such as anemia or cancer.

○ *Is your dog urinating more frequently, or urinating inside the house?* Frequent urination often goes hand in hand with excessive thirst. It can indicate a bladder or kidney infection or diabetes.

Some of these signs indicate a need for a veterinary exam so that problems causing the changes can be stopped before they become serious. If you answer yes to one or more of these, schedule a geriatric exam for your dog. Or even better, schedule a geriatric exam *before* you see any of these problems to establish a basis for comparison if your dog later becomes ill. Besides a physical exam to check for stiffness, heart murmurs, bad breath, skin lesions, and other typical signs of aging, a geriatric exam usually includes blood work or other diagnostic tests to determine the status of your dog's organ function and body chemistry. Regular blood testing can help identify diseases in their earliest and most treatable stages. Your veterinarian may also ask if you've seen signs of disorientation or other behavioral changes and may recommend lifestyle changes such as a different diet, an increase in exercise, or minimizing stress by creating a more stable routine.

How to Keep Your Older Dog Comfortable

No doubt your dog has been living in comfort all his life, but you can still do extra things to make life easier for him as he ages. Here are a few suggestions:

○ *Make sure his bedding is extra comfy.* Those old bones need warmth and cushioning more than ever. If your dog doesn't already have a heated bed, consider purchasing one to keep the shivers away. Heated beds are sometimes available at pet stores but are most often found in pet supply catalogs or through Internet pet suppliers (do a search for dog beds). Choose a bed that comes with safety features to prevent overheating (most do).

When Lulu, a Miniature Pinscher, turned 10 years old, her people noticed that the pampered senior citizen was sleeping more than she used to. Lulu had always loved the sunshine, so her owners made it a habit to move her lambswool sleeping pad to various areas of the house throught the day so that Lulu would always be able to warm her aching joints in the healing rays of the sun.

○ *Make it easier for him to get up on the furniture, if that's allowed.* Provide a stepstool or ramp up to the sofa or bed so he doesn't have to leap quite so high. (Assist your dog getting in and out of the car, too.) Giving him a step up will also lessen the likelihood of a broken bone from a fall.

○ *Give him plenty of opportunities to go out to eliminate.* The aging bladder doesn't have the holding capacity of its younger years, so spare your dog the embarrassment of having an accident in the house. Take him out several times a day or put down papers in the house.

○ *Provide mental and physical stimulation.* Just because your dog is old doesn't mean he won't still enjoy a fun game or a short walk. Exercise maintains muscle tone, enhances circulation, promotes digestion, and helps maintain proper weight. Reduce your pace a little so Buster doesn't have to strain to keep up.

Molly, a 13-year old Shetland Sheepdog, began limping a few years ago and had trouble negotiating the stairs. Her owners took her to the veterinarian, who prescribed a pain reliever that had her feeling better in no time. Nevertheless, she has slowed down quite a bit, but her owners

Did You Know?

The old rule of multiplying a dog's age by seven to find the equivalent human age is inaccurate. A better measure is to count the first year as 15, the second year as 10, and each year after that as 5.

make sure she still gets a brief period of exercise every day. They are also more likely to leave her at home instead of taking her on day trips, because the exertion and excitement of going out can leave her exhausted for the next day or so.

○ *Keep brushing those teeth.* Dental disease is the scourge of the old dog. You don't want your dog to have to gum his food.

Age-Related Disorders

As dogs get older, they are more prone to disease; but when problems are caught early, they can often be successfully treated, ensuring your dog a long and comfortable life. Among the commonly seen problems of middle-aged and older dogs are arthritis, cancer, cognitive dysfunction syndrome, dental disease, hypothyroidism, heart disease, hearing and vision loss, and kidney disease.

A diagnosis of cancer used to be considered a death warrant, but today it can often be successfully treated if caught in time.

Cancer occurs when cells grow uncontrollably on or inside the body. These uncontrolled growths may remain in a single area or spread to other parts of the body. Most forms of cancer are diagnosed through a biopsy, the removal and examination of a section of tissue. Blood tests, x-rays, and physical signs can also indicate cancer. Among the types of cancer that are commonly seen in dogs

are skin tumors, breast cancer, testicular cancer, cancers of the mouth or nose, and lymphoma. Lots of older dogs develop lumps and bumps on or beneath their skin. Fortunately, these growths are usually harmless, but they should always be checked out by your veterinarian when you notice them. Be concerned if the tumor increases in size or changes in color or texture.

Signs of Cancer

The signs listed below don't always mean cancer. Some of them are just part of getting old, but they should be checked out any time you notice them. Whatever your dog's health problem, early detection promises a much better chance of treatment and recovery. Don't ignore any of these potential cancer signs:

○ Abnormal swellings that persist or continue to grow

○ Sores that don't heal

○ Unusual or excessive weight loss

○ Extended lack of appetite

○ Bleeding or discharge from any body opening

○ Offensive odor

○ Difficulty eating or swallowing

○ Hesitation to exercise or loss of stamina

○ Persistent lameness or stiffness

○ Difficulty breathing, urinating, or defecating

Half of all breast tumors in dogs are malignant, but spaying your dog before her first heat will greatly reduce the risk of breast cancer. Breast tumors are usually removed surgically.

Testicular tumors are common in dogs, and dogs with retained testicles (testicals that have not descended) may be especially prone to them. Testicular tumors are removed surgically and can be prevented altogether with neutering.

Signs of mouth cancer are a mass on the gums, bleeding gums, bad breath, or difficulty eating. Bleeding from the nose, difficulty breathing, or facial swelling may indicate nasal cancer. Early, aggressive treatment is important for these types of cancer, so don't delay a veterinary visit if your dog exhibits these signs.

Lymphoma is characterized by enlargement of one or more lymph nodes. This type of cancer is usually treated with chemotherapy, which has a good rate of effectiveness. Fortunately for dogs, they don't suffer the same side effects from chemotherapy as people; there's no nausea or hair loss, although the dog may be tired for a few days afterward.

Arthritis is a painful degenerative joint disease that commonly affects dogs seven years or older. It's a progressive condition that may start out with subtle signs such as decreased activity or lagging behind on walks and progress to more obvious ones: reluctance to run, jump, or climb stairs; stiffness; soreness when touched; and behavioral changes such as aggression or withdrawal. Weight loss can help relieve stress on joints, and new medications are available to relieve the pain and inflammation caused by osteoarthritis. These medications are generally safe for long-term use, but be aware of possible side effects involving the digestive system, kidneys, or liver.

A newly recognized disorder in dogs is called cognitive dysfunction syndrome. It's any age-related mental decline that can't be attributed to a condition such as a tumor, organ failure, or hearing or vision loss. Signs of CDS are disorientation or confusion, such as aimless wandering, staring into space, or seeming lost in the house; fewer or less enthusiastic interactions with family members; changes in sleep and activity patterns, such as sleeping more during the day or pacing the house in the middle of the night; and breaking housetraining.

English Cocker Spaniel Holly, who was 10 years old when she was diagnosed with CDS, showed many of these symptoms. Her owner would go out looking for Holly in the backyard and find her sitting under a bush, looking as if she didn't know where she was. At breakfast time, Holly would sit in a corner and whine until a family member showed her where her dish was. Holly's veterinarian diagnosed CDS and placed her on medication that helped return the dog to her former happy self.

If your dog shows signs of CDS, talk to your veterinarian. He can prescribe medication that can help. Possible side effects to watch for are vomiting, diarrhea, hyperactivity, or restlessness.

Dental disease is a serious problem in most older dogs. Signs of dental disease are bad breath, a buildup of brown plaque on the teeth, and inflammation of the gums. Left untreated, the mouth becomes a breeding ground for bacteria, which enter the bloodstream and can go on to infect organs such as the heart or kidneys. Keep your dog's mouth healthy by brushing his teeth regularly, providing chew toys and hard biscuits to help remove plaque, and taking him in for an annual veterinary cleaning. After a cleaning, your veterinarian may prescribe a course of antibiotics to help prevent bacterial infections.

Hypothyroidism is the underproduction of thyroid hormones T3 and T4 and is a common hormonal disorder in all dogs. A decrease in thyroid function usually occurs because of damage to or destruction of the thyroid gland. Potential causes of such damage are cancer or immune-mediated inflammation of the thyroid gland. Hypothyroidism can also be congenital, meaning it has existed since birth.

Dogs with hypothyroidism often seem low on energy or mentally lethargic. They may gain weight, even though they aren't eating more, or develop a dull, dry coat. Other signs of hypothyroidism include a darkening of skin pigmentation, hair loss or scaly skin. Your veterinarian can diagnose it with a blood test.

Did You Know?

The oldest dog ever documented was an Australian Cattle Dog named Bluey, who was put to sleep at the age of 29 years and 5 months.

In many breeds, hypothyroidism doesn't develop until middle age or the geriatric years, but in others it can occur at a fairly young age. Dogs with hypothyroidism are treated with synthetic thyroid hormone, which is usually given in pill form twice daily. The medication must continue for the rest of the dog's life.

Hearing Loss

We often accuse dogs of having selective hearing, but as they age their ability to hear does indeed decrease. They aren't just faking it when they don't hear you call them to come in. To test whether your dog's sense of hearing has declined, stand behind him and clap your hands. If he doesn't respond, he may have suffered some hearing loss.

Deafness can result from a history of ear infections or simply from degeneration of the sound receptors in the ear. Your veterinarian should examine the dog to make sure his problem isn't related to an ear infection or neurologic disease.

> We often accuse dogs of having selective hearing, but as they age their ability to hear does indeed decrease.

Deaf dogs usually adjust to their conditions by making better use of their other senses. You can communicate with a deaf dog by using hand signals instead of verbal commands. When you approach him, be sure he sees you or feels the vibrations from your footsteps so you don't startle him into biting.

Loss of Vision

One of the most visible signs of aging in dogs is called nuclear sclerosis, a condition in which the nucleus, or center, of the lens becomes a hazy gray color. Nuclear sclerosis eventually occurs in all old dogs, but it doesn't affect their vision significantly.

Another eye condition associated with old age is cataracts, an opacity of the lens. Cataracts are common in dogs and cause gradual loss of vision. Every case is different, but many times cataracts can be surgically removed by a veterinary ophthalmologist. If that's not possible or cost-effective, be aware that most dogs learn to adapt to sightlessness without much problem, especially if they're in a familiar environment. Rearranging the furniture might cause a slight problem, but dogs are good at using their sense of smell to navigate, and you can help him learn

> Visually impaired dogs are sometimes fearful of going down stairs. It may be necessary to keep them on the ground floor only or to carry them downstairs.

the new arrangement by guiding him around the room. Another tip is to scent the furniture with perfume at the dog's nose level so he can use the smell as a "map." Visually impaired dogs are sometimes fearful of going down stairs. It may be necessary to keep them on the ground floor only or to carry them downstairs. When Jerry's Greyhound, Savanna, lost her eyesight, he and his wife took turns carrying the 45-pound dog up and down the stairs of their second-floor condominium several times a day. It was a great biceps-builder for both of them.

Kidney Disease and Kidney Failure

Kidney function can gradually deteriorate with age, but if it's identified it can be managed through diet and sometimes medication. It's a good idea to make routine screening tests for kidney function part of your older dog's annual exam, particularly if his water consumption appears to have increased. If your dog develops kidney disease, your veterinarian will probably prescribe a low-protein diet that won't overwork the kidneys. That doesn't mean, however, that you should automatically give an old dog a low-protein diet. If the kidney function of a normal, healthy old dog is still good, reduction of protein levels won't prevent the development of kidney disease.

Kidney failure is the loss of 65 percent or more of the functional tissue in both kidneys. Chronic kidney failure occurs in approximately one-half of one percent of pet dogs in the United States, about 265,000 dogs annually, so it's certainly of concern to dog owners and veterinarians. The signs of kidney failure are subtle to nonexistent in the beginning, when it can best be managed, so regular testing to detect the buildup of nitrogen wastes in the blood can help you and the veterinarian keep tabs on your dog's condition and institute treatment before the problem gets serious. Later signs of failure are greater than normal intake of water and output of urine. The dog may begin to have accidents in the house or be unable to hold his urine through the night.

If kidney failure isn't detected and continues to progress, the dog will become depressed, lose his appetite, and develop a dry hair coat and an ammonialike odor to his breath.

Like kidney disease, chronic kidney failure can be managed with a protein-restricted diet. A change in diet can slow the progression of the disease.

Prostate disease isn't limited to men; it also occurs in unneutered male dogs. The prostate gland, which plays a role in semen production, surrounds the neck of the bladder. With age, it can gradually become enlarged and more susceptible to infection or structural abnormalities.

Signs of prostate disease are a bloody discharge from the tip of the penis, difficulty passing feces, and feces that are smaller than normal in diameter. Your veterinarian may prescribe antibiotics and in some cases will recommend neutering after the infection is eliminated.

Many large and giant breeds have a high incidence of cardiomyopathy, or enlargement of the heart. The cause of cardiomyopathy is unknown, but veterinary researchers believe it is a genetic problem. Cardiomyopathy is difficult to detect unless the dog receives a cardiac ultrasound exam, but if diagnosed in its early stages, it can be controlled for a time with medication.

Saying Goodbye

Few things in this life are more difficult than losing a beloved pet. It's grievous when human friends or relatives die, but rarely do we make the decision that it's time for them to go. As caring pet owners, though, that's often what we must do for our animals. As much as we'll miss them, it's not fair to extend their lives when they are in pain or no longer find pleasure in their daily activities. A painless exit from their misery is the greatest gift we can offer.

> ## Did You Know?
>
> The average life-span for a dog is 12 years.

How to Know When to Let Go

It's never easy to decide when to end your best friend's time on this Earth. The decision is made for some lucky owners, whose dogs die peacefully in their sleep. Unfortunately for the rest of us, a time may come when we'll each have to decide when our dog's life is no longer worth living. This is an extremely personal decision that you and you alone must make.

What to Expect

When you decide it is time to alleviate your dog's suffering, call your vet. Some vets will make house calls for euthanasia, whereas others will ask you to bring in your dog. Make sure the clinic staff knows the reason for your visit. Most veterinary practices will let you move immediately into an exam room upon your arrival, where you can be alone with your pet, rather than spending your last moments together in a crowded waiting room.

Your vet will describe the procedure to you and will answer any questions you have. Don't feel you need to hold back your tears. Your vet realizes what a difficult time this is and will understand the flood of emotions that comes with the death of a beloved pet. Talk to your dog. Stroke her head and tell her how much you love her. We don't know what animals can understand in a situation like this, but your pet surely will feel comforted by your soothing voice and your presence.

If you feel you absolutely cannot be in the room with your dog during her last moments, don't feel guilty. Each person handles saying good-bye to a pet differently. There is no right or wrong way to face death. Know that your need to distance yourself from your dog's final passing will not wipe away or diminish years of loving care.

At that point, your vet may sedate your pet. He or she then will inject a drug into your dog's blood stream that causes unconsciousness and heart failure. Your dog may appear to gasp for breath and may lose control of her bladder. Remember, these are reactions to the drug—your dog will experience no pain.

Remembering Your Pet

Once you say good-bye, you can ask your veterinarian to take care of your dog's remains. Other owners ask to have their dogs cremated and request the ashes. A burial, either in your backyard (if local ordinances allow) or in a pet cemetery, is another option. For some, a favorite toy buried under a backyard tree provides the perfect memorial, while others choose to give a donation to an animal charity in their dog's honor. Whichever you choose, make sure you do what feels right for you and your family. The most important thing to remember is that emotional pain and grief are natural and must be experienced before the healing can begin.

Stages of Grief

Right after you lose your pet, you'll probably feel numbness, which often accompanies shock and denial. This first stage usually lasts longer for those whose pet's death was unexpected. The death of a senior dog that seemed fine one day, then rapidly declined, may leave his owner feeling like this couldn't possibly have happened.

During the middle stage of grief, you'll likely be filled with depression and anger. You may wake up in the morning expecting to find your dog at your feet,

> The most positive way of coping with a dog's death is to celebrate his life. Concentrate on what was wonderful about your dog, the special moments you shared, and the ways in which you enriched each others' lives.

only to be hit with a rush of emotion as you remember your dog is no longer with you. You may feel guilty for not trying an experimental procedure, or you may feel angry with the veterinarian for not being able to cure your dog. You may find it difficult to make

Veterinary Teaching Hospital Grief Hotlines

○ University of California, Davis, California, (916) 752-4200, 6:30–9:30 P.M. PST, Monday through Friday

○ Colorado State University, Fort Collins, Colorado, (970) 491-1242

○ University of Florida, Gainesville, Florida, (352) 392-4700 (ext. 4080); takes messages 24 hours a day; someone will call back between 7:00 and 9:00 P.M. EST

○ Michigan State University, East Lansing, Michigan, (517) 432-2696, 6:30–9:30 P.M. EST, Tuesday, Wednesday and Thursday

○ Ohio State University, Columbus, Ohio, (614) 292-1823; takes messages 6:30–9:30 P.M. EST, Monday, Wednesday and Friday

○ University of Pennsylvania, Philadelphia, Pennsylvania, (215) 898-4529

○ Tufts University, North Grafton, Massachusetts, (508) 839-7966, 6:00–9:00 P.M. EST, Monday through Friday

○ Virginia-Maryland Regional College of Veterinary Medicine, Blacksburg, Virginia, (540) 231-8038, 6:00–9:00 P.M. EST, Tuesday and Thursday

○ Washington State University, Pullman, Washington, (509) 335-4569

it through the day without crying, and you may have a hard time concentrating at work. It is important at this time to surround yourself with other pet lovers who will understand your grief and not criticize, wondering how you could be so upset over the death of an animal.

The final stage of grief is acceptance. At that point, you'll believe and understand the death of your pet, and the pain may begin to fade. Still, a tug at your heart may continue to accompany memories of your beloved dog.

If you experience difficulty reaching this final stage, you may need to seek outside help. Several veterinary schools across the nation offer grief-counseling hotlines. You also can check with your veterinarian for the numbers of local pet-loss counseling services, which humane societies often offer. Books and Internet sites on dealing with the death of a pet can also offer some solace.

Now is the time to leave the guilt and the negative experiences behind. Celebrate what was, and soon maybe you'll be ready to invite a new canine companion into your home and into your heart. The most positive way of coping with a dog's death is to celebrate his life. Concentrate on what was wonderful about your dog, the special moments you shared, and the ways in which you enriched each others' life.

Appendix A: Age-Related Developmental Stages

Body System Age Developmental Stages

Eyes	Birth-13 days	Eyelids are closed, but puppies respond to a bright light with a blink reflex. This reflex disappears at 21 days likely due to development of accurate pupil control. Palpebral reflex is present at 3 days, becoming adult-like by 9 days.
	5-14 days	Menace reflex is present, but slow. Eyelids separate into upper and lower lids. Pupillary light responses are present within 24 hours after eyelids separate. Reflex lacrimation begins when eyelids separate. Corneal reflex is present after eyelids separate.
	3-4 weeks	Vision should be normal.
Ears	Birth-5 days	External ear canals are closed. Hearing is poor.
	10-14 days	External ear canals open(should be completely open by 17 days). For the first week after the ear canals are completely opened there is an abundance of desquamated cells and some oil droplets, which is normal as the ear canals remodel to the external environment.
Teeth	4-6 weeks	Deciduous incisors erupt, followed by deciduous canines.
	4-8 weeks	Deciduous premolars erupt.
Circulatory	Birth-4 weeks	Lower blood pressure, stroke volume and peripheral vascular resistance present. Increased heart rate (<220 bpm), cardiac output and central venous pressure present. Heart rhythm is regular sinus.
Respiratory	Birth-4 weeks	Respiratory rate is 15 to 35 breaths per minute.

Neuromuscular	Birth	Flexor dominance is present at birth, with extensor dominance starting as early as 1 day. Seal posture reflex can last up to 19 days. Sucking reflex is present, but disappears by 23 days. Anogenital reflex disappears between 23-39 days. Cutaneous pain perception is present, but withdrawal reflex is noticeable at about 7 days. Tonic neck reflexes are present until 3 weeks of age. Can raise head. Righting response is present. Myotatic reflexes are present at birth, but difficult to elicit in newborns. Panniculus reflex is present at birth.
	5 days	Nystagmus associated with rotatory stimulation appears at the end of the first week. Cross extensor reflex ends between 2-17 days—persistence of this reflex indicates upper motor neuron disease. Direct forelimb support of body weight.
	14-16 days	Puppies are crawling. Rear limb support of body weight.
	20 days	Puppies can sit and have reasonable control of distal phalanges.
	22 days	Puppies are walking normally. Vestibular nystagmus becomes adult-like.
	23-40 days	Puppies are climbing and have air righting response.
	3-4 weeks	Hemiwalking response, but may not be fully developed in rear limbs until 6 weeks old.
	6-8 weeks	Postural reactions are fully developed

Note: The time frame is an approximation for normal development, with variances occurring with some individuals.

Developmental chart provided courtesy of Johnny Hoskins, D.V.M., Ph.D.

Appendix B: Common Congenital Defects

Defect	Breeds
Epilepsy	Beagle, Belgian Shepherd, keeshond, collie, dachshund, poodle, German shepherd, setters, retrievers, spaniels
Cerebellar hypoplasia	Chow chow, Irish setter, wirehaired fox terrier
Narcolepsy-cataplexy	Beagle, dachshund, doberman pinscher, Labrador retriever, Saint Bernard
Myasthenia gravis	Jack Russell and smooth coated fox terriers, springer spaniel
X-Linked muscular dystrophy	Belgian shepherd, golden retriever, Irish terrier, rottweiler, Samoyed
Cryptorchidism	Boxer, cairn terrier, Chihuahua, dachshund, English bulldog, Maltese, miniature schnauzer, Pekingese, Pomeranian, Shetland sheepdog, toy and miniature poodles, Yorkshire terriers
True hermaphrodite	Many breeds
Stenotic nares	Brachycephalic breeds
Collapsing trachea	Brachycephalic and miniature breeds, (Chihuahua, Pomeranian, poodle)
Aortic stenosis	Boxer, German shepherd, German shorthaired pointer, golden retriever, Newfoundland
Patent ductus arteriosus (PDA)	Collie, German shepherd, Pomeranian, poodle, Shetland sheepdog
Persistent Right Aortic Arch (PRAA)	German shepherd, Irish setter
Pulmonic stenosis	Beagle, Chihuahua, English bulldog, fox terrier, miniature schnauzer, Samoyed
Tetralogy of Fallot	Keeshond
Ventricular septal defect	English bulldog
Umbilical hernia	Airedale terrier, basenji, Pekingese, pointer, Weimaraner
Inguinal hernia	Basenji, Basset hound, Cairn terrier, West Highland white terrier
Hip dysplasia	Mainly large/giant breeds, plus cocker spaniel, and Shetland sheepdog

Elbow dysplasia	Basset hound, bull mastiff, French bulldog, German shepherd, Great Dane, Great Pyrenees, Irish wolfhound, Labrador retriever, Newfoundland, Weimaraner
Panosteitis	Basset hound, German shepherd, and many other breeds
Luxating patella (knee cap)	Many toy breeds
Spina bifida	Beagle, English bulldog
Dwarfism	Alaskan malamute, Labrador retriever, Shetland sheepdog
Cleft palate/ cleft lip	Beagle, Brachycephalic breeds, cocker spaniel, dachshund, German shepherd, Labrador retriever, schnauzer, Shetland sheepdog
Meckel's diverticulum	Many breeds
Deafness	Akita, American Staffordshire terrier, Australian heeler and shepherd, Australian cattle dog, beagle, Boston terrier, boxer, border collie, bull terrier, Catahoula, cocker spaniel, collie, Dalmation, dappled dachshund, doberman pinscher, English setter and bulldog, foxhound, fox terrier, German shepherd, Great Dane, Great Pyrenees, Ibizan hound, Kuvasz, Maltese, poodle, Old English sheepdog, pappillon, pointer, Rhodesian ridgeback, rottweiler, Saint Bernard, Scottish and Sealyhan terriers, Shetland sheepdog, Walker American hound, West Highland white terrier
Cataracts	Afghan hound, Australian shepherd, beagle, Bedlington and Sealyham terriers, Boston terrier, Chesapeake Bay retriever, cocker spaniel, German shepherd, golden retriever, miniature schnauzer, Old English sheepdog, Siberian husky, Staffordshire terrier, standard poodle, Welsh springer spaniel
Ectropion	Basset hound, bloodhound, cocker spaniel, Saint Bernard
Entropion	Many breeds
Glaucoma	Alaskan malamute, basset hound, beagle, Bouvier des Flandres, cocker and English springer spaniels, poodle, Samoyed, wirehaired terrier
Trichiasis	Many dog breeds
von Willebrand's disease	Many dog breeds

Developmental chart provided courtesy of Johnny Hoskins, D.V.M., Ph.D.

Appendix C: Important Phone Numbers and Addresses _____

Boarding, Pet Sitting, Traveling

books

Dog Lover's Companion series
Guides on traveling with dogs
   for several states and cities
Foghorn Press
P.O. Box 2036
Santa Rosa, CA 95405-0036
(800) FOGHORN

Take Your Pet Too!: Fun Things to Do!,
   Heather MacLean Walters
M.C.E. Publishing
P.O. Box 84
Chester, NJ 07930-0084

Take Your Pet USA, Arthur Frank
Artco Publishing
12 Channel St.
Boston, MA 02210

*Traveling with Your Pet 1999: The AAA
   Petbook*, Greg Weeks, Editor
Guide to pet-friendly lodging in the
   U.S. and Canada

Vacationing With Your Pet!, Eileen
   Barish
Pet-Friendly Publications
P.O. Box 8459
Scottsdale, AZ 85252
(800) 496-2665

...other resources

The American Boarding Kennels
   Association
4575 Galley Road, Suite 400-A
Colorado Springs, CO 80915
(719) 591-1113
www.abka.com

Independent Pet and Animal
   Transportation Association
5521 Greenville Ave., Ste 104-310
Dallas, TX 75206
(903) 769-2267
www.ipata.com

National Association of
   Professional Pet Sitters
1200 G St. N.W., Suite 760
Washington, DC 20005
(800) 286-PETS
www.petsitters.org

Pet Sitters International
418 East King Street
King, NC 27021-9163
(336)-983-9222
www.petsit.com

Breed Information, Clubs, Registries

American Kennel Club
260 Madison Avenue
New York, NY 10016

(212) 696-8800
Customer Service: (919) 233-9767
www.akc.org/

Canadian Kennel Club
Commerce Park
89 Skyway Ave., Suite 100
Etobicoke, Ontario, Canada M9W 6R4
(416) 675-5511
www.ckc.ca

InfoPet
P.O. Box 716
Agoura Hills, CA 91376
(800) 858-0248

The Kennel Club
(British equivalent to the American
   Kennel Club)
1-5 Clarges Street
Piccadilly
London W1Y 8AB
ENGLAND
http://www.the-kennel-club.org.uk/

National Dog Registry
Box 116
Woodstock, NY 12498
(800) 637-3647
www.natldogregistry.com/

Tatoo-A-Pet
6571 S.W. 20th Court
Ft. Lauderdale, FL 33317
(800) 828-8667
www.tattoo-a-pet.com

United Kennel Club
100 East Kilgore Rd.
Kalamazoo, MI 49001-5598
(616) 343-9020
http://ukccdogs.com

Dog Publications

AKC Gazette and AKC Events
   Calendar
51 Madison Avenue
New York, NY 10010
Subscriptions: (919) 233-9767
www.akc.org/gazet.htm
www.akc.org/event.htm

ARK, quarterly newsletter of the American Rottweiler Club
Marilyn Piusz
339 County Highway 106
Johnston, N.Y. 12095

Direct Book Service
(800) 776-2665
www2.dogandcatbooks.com/directbook

Dog Fancy
P.O. Box 6050
Mission Viejo, CA 92690
(714) 855-8822
www.dogfancy.com/

Dog World
500 N. Dearborn, Suite 1100
Chicago, IL 60610
(312) 396-0600
www.dogworldmag.com/

Fun, Grooming, Obedience, Training

American Dog Trainers Network
www.inch.com/~dogs/index.html
(212) 727-7257

American Grooming Shop Association
(719) 570-7788

American Herding Breed Association
1548 Victoria Way

Pacifica, CA 94044
www.primenet.com/~joell/abba/main.htm

American Kennel Club (tracking,
   agility, obedience, herding)
Performance Events Dept.
5580 Centerview Drive
Raleigh, NC 27606
(919) 854-0199
www.akc.org/
American Pet Dog Trainers
P.O. Box 385
Davis, CA 95617
(800) PET-DOGS

Animal Behavior Society
Susan Foster
Department of Biology
Clark University
950 Main Street
Worcester, MA 01610-1477

Association of Pet Dog Trainers
P.O. Box 385
Davis, CA 95617
(800) PET-DOGS
www.apdt.com/

The Dog Agility Page
http://www.dogpatch.org/agility/
Grooming supplies

Pet Warehouse
P.O. Box 752138
Dayton, OH 45475-2138
(800) 443-1160

Intergroom
76 Carol Drive
Dedham, MA 02026
www.intergroom.com

National Association of Dog Obedience
   Instructors
729 Grapevine Highway, #369
Hurst, TX 76054-2085
http://www.nadoi.org/

National Dog Groomers Association of
   America
P.O. Box 101
Clark, PA 16113
(724) 962-2711

North American Dog Agility Council
HCR 2 Box 277
St. Maries, ID 83861
www.nadac.com

North American Flyball Association
1400 W. Devon Ave, #512
Chicago, IL 60660
(309) 688-9840
http://muskie.fishnet.com/~flyball/

United States Dog Agility
   Association, Inc.
P.O. Box 850955
Richardson, Texas 75085-0955
(972) 231-9700
www.usdaa.com/

United States Canine Combined
   Training Association
2755 Old Thompson Mill Road
Buford, GA 30519
(770) 932-8604
http://www.siriusweb.com/USCCTA/

Grief Hotlines

Chicago Veterinary Medical Association
(630) 603-3994

Cornell University
(607) 253-3932

Michigan State University
College of Veterinary Medicine
(517) 432-2696

Tufts University (Massachusetts)
School of Veterinary Medicine
(508) 839-7966

University of California, Davis
(530) 752-4200

University of Florida at Gainesville
College of Veterinary Medicine
(352) 392- 4700

Virginia-Maryland Regional College of
Veterinary Medicine
(540) 231-8038

Washington State University
College of Veterinary Medicine
(509) 335-5704

Humane Organizations and Rescue Groups

American Humane Association
63 Inverness Drive E
Englewood CO 80112-5117
(800) 227-4645
www.americanhumane.org

American Society for the Prevention of
Cruelty to Animals (ASPCA)
424 East 92nd Street
New York, NY 10128-6804
(212) 876-7700
www.aspca.org

Animal Protection Institute of America
P.O. Box 22505
Sacramento, CA 95822
(916) 731-5521

Humane Society of the United States
2100 L Street, NW
Washington, DC 20037
(301) 258-3072, (202) 452-1100
www.hsus.org/

Massachusetts Society for the
Prevention of Cruelty to Animals
350 South Huntington Avenue

Boston, MA 02130
(617) 522-7400
http://www.mspca.org/

SPAY/USA
14 Vanderventer Avenue
Port Washington, NY 11050
(516) 944-5025, (203) 377-1116 in
Connecticut
(800) 248-SPAY
www.spayusa.org/

Medical and Emergency Information

American Animal Hospital Association
P.O. Box 150899
Denver, CO 80215-0899
(800) 252-2242
www.healthypet.com

American Holistic Veterinary Medicine
Association
2214 Old Emmorton Road
Bel Air, MD 21015
(410) 569-2346

American Kennel Club Canine Health
Foundation
251 West Garfield Road, Suite 160
Aurora, OH 44202
(888) 682-9696
www.akcchf.org/main.htm

American Veterinary Medical
Association
1931 North Meacham Road, Suite 100
Schaumburg, IL 60173-4360
(847) 925-8070
http://www.avma.org/

Canine Eye Registration Foundation
(CERF)
Veterinary Medical Data Program
South Campus Courts, Building C

Purdue University
West Lafayette, IN 47907
(765) 494-8179
www.vet.purdue.edu/~yshen/cerf.html

Centers for Disease Control and
    Prevention
1600 Clifton Road NE
Atlanta, GA 30333
(404) 639-3311 (CEC Operator)
(800) 311-3435 (CEC Public Inquiries)
www.cdc.gov

Complementary and Alternative Veteri-
    nary Medicine
www.altvetmed.com

National Animal Poison Control Center
1717 S. Philo, Suite 36
Urbana, IL 61802
(888) 426 4435, $45 per case, with as
    many follow-up calls as necessary in-
    cluded. Have name, address, phone
    number, dog's breed, age, sex, and type
    of poison ingested, if known, available
www.napcc.aspca.org

Orthopedic Foundation for Animals
    (OFA)
2300 E. Nifong Blvd.
Columbia, MO 65201-3856.
(573) 442-0418
www.offa.org/

PennHIP
c/o Synbiotics
11011 Via Frontera
San Diego, CA 92127
(800) 228-4305

Pet First Aid: Cats and Dogs, by Bobbi
    Mammato, D.V.M
Mosby Year Book

*Skin Diseases of Dogs and Cats: A
    Guide for Pet Owners and Profes-
    sionals,* Dr. Steven A. Melman
Dermapet, Inc.
P.O. Box 59713
Potomac, MD 20859

U.S. Pharmacopeia
vaccine reactions: (800) 487-7776
customer service: (800) 227-8772
www.usp.org

Veterinary Medical Database/Canine
    Eye Registration Foundation
Department of Veterinary Clinical Science
School of Veterinary Medicine
Purdue University
West Lafayette, IN 47907
(765) 494-8179
http://www.vet.purdue.edu/~yshen/

Veterinary Pet Insurance (VPI)
4175 E. La Palma Ave., #100
Anaheim, CA 92807-1846
(714) 996-2311
(800) USA PETS,
    (877) PET HEALTH in Texas
www.petplan.net/home.htm

Nutrition and Natural Foods

California Natural, Natural Pet Products
P.O. Box 271
Santa Clara, CA 95052
(800) 532-7261
www.naturapet.com

Home Prepared Dog and Cat Diets,
    Donald R. Strombeck
Iowa State University Press
(515) 292-0140

Infectious Diseases of the Dog and Cat,
  Craig E. Greene, Editor
W B Saunders Company
PHD Products Inc.
P.O. Box 8313
White Plains, NY 10602
(800) 863-3403
www.phdproducts.net/

Sensible Choice, Pet Products Plus
5600 Mexico Road
St. Peters, MO 63376
(800) 592-6687
www.sensiblechoice.com/

Search and Rescue Dogs

National Association for Search and
  Rescue
4500 Southgate Place, Suite 100
Chantilly, VA 20151-1714
(703) 622-6283
http://www.nasar.org/

National Disaster Search Dog Foundation
323 East Matilija Avenue, #110-245
Ojai, CA 93023-2740
http://www.west.net/~rescue/

Service and Working Dogs

Canine Companions for Independence
P.O. Box 446
Santa Rosa, CA 95402-0446
(800) 572-2275
http://www.caninecompanions.org/

Delta Society National Service
  Dog Center
289 Perimeter Road East
Renton, WA 98055-1329
(800) 869-6898
http://petsforum.com/deltasociety/
  dsb000.htm

Guiding Eyes for the Blind
611 Granite Springs Road
Yorktown Heights, NY 10598
http://www.guiding-eyes.org/

The National Education for Assistance
  Dog Services, Inc.
P.O. Box 213
West Boylston, MA 01583
(508) 422-9064
http://chamber.worcester.ma.us/neads/
  INDEX.HTM

North American Working Dog Association
Southeast Kreisgruppe
P.O. Box 833
Brunswick, GA 31521

The Seeing Eye
P.O. Box 375
Morristown, NJ 07963-0375
(973) 539-4425
http://www.seeingeye.org/

Therapy Dogs Incorporated
2416 E. Fox Farm Road
Cheyenne, WY 82007
(877) 843-7364
www.therapydogs.com

Therapy Dogs International
6 Hilltop Road
Mendham, NJ 07945
(973) 252-9800
http://www.tdi-dog.org/

United Schutzhund Clubs of America
3704 Lemay Ferry Road
St. Louis, MO 63125

Appendix D: Poisonous Plants _____

Below is a list of commonly found plants both inside and outside of the home. Please note that this list is not inclusive and that the toxicity level varies from plant to plant.

Aloe Vera
Amaryllis
Apple (seeds)
Apple Leaf Croton
Apricot (pit)
Asparagus Fern
Autumn Crocus
Avocado (fruit & pit)
Azalea (Philodendron Pertusum)
Baby's Breath
Bird of Paradise
Bittersweet
Branching Ivy
Buckeye
Buddhist Pine
Caladium
Calla Lily
Castor Bean
Charming Dieffenbachia
Cherry (seeds & wilting leaves)
Chinese Evergreen
Christmas Rose
Cineraria
Clematis
Cordatum
Corn Plant
Cornstalk Plant
Croton

Cuban Laurel
Cutleaf Philodendron
Cycads
Cyclamen
Daffodil
Devil's Ivy
Dieffenbachia
Dieffenbachia
Dracaena Palm
Dragon Tree
Dumb Cane (Dieffenbachia)
Easter Lily (esp. cats)
Elaine
Elephant Ears
Emerald Feather
English Ivy
English Ivy
"Exotica Perfection"
Fiddle-leaf Fig
Florida Beauty (especially cats)
Foxglove
Fruit Salad Plant
Geranium
German Ivy
Giant Dumb Cane
Glacier Ivy
Gold Dieffenbachia
Gold Dust Dracaena

Golden Pothos
Hahn's Self-Branching
Heartleaf Philodendron
Hibiscus
Holly
Hurricane Plant
Indian Laurel
Indian Rubber Plant
Janet Craig Dracaena
Japanese Show Lily (especially cats)
Jerusalem Cherry
Kalanchoe (Panda Bear Plant)
Lacy Tree Philodendron
Lily of the Valley
Madagascar Dragon Tree
Marble Queen
Marijuana
Mexican Breadfruit (Split Leaf Philodendron)
Miniature Croton
Mistletoe
Morning Glory
Mother-in-Law's Tongue
Narcissus
Needlepoint Ivy
Nephthytis
Nightshade
Oleander

Onion
Oriental Lily
Peace Lily
Peach (wilting leaves & pits)
Pencil Cactus
Plumosa Fern
Poinsetta (low toxicity)
Poison Ivy
Poison Oak
Pothos
Precatory Bean
Primrose (Primula)
Red Emerald

Red Princess
Red-Margined Dracaena
Rhododendron
Ribbon Plant
Saddle Leaf Philodendron
Sago Palm
Satin Pothos
Schefflera
Silver Pothos
Spotted Dumb Cane
String of Pearls/Beads
Striped Dracaena
Sweetheart Ivy

Swiss Cheese Plant
Taro Vine
Tiger Lily (especially cats)
Tomato Plant (green fruit, stem & leaves)
Tree Philodendron
Tropic Snow Dieffenbachia
Variegated Philodendron
Variegated Rubber Plant
Warneckei Dracaena
Weeping Fig
Yew

Glossary of Terms _____

Anemia. The condition in which the number of circulating red blood cells is reduced. Anemia is a symptom of many diseases but not a disease itself.

Antibodies. Protein substances normally produced by the body in response to foreign agents. Antibodies serve to protect the body against disease.

Ascites. The accumulation of fluid within the abdominal cavity.

Benign. A term used to designate that a growth, tumor, or cells are not malignant or cancerous.

Blood titer. The blood level measured on any substance. A volumetric measure of concentration.

Elbow Dysplasia. Any of three conditions that effect the dog's elbow and which result in secondary osteoarthritis. Usually seen in rapidly growing young dogs.

Enteritis. Simply an infection of the intestines.

Estrus. Most commonly known as a stage of the "heat" cycle in dogs. The period sexual activity in dogs which is characterized by swelling of the vulva, blood tinged discharge, ovulation and acceptance of the male dog.

Euthanasia. The humane act of ending a dog's life usually with the overdose of a barbituate.

Fecal. Having to do with the microscopic examination of the dog's stool. The fecal exam is used to identify the presence or absence of intestinal parasites.

Feco-oral route. The transmission of disease by way of exposure to feces through the dog's oral cavity.

GDV. A commonly used acronym for Gastric Dilatation-Volvulus. A life threatening emergency that involves the bloating of the stomach and sometimes results in the twisting of the stomach that can involve the spleen.

Hip Dysplasia. A developmental disease of dogs in which the hip joint becomes unstable due to head of the femur, (the ball), not being properly seated into the acetabulum, (socket).

Hypertrophic Osteodystrophy Commonly known as HOD. A developmental disease of young and rapidly growing dogs that belong to giant or large breeds. HOD is usually characterized by lameness, swelling and inflammation of the long bones. It generally occurs at or near the growth plate region.

Lethargy. Just as in people, it is a condition in which the dog is extremely sluggish and has no energy.

Malignant. Refers to growths or cells that are classified as cancerous.

Myocarditis. An inflammation of the cardiac (heart) muscle.

OCD. The often used acronym for Osteochondritis Dissecans. A condition in which the end cartilage of the bone has a defect.

Palpate. To examine by feeling or touch.

Panosteitis. A disease of rapidly growing large breed or giant breed dogs. The symptoms are lameness, pain on palpation of the legs and areas of increased bone density that can be observed on X-ray.

pH. Refers to the hydrogen ion concentration in a solution. A low pH (below 7.0) indicates an acidic condition while a high pH (above 7.0) indicates an alkaline condition.

Physiology. The study of the body's complex functions and how the body systems work together.

Radiograph. Simply another term for an X-ray.

Sepsis. Any microbial infection of the blood.

Wobblers. Disease characterized by a malformation of the lower cervical vertebrae that results in varying degrees of spinal cord compression. Most commonly seen in Dobermans and Great Danes. The dogs exhibit a wide range of uncoordinated movement and at times paralysis.

Zoonotic. Having to do with diseases that can be transmitted from animals to humans.

Index

A

Abscesses, tooth, 255
Accidents, elimination, 220–221
Acetabulum, 155
Acetaminophen poisoning, 199
Activity, 6
Adolescent dogs, 34
Adult dogs. *See also* Aging dogs
    foods for, 70
    puppies *vs.*, 17–18, 34
    supplements for, 98
    training, 219
    welcoming home, 64–65
Ages of dogs, 301
Aggression
    play and, 234
    in puppies, 45
    sudden aggressiveness, 141
Agility training, 269–270
Aging dogs, 298–300
    arthritis, 304
    cancer, 302–304
    cognitive dysfunction syndrome
        (CDS), 304–305
    comfort of, 300–302
    dental care for, 299, 305
    disorders of, 302–309
    dry eye, 205
    foods for, 71
    hearing loss, 306
    hypothyroidism, 305–306
    kidney disease/failure, 307–309
    mental/physical stimulation, 301
    old-dog encephalitis (ODE), 116

vision, loss of, 306–307
Agriculture Department, 284
Air travel, 285–287
    in cargo bays, 286
    crates for, 226
Alaskan Malamutes, 270
Alcohol, 47
Allergic inhalant dermatitis, 203
Allergies, 9–10
    flea allergy dermatitis, 165–166
    food allergies, 203
    reactions, treating, 202–203
All-natural foods, 80–81
Alpha dogs, 229–230
Alzheimer's patients, 2
American Animal Hospital Association,
    268
    naming pets, 51
American Boarding Kennel Association,
    289
American dog tick, 169–170
American Eskimos, 46
American Grooming Shop Association, 265
American Humane Society, 286–287
American Kennel Club (AKC)
    breeder referrals, 29
    breed standards, 16
    Canine Good Citizen (CGC) test,
        274–275
    description of, 15–16
    herding titles, 273
    registered breeds, 12
American Mixed Breed Registry,
    273–274

About the Author

Tracy Acosta, D.V.M. is a Mississippi native and a graduate of the Mississippi State University College of Veterinary Medicine. Although her first love is dogs, she deals with all kinds of furry friends in her daily work as a small animal practitioner. Her goal as a veterinarian is to educate her clients about their pets' needs through all stages of life and to encourage them to take a proactive role in their animals' care. In her "spare" time, Tracy writes a newspaper column called Pet Doctor and visits schools to discuss proper pet care with children. "I fully support the studies that have demonstrated that children raised with animals carry on a lifelong greater respect for animals and fellow humans as well," she says. An avid Mississippi State Bulldogs fan, Tracy lives in Gulfport, Mississippi, where she is blessed with the companionship of Bacchus, a black Lab; Cairn Terriers Murphy and Mongo; and her cat, Oreo.